# MY STORY, FROM VICTIM TO SURVIVOR

*Mary Bernard Shay*

PublishAmerica
Baltimore

First printing

Hardcover 978-1-4560-0448-4
Softcover 978-1-4560-0447-7
PUBLISHED BY PUBLISHAMERICA, LLLP
www.publishamerica.com
Baltimore

Printed in the United States of America

I was born in the "baby boomer age" in the middle of March 1949. It was called the "baby boomer age" because the GIs had just returned from overseas, and I guess you can figure the rest out. I was born in a hospital in central Connecticut. On the way home, my Dad gave me a nickname. He called me "Button" because he said my nose was flat just like a button. A popular song of the era was called "Buttons and Bows". My family consisted of a maternal grandmother who was full Apache Indian, her male fried Uncle Phil. Uncle Phil lived in Philadelphia and came to grandma's every two weeks. My paternal grandparents immigrated from Poland in 1917, escaping Hitler's reign of terror. Also there were aunts, uncles, and cousins. Pretty normal family you'd say, well not exactly. Shortly after I was home from the hospital my mother decided that she couldn't share my Dad's love with me.

My Dad began noticing bumps and bruises on me. He questioned my mother about them, and she explained it away as "accidents", such as falling off a chair or my rocking horse. Strange thing was, I wasn't old enough to climb. At about four months old, my Dad noticed that my arm wasn't laying right, and that I was crying more than usual. He brought me to the doctor. My left shoulder was dislocated. Dad wasn't the only one that saw the bruises, so did my relatives. Back in the 50's there was a saying, "What went on in your house, stayed in your house. "It meant mind your own business.

# CHAPTER ONE

When I was three years old, we moved to Tariffville. My Aunt Emma and Uncle Bill got married. It was my aunt's second marriage. My parents babysat my four cousins while they went on a honeymoon. We lived on a dirt road, and across the road was a cemetery. My cousins and I played hide-and-seek between the grave stones. I would fall often on the rocks, always the same knee, and the same spot. I still have the scar today. Once my mother cut out a mask from the back of a cereal box. She put it on me and told me to scare the little boy that lived upstairs. Down the road was the high school. They used to fly gas-modeled airplanes there. I would watch them soar, dip, and spin from my backyard.

My aunt and uncle moved into the first floor apartment of my grandparents house. It was only four rooms, but rent free, my grandparents lived upstairs. My grandfather learned English by working, but my grandmother never did. She could swear like a trooper in English though. Every time she was angry with my grandfather, he would go outside and sit on the front veranda. My grandmother would throw anything she could get her hands on out the windows of the sun porch and down on the ground at him. People walking down the street would stop and watch her. My grandmother had gone senile many years before, but never got medical care. My grandparents didn't believe in doctors. In Poland, when you got sick, you called the priest. Many priests had some medical training. I'm mentioning my paternal grandparents because they played important roles in the early years of my life.

# CHAPTER TWO

Shortly after my aunt and uncle got married, my mother left Dad and me. I was three years old. My Dad and I moved in with my Aunt Emma and Uncle Bill and four cousins. My aunt and uncle were my godparents. Now there were five children and three adults living in four small rooms. My grandfather often came downstairs with hard candy in his pockets. It must have been old, because the candy always stuck to the paper. We five kids slept in one bedroom, even though one of my cousins was a boy. Buddy used to like to tease me about the boogey man. One time I ran into the bathroom to get away from the boogey man. The linoleum got stuck under the bathroom door and it wouldn't open. I had to stay in the bathroom until Dad came home from work. He had to take the door off the hinges to get me out. Of course Buddy got a spanking and sent to bed. My Aunt Emma was a strict parent, Uncle Bill on the other hand was a very quiet man. All the time I lived with them, I never heard them argue. If my aunt was having a bad day, he'd go outside in the summer or down to the basement in winter. They always went for a ride by themselves after Sunday dinner.

I used to like raw potatoes. Aunt Emma would give me a couple of pieces while she fixed supper. She always made cooked pudding with the skin on top with whipped cream for dessert. Around Christmas time that year, Aunt Emma was trying to teach me to tie my shoes. I was having trouble learning. Just before Christmas, there was a Christmas party at the Polish Club. Aunt Emma told me that if I got my shoes tied, I could go with my cousins. I kept trying, but I couldn't get them tied. I didn't go to the party. My cousins brought me my gift and

Christmas stocking. One Saturday afternoon my aunt dropped me and my cousins off at the movies. I was helping people coming in by trying to hold the door open. In the process, my pinky finger got caught in the door. The owner took me and my cousins into his office. He bandaged my finger, and we had free refreshments until the end of the show

Dad and I lived with my Aunt Emma until the summer before I started kindergarten. Three years before, my father's other sister and her husband and my four male cousins left Connecticut and had bought an old farm in Lake Sunapee, New Hampshire. I went to spend the summer with my Aunt Esther and Uncle Harold on the farm. My dad still lived with Aunt Emma. The farmhouse dated circa before the Revolutionary War. The king of England had grazed his horses on her 350 acres of land. It was also said that one of George Washington's cousins had slept in the house. The way the house was built, I also believe that at one time there had been slaves working the land. When I was doing the research for my last book "Forbidden Love" which deals with the issues of slavery and The Civil War, I believe it was part of the Underground Railroad. I'll explain more about that a little later in this chapter. The house was a two story square building, covered with asbestos shingles. If you went into the house by the side entrance, you entered a large room, that my uncle and cousins used as a workshop. At the far end of the room was a short hallway and at the end was a "indoor" outhouse. At the other end which I believe had been the slave quarters, my uncle had gutted out to store wood. At the opposite end was the door leading into the kitchen. Each room had a fireplace, that my uncle had cemented in, except for the one in the kitchen. There was no running water. Water was piped into a copper-lined tub in the kitchen from a spring. The water continuously flowed from a short pipe on he side of the tub into an enamel kitchen sink. You had to turn off the main road and go up a dirt road to reach the farm. If you stayed on the main road, about a quarter mile down was a white Protestant church with a square belfry There was a large wooden porch on the front of the house. In the evening, we would sit on the porch and watch the deer graze in the field across the road. We would also catch fireflies ina jar and watch them light up. As you looked straight ahead, there was a large pasture. The square belfry from the church looked like it was in the center of a mountain. One night I saw a baby rabbit on the lawn. I wanted to catch it, but my uncle told me that if I touched the baby rabbit, its mother wouldn't take care of it anymore. I remember thinking, my mother touched me, is that why she didn't want to take care of me anymore.

I. loved being on the farm. My aunt was up every morning at four AM to make breakfast for her men when they came in from milking the cows. My bedroom was at the back of the house and faced the barn. The smell of manure and the cows going into the barn woke me up every morning. I would run out to the barn and watch my cousins and uncle milk the cows, then send them back out to pasture. My aunt told me that I would sit on the top step and sing to the cows. After breakfast I rode in the back of the pickup truck with the milk cans for the eight mile ride to the creamery. There was always a large can of Nestle's Quick on the counter for fresh chocolate milk. My aunt had a saying, "no work, no eat" though she didn't mean it. Even as young as I was, I had to do simple chores. I got to ride on the end of the baler, and of course on top of the hay wagon. Paul would sometimes let me sit in front of him on the tractor, and help him steer. I even had a one-legged chicken that I named "Pecky". She was born with only one leg. Aunt Esther had to separate her from the other chickens or they would have killed her. She'd follow me all over the yard. My cousin Paul built her a small coop and surrounded it with chicken wire, and put in the workshop. That's where she slept at night. Once I helped my uncle deliver a calf. She was black and white. I don't know why, but I named her "Veronica Lake." A few days later, my uncle and I were watching a movie on television starring "Veronica Lake". My uncle laughed, saying wouldn't she be insulted if she knew you named a cow after her. Because my aunt was up so early every morning, she would lay down from noon to one everyday. Nothing could get her up before that hour was over. It was usually during this time that I would get into mischief. Somehow, she'd always find out. One time I asked her how she knew that I did something. She told me that "a little birdie told her." The next time I wanted to do something, I'd look around to see if I could find that stupid bird. That "bird were four boy cousins that tattled on me. I got even with them though, my aunt didn't want her boys to have comic books. She wanted them to get a good education, so that they wouldn't have to work hard all their lives. They had them though. I'd threaten to tattle on them if they wouldn't let me do something with them. It usually worked! My aunt was right. My oldest cousin Earl got a citation from President Nixon for his research on cancer. My second cousin Harold became a doctor. Paul took up auto mechanics. He built himself a motorcycle from a frame he found at the dump. My youngest cousin Peter became a teacher of foreign languages. He moved back to New London, Ct. to teach.

My aunt had another rule, if I remember we went to town, I had to wear a dress. She said that I had to look like a young lady if I wanted to go to town with her. I remember going into the Ann Page grocery store, and as soon as you were inside all you could smell was the aroma of their eight o'clock coffee. Now I'll tell you why I believe that my aunt's house might have been a "station" for the Underground Railroad. It wasn't all work on the farm. on rainy days, we got to play inside. One rainy day, my cousins and I were upstairs playing hide-and-seek. I went into a bedroom closet to hide and the back wall gave way. There was a passage way between the wall that gave away and the other wall which was the back wall of a closet in the next bedroom. I tried to research this but the town my aunt and uncle lived in was under a different name in the 1800's.

I also craved a lot of attention. I'm terrified of snakes. Sometimes I'd lie and tell my cousins that I saw a snake. They would come running to kill the snake that wasn't there. It was negative attention, but by doing this, I was the center of attention.

The summer went all too fast. At the end of August, Aunt Esther told me that my parents were coming to bring me home. I was terrified about going home. I missed my Dad, but my mom and him were back together. Finally the day came, and my parents were there. They told my aunt and uncle of the big 1955 flood caused by a hurricane. Many families from the northern New England states were moving to Connecticut to get work on cleaning up and repairing after the flood. Most of them stayed. My parents also told me that I had a new baby sister at home. I cried almost all the way home. My Dad kept telling me "that all good things had to come to an end."

# CHAPTER THREE

I told you how my Dad had given me the nickname "Button". Now that I was starting school. he told me that Ann Marie was my "real" name. Actually I was named after Aunt Emma's oldest daughter. My aunt wanted a name for her daughter that wasn't very common. She named her daughter Marie Ann. My Dad liked the name and just switched it around. My aunt was kind of upset that my Dad had taken her name for me

The "accidents" began again. Like my walking into mom's cigarette right between my fingers. Cynthia splitting my head open with a beer can. My mother didn't like that I had picked up the New Hampshire accent, especially the way I said the word "spaghetti. She fed me a name brand can of spaghetti until I said it in a way that satisfied her. She told Dad that it was my favorite meal. One afternoon while Mom was taking a nap, I wrote all over her bedroom mirror with lipstick. I got a beating with the strap, and I had to clean the mirror. Dad's way of trying to stop her beating me, was by beating her. Sometimes when she woke me up, she'd have a bruise on her cheek. But it only made it worse. She punished me for the beating she got

# CHAPTER FOUR

I remember my first day of school many of the kids were crying because their moms couldn't stay. I was glad that my mom had to go home. I also got into an argument with my kindergarten teacher. She asked me what my first name was, I told her that I didn't have one. She said oh yes I did. I told her no, that I didn't. She told me that Ann Marie was my first name. I told her that Ann Marie was my real name. Soon the first day of school was over, and I had to go home. There was no mom happy to see me, or ask me how my first day of school went. She didn't put my pictures on the refrigerator either. She'd send me straight to my room. My Dad would ask my mom why I was in my room. She always told him that I was being punished. Then he would go across the street to the tavern until my mom sent me to get him for supper. After supper he'd go back to the tavern. Mom would tell me to tell him when he came home, that I was tired and wanted to go to bed. I was to terrified not to tell him. She would make me take milk of magnesia every night. I had to say the prayer "Now I lay me down to sleep" I was terrified of the line, "If I should die before I wake" I was terrified that she would come into my room during the night and stab me. I taught myself to stay awake. I had a double bed. I would go down the bottom of the bed, and count the cars as they went by. I would dread to have her open my bedroom door. She get me up by giving me the strap or an enema.

My baby sister was beautiful, except she had a purple mark on her left cheek. Dad said it was a birthmark. He had talked to a doctor about covering it up with a skin graft. Dad was told that the skin graft would have to wait until she stopped growing. Her name was Cynthia.

I remember the apartment we lived in. It was four rooms. The kitchen had red and gray tiles on the floor. The bathroom was off the kitchen. You had to step up to reach the bathtub, sink, and toilet. My and Cynthia's bedroom was off the kitchen. My parents room was off the living room. also at the other end of the living room was a walk-in closet with no door. We lived across the street from a tavern in the center of town. We lived in a large apartment house on the corner. At the corner was a canteen. Across from the canteen was the firehouse. At six o'clock every evening the fire whistle would blow. The was an old colored bum named Benny who lived behind some garages down the street. At six o'clock when the whistle blew, after just leaving the tavern, he'd be standing in the middle of the road swearing his head off. All the neighborhood kids were afraid of him, including me. At five o'clock the street was almost free of kids. They'd be in their homes watching the "Mickey Mouse Club." My maternal grandmother and my aunt Penny(mom's sister) lived down the street from us, over a mom and pop grocery store. In the back were the garages. The dirt always smelled of motor oil. There was a wooden table and a bench on each side covered with grape vines. The grapes were green and sour. We kids would collect soda bottles to buy penny candy at the mom and pop store. My grandmother had to share a bathroom with the apartment next door to her. I can remember the strong smell of pine coming from the Airwick air fresher. I spent a lot of time at grandma's. In her dining room was a large buffet. At the end of the buffet was a large glass cookie jar with a green cover. It was always filled with oatmeal raisin cookies. When grandma's boyfriend Phil came for the weekend, we had the best spaghetti dinner.

Dad tried to make Mom happy. He took her out one night a week. Aunt Penny would baby-sit us. Most kids cry when their

Mom leaves. I cried when mine came back. I loved it when Aunt Penny baby-sat. Aunt Penny was a teenager. She taught me how to bebop with "American Bandstand." She taught me to love Elvis Presley. Sometimes we'd order a pizza from the tavern across the street. She also paid for me to take tap dancing and acrobatic lessons. That didn't work out. I was just too uncoordinated. Dad had a green Ford Ranchwagon. We used to go to the drive-in on buck night. They would show movies from dusk to dawn. Dad would put the back seat down and make a bed for Cynthia and me. I would peek through the crack between the front seat and watch the movies. Dad even let Mom have jewelry demonstrations. I got to try on the jewelry. She played the perfect Mom in front of the women who came to the demonstrations. I only have one good memory of Mom. That Christmas she played "Ring Around the Rosie" with me. When it came to "all fall down" her ring accidentally scratched me.

When Cynthia was fourteen months old, I had another new baby sister. Again, Dad named her after another one of Aunt Emma's daughters, Victoria Elizabeth. Again Aunt Emma was upset. The only name he picked out himself was Cynthia's. Her middle name was Penelope after Aunt Penny. Victoria was a beautiful baby. She had curls just like Shirley Temple. I used to walk my baby sisters up and down the street in their stroller. People would comment on how beautiful she was, and most avoided asking me about the purple mark on Cynthia's cheek.

That Easter, Aunt Penny bought the three of us three dyed live baby chicks. We kept them in a box in the walk-in closet. We named them Tom, Dick, and Harry. Aunt Penny's boyfriend wanted to know who she named them after. When they grew too big for the box, Dad gave them to a friend of his at work who had a chicken farm. They grew up to be three white roosters.

Mom began taking Dad to work so that she could have the car. We always went to Hartford. I wasn't supposed to tell Dad where we went. She would try to find a baby-sitter among her

14

friends in Hartford. When she couldn't, she'd leave us in the car while she went into a bar. She'd come out to check on us once in a while. I changed the babies and gave them their bottles if she didn't come out in time. We had to pick up Dad at four o'clock. He worked on the top floor of the factory. He'd go down to the last window and wave down to us.

# CHAPTER FIVE

I'm in the first grade now. I've taught myself to stay awake most of the night. I would hear Mom and Dad arguing over me and Mom's brother my Uncle Bob. He would only come to see Mom when he wanted her to ask Dad for money, that he never paid back. Mom woke me like always, with the strap or an enema. Sometimes I'd be so upset, that I threw up my breakfast. She would make me eat my vomit. After I was dressed for school, I had to stand in the doorway of my room, shoulders back and head straight. I had to stand like this until it was time to leave for school. Then she'd make me run and stand in the doorway to make sure I did. I would run until I knew that she couldn't see me anymore. I thought about running away. I thought that I could walk to the farm. It didn't take that long by car. I thought I knew the way there., but I never tried. I knew what would happen to me if I got caught. I was also starting to lose my baby teeth. When they were loose, Dad pulled them out with pliers.

One day Mom got Aunt Penny to baby-sit us. She told her a friend was picking her up to go shopping. But Mom never came home. Aunt Penny babysat us while Dad worked. Then One Saturday Dad asked Grandma and Aunt Penny to come with us to Hartford to find Mommy. I remember going into the bar with Dad to show him the man Mom went to see. Mom was there. I went back out to the car where Grandma and Aunt Penny were waiting. Dad was in the bar for awhile, then he and Mom came out to the car. Mom told Dad that she had to go to her apartment to get her things. We drove to this large apartment house. Dad asked me to go in with her. Mom and I went inside and climbed a flight of stairs. She told me to wait for her on the top step while she went into the bathroom at the end of the hall. I waited and waited. People coming into the building were asking me if I was lost. I would tell them that I was waiting for my mother. After awhile Dad came in. I told him that Mom was in the bathroom. He knocked on the door, then went in. The bathroom window was open and there was a fire escape. Dad began knocking on doors, showing those that answered her picture. Nobody recognized her. She never lived there. We drove back home. For the next three Saturdays, Dad drove to Hartford looking for Mom. On the third Saturday, Dad came home with her. Shortly after she came home, Victoria had to be admitted to the hospital. Dad said that she had pneumonia.

One day in second grade, the school nurse sent me home from school. She thought that I had the mumps. I was too terrified to go home. I walked around town, sat on the green and went in and out of stores. I didn't know how to tell time yet. I finally figured that school must be over by now, so I went home. When I got there, the lady next door was coming for coffee. I was so happy to see her. I knew Mom wouldn't beat me in front of her, but she did when the lady left. Dad called the doctor. They still made house calls then. All I had was swollen glands.

Aunt Penny and her boyfriend got married. Aunt Penny went to work in a small factory in the next town. One day Mom told Dad that she wanted to go to work at the same factory. Dad didn't want Mom to work. They had a big argument about her working that night. Dad must have gave in. The next day she left us with Grandma and took Dad to work so that she could have the car. When Dad got out of work, the car was in his parking spot, but no Mom. That morning was the last time I would see or hear from her for twenty years. Aunt Penny was now pregnant and her and her husband were moving to Maine. Dad went to Aunt Emma again, but she wouldn't help him out this time. She told him that he should have learned his lesson after me, but he didn't. She also said that she couldn't raise seven kids. Dad went to Mom's friends in the neighborhood to baby sit. Some would baby-sit for awhile then quit, saying it was too much for them to take care of three plus their own. Some wanted too much money. Even the nuns at the orphanage wouldn't take all three of us because Victoria wasn't potty trained. Finally, Dad left us alone while he worked. He would fix their bottles before he left for work. I knew how to change them. Mom used to make me do sometimes. Dad told me to keep perfectly quiet and keep the girls from crying, so that nobody would know that we were alone. I remember that the girls slept most of the day. Dad told them at school, that I was living with his parents. I only went to school three months in second grade. Dad brought me to school the last day for the party and to get my report card. Believe it or not, they passed me!

During that summer Dad met a man who was a widower with two daughters. He told Dad that they lived in a good foster home during the week, and he took them on weekends. He gave Dad the name and address of this foster mother. Dad took us there to meet her, but she didn't have room in her house for three more children, and Dad wouldn't split us up. She gave Dad the name of her sister who lived down the street and also took in foster children. We went to see her and she and her husband agreed to take us in for thirty-six dollars a week. They seemed real nice, and after we got home, Dad asked me if I wanted to live there. I was old enough to remember how many places Dad tried and who wouldn't take the three of us, so I said yes. So Victoria, Cynthia, and I went to live with Mr. and Mrs. Foster. Dad moved in with his youngest brother, my Uncle Stan. They lived downstairs from my grandparents, because by then, Aunt Emma and Uncle Bill had bought a house across the street. Dad came to visit on Friday nights, and took us to his place on Sunday afternoons. Dad had to have us back by six o'clock, because seven o'clock was our bedtime.

# CHAPTER SIX

Mr. and Mrs. Foster wanted us to call them Gram and Grandpa They were both in their late sixties. They had a large two story yellow and green house with a closed in front porch. A green awning covered the window of the second floor front bedroom. There was a large front yard with a long sidewalk in the center leading to the front door. They had a long driveway that had a gigantic pine tree on one end. The driveway led to a two door garage, that had a side door. a sidewalk led from this side door and ran alongside the garage. It turned off at the outhouse that was in back of the garage. A small closed in porch led to the side door, where you entered the kitchen. There was a large back lawn. At the end of the lawn was a white arbor where red roses bloomed. On the other side of the arbor was a tulip bed. Behind the tulip bed was a large vegetable garden. It ran alongside of what we called "the hill" this was where we had to play. There were two huts on the hill, one across from the vegetable garden and the other at the top of "the hill".

On the first floor was a large kitchen, living room, piano room, and dining room. You went upstairs from the dining room. Gram and Grandpa's bedroom was across the hall from the top of the stairs. On the end of the hall was the bathroom that we could only use at night or to take a bath during the colder months. Our room was bright yellow. It had two windows and a large walk-in closet. It had a double bed on one end. Two extra kitchen chairs were side by side of the first window. A single bed was at the other end alongside the other window. Gram put Cynthia and I in the double bed, with Cynthia on the inside near the wall Victoria was in the single bed, which she was too young for. She kept falling out of bed, so Gram put the two girls in the double bed and me in the single bed Sometimes my sisters would cry, wanting Daddy to come and get us. I wanted that too. I would hold them until they fell asleep. If Gram had caught me in their bed, I would have gotten a beating. At the other end of the hall was a large room whose door was closed most of the time. Gram kept plants in there. Gram loved flowers, and had a green thumb.

When we were inside, we had to sit on the floor in the corner of the kitchen by the closet door. We had to whisper to each other. When it was time to go to bed, our clothes had to be folded neatly in the corner, as well as our toys. The girls were two young to do this, so I did it for them, despite the fact that Gram wanted them to do their own. When we were outside, we had to play "on the hill". We had to use the outhouse to go to the bathroom. We couldn't come in the house until Gram called us in to eat. When it was cold, we took our time eating lunch so that we could warm up before going back outside. Gram called us in at five o'clock for supper. In the fall we sat in the hut in the dark because it got dark before five. In the winter we sat on each other's feet and close together to try to be warm. Sometimes, we would talk Victoria into going in the house and ask Gram if we could come in. Sometimes Gram would let her stay in, but not me and Cynthia. That first winter was very cold. Gram had a thirteen year old cocker spaniel named "Bootsie" One cold night, I asked Gram if Bootsie could come in the house. She was always outside. Gram told me no, and just to open the side door of the garage so she could get in. There was no heat in the garage, and the floor was cement. The next morning I went to give her her food. I found her standing frozen stiff in the middle of the sidewalk. We couldn't tell Dad about how Gram was treating us when he came to visit, because Gram would be listening from the living room. She would have told him that I was lying anyway.

I went to the same school that Gram had gone to. It was a large gray building with a belfry on top. It had nine classrooms from kindergarten to sixth grade. This is where I began third grade. Third grade was a little hard for me because I had only three months of second grade. I tried hard, I didn't dare bring home a bad report card. I was the only student that had perfect attendance that year.

I developed a habit that would drive Dad nuts. If someone just raised their voice to me, I would burst into tears. I would get hysterical if I had to stay after school. Before we went to live at Gram's, Dad had bought me a necklace and bracelet with a four leaf clover and a fake pearl in the center. Gram wouldn't allow me to wear it. One day, I sneaked and wore the necklace and bracelet to school. During the day, I noticed the pearl in the bracelet was missing. I became uncontrollably hysterical The principal took my bracelet to a jeweler and had a diamond chip put in the center

Dad had given Aunt Emma money to take me school clothes shopping. Gram wouldn't let me wear them. Three of her seven married children lived down the street from her. She would make me wear their hand-me-downs that were too large for me. A pair of brown and white saddle shoes were handed down to me. One day when I was tying my shoes for school, Gram noticed that the tongue on one of the shoes was missing. She made me look for it. I looked all over the school and playground and even along the sidewalks that I took school, but I couldn't find it. Gram gave me a beating and took the shoe to the shoemaker to get it fixed.

Then came Halloween. Dad had bought us Halloween costumes. We had to dress up at school for the Halloween party. One of Gram's granddaughters took dance classes. Gram made me wear one of her dance costumes. It had a top hat, black leotards, red shorts, a black coat with tails and fishnet stockings. Much too provocative an eight year old. All the boys were giving me wolf whistles and some of the other teachers and principal came in to look at me. Halloween was a nightmare. Gram wouldn't let us go out treat or treating. She said that it was begging. We had to sit in our corner and watch the other kids come for candy. Finally, Auntie Pat, Gram's daughter came and talked Gram into letting us go out. Auntie Pat took us to her house and dressed us up, then took us and her son Denny out trick or treating.

When I was about nine, Grandpa would start coming into my room while I was changing my school clothes if Gram wasn't home. He'd try to touch my private parts. He even came into the outhouse if I was in there. I would try to fight him off, but once in awhile, I'm ashamed to say, I let him sometimes. It was a form of attention and I wasn't getting beat. He would try to enter me by using Vaseline, but he never could. If we came down with a cold, Gram made us eat Vicks Vapor Rub. Victoria got the measles and had to stay on a daybed in the dining room with the shades down. She also got stung my a yellow jacket while we were playing on the hill. There was an apple tree so there were many yellow jackets. Victoria began to swell up all over after she was stung. Gram rushed her to the emergency room. Apparently she was allergic to bees. I couldn't tell Dad, about the way Gram and Granpa were treating us, because I knew he'd take us out of there, and maybe my sisters and I would have to be separated.

In the winter time, Gram made us jumpers to wear with our tights. She would darn the runs in our tights. At Christmas every year we were there she would always buy us the same gifts, tights and mittens. In fourth grade Gram made me a beautiful white with a rose-patterned dress. It had lace around the collar and the cuffs. There were three red buttons in a row on the bodice. I loved that dress.

One of Gram's sons that lived a couple of houses down the street had three children, a girl and two boys. They were about our age. "Carrot top" was my age, and Robbie and Ricky were near my sisters' age. They would come to Gram's often to play with us on the hill. If we were making too much noise, Gram would holler at us from her bedroom window. "Carrot top" loved raw carrots, which was probably how she got her nickname. She would pull them out of the garden, wash them with the garden hose and eat them. Sometimes we went to play at their house. In bad weather we played downstairs in their rec room. We really liked going to Auntie Pat's house. Denny, being an only child, and Auntie Pat being told she couldn't have anymore children, had everything a child could wish for. He had two rooms full of toys, plus the basement. There was a huge a electric train and village set up on a train table down there. Auntie Pat also had a large swimming pool that she and Uncle Walter set up in the summertime. At Auntie Pat's we could play like normal children. She'd have cookouts also, which were fun, unless Gram came. There was also a large hill across from a dirt road that was excellent for sliding We could also slide down the dirt road because there was a hill at the end. Sometimes Gram would make me go sliding even if nobody else was outside. The hill ended into a field where we played softball in the spring and summer. Even though there were still kids playing outside in the summer, we had to come in at seven thirty to be in bed by eight, even though sometimes we'd be in the middle of a game. Even though Dad bought us sneakers to wear in the summer, Gram mainly made us go barefoot. We would wash our feet in an old dishpan before going into the house. When we had to take a bath, in the summer she would fill a large wash tub on the back lawn with water from the garden hose. We had to go to bed without underpants. Grandpa knew this, and would sometimes try to sneak in our room. Once again, I was afraid to fall asleep.

It took me a long time, because I wasn't athletically inclined to be able to hit a softball, but once I did, I could really hit it out there. I was lousy in the field though, I couldn't catch a fly ball if my life depended on it. This would have an impact a little later on. At the top of the hill where we went sliding began the woods Carrot top, her brothers, my sisters and I used to play in the woods. One day we found a three-sided cement wall, that might have been the basement to someone's house once. We cleaned out the leaves and dirt. We found logs to lay across the top for a roof. There was also some metal shingles that we put on top of the logs. We would eat our lunch and snacks there sometimes. Sometimes in the winter, the six of us would build a snow fort out of snowballs on the hill. I used to get mad at Robby and Ricky sometimes, because they would make fun of Dad and call him "beer belly."

I would have to mow both lawns in the summer and rake the leaves in the front and back yards to the road and put them in piles in the fall. We weren't allowed to jump and play in the leaves like normal children would want to do. Then you were able to burn the leaves. I loved the smell of them burning in the dusk air. Some Gram had me put in trash bags and dump them on the tulip bed. She said it kept the bulbs from freezing. Connecticut used to have winters with a lot of snow. I had to shovel the sidewalks and a path along the side of the driveway to the side door. Sometimes the snow was so deep, that I'd have to cut it in half first.

# CHAPTER SEVEN

Monday was laundry day. Gram had a wringer washing machine so it took most of the day. After the clothes were washed, they had to go through the wringer and the whites into a large washtub of bluing. Then rinsed and put through the wringer again, then finally on the clothesline. Gram ironed everything except the underwear. She even ironed sheets and pillowcases. When I wasn't in school, I had to help her. My ability to use a wringer washing machine would come in handy many years later. When automatic s machines came out, Gram bought one. A leading detergent company made their detergent in the shape of tablets. Gram had a habit of keeping the box inside the washing machine. One day I came home from school, and as soon as I was in the door, she began to beat me across the back with the broom handle. She said that I left Kleenix in the pockets of my clothes. Later she realized that she hadn't taken the box of detergent out of the machine before she started it. She never apologized though. After that I dreaded coming home from school. I kept thinking all day at school what Gram would think of to beat me for. Sometimes it was our messy bedroom closet or dresser drawers. They were never messy, because I didn't dare let them get that way. Mostly, Gram put our clothes away. Saturday, my sisters and I had to polish all the furniture. Back then they had large wooden furniture. I still have the scar on my right eyebrow from where I cut it on the corner of the dining room table. I wasn't very popular. Most of the kids thought that I was ugly. The boys in the neighborhood called me "fish lips" because of my full lips. My own sisters called me "nigger lips". I think Gram abused me because she believed that I was half Puerto Rican or Negro because of my dark complexion. My Dad was very dark complected even though he was full-blooded Polish. There was a lot of prejudice back then. My sisters were fair-skinned, blonde hair and blue eyes. Gram even got Cynthia to believe that Dad caused her birthmark. She told Cynthia that Dad hit Mom in the stomach when she was pregnant with her and left a mark on her.

Once Gram sent me to the village grocery store to buy cold cuts. I didn't even know what cold cuts were, and she didn't give me a list. Johnny at the store gave me what he thought Gram wanted. I got home and handed her the package, but it wasn't what she wanted. She sent me back to the store. This time Johnny called her to find out what she wanted.

One night after we went to bed, I got my sisters to save their spit so I could set my hair in pincurls. I didn't dare take the chance of Gram hearing me in the bathroom to wet my hair down. The next morning when I came downstairs for breakfast, Gram noticed that my hair was curly. She made me wet it down. About that time, putting glitter in your hair was the latest fad. I had a tube of glitter in my purse. Before I left for school, I went into the garage. There was a mirror in there from an old medicine cabinet. I put the glitter in my hair and started walking down the driveway. Gram was watching from the kitchen window. The sun made the glitter show. Gram came outside and pulled me into the house. She brushed my hair till it hurt. I was late for school. I became hysterical when the teacher told me that I had to stay after school for being late.

When I was in the sixth grade, Carrot top decided she wanted to try smoking. We tried rolling pine needles in toilet paper from the outhouse, but of course it just burned down. Dad kept a carton of Marlboros on his dresser. One Sunday when we went to visit, I took a pack from his carton and put them in my purse. One morning Gram grabbed my purse and dumped its contents on the kitchen table. Out came the pack of cigarettes. Naturally I got beat, but she just couldn't wait to tell Dad when he came to visit on Friday night. It was the first time my Dad ever hit me. He slapped me across the face. He remarked that I even smoked his brand. Carrot top hardly got punished at all.

About this time, I really believed that I wanted to become a nun. I read everything I could about nuns and life in a convent. My favorite book was "The Nun's Story." I drew pictures of nuns and rosary beads on my book covers. When I told Dad he laughed and told me that I would never be able to keep the vow of silence. He said that I was born with the gift of gab. I think he would have been proud of me though. I know now, that I wanted the religious life because it was safe,

I had my first male teacher in the sixth grade. They were building a new school at the end of the playground. One day while out for recess, a boy had found a small black snake with a yellow ring around its neck. He brought it in after recess. The teacher had it crawling up the sleeve of his white shirt. He didn't know that I was terrified of snakes. He stopped at my desk and told me to feel how dry the skin was. I flew out of the classroom, out of school, and was halfway home before I realized I had to go back to school. The teacher put it in a fish take and placed it on the window sill. It was too hot there and the snake died. Even though it was dead, I still couldn't touch it.

Around Christmas time, Gram ordered something for her daughter-in-law from Spiegel's catalog. She did most of her shopping from saving green stamps and catalogs. When she was notified by the post office that her order was in, she sent me to pick it up. She didn't tell me that there was two packages. It was very cold, so on the way home, I put my mittened hand in my coat pocket grasping the package underneath my coat. When I got home, I gave Gram the package. She asked me where the other one was. I was scared, so I lied and told her the post office had only given me one package. She sent me back to the post office to get the other one. They told me that they were sure they had given me both of them. I lied again, telling them that I had only gotten one. Gram kept sending me back to the post office everyday, telling them they must have lost it. They turned that post office upside down, and of course never found it. Spring was coming, and the snow began to melt. On our way home from school one day, Ricky picked up a soggy package off someone's lawn. He brought it home. It was the robe to the nightgown Gram had ordered for Aunt Fran. I must have dropped it when I put my hand in my coat pocket. Since then, I try very hard not to lie to anyone.

# CHAPTER EIGHT

We still went to Aunt Emma's farm every summer during Dad's vacation. Gram never packed us any dresses. She said that we didn't need a dress on a farm. Aunt Emma had to make us some dresses so that we could go to town and for rides with her. She took us to "The Cathedral of the Pines" The first summer was after we had been at Gram's a year. Somehow I had caught lice in school. Gram gave us all boy haircuts. Victoria was only three. My cousins would tease her and call her Victor. One day, the cows were in the barn for the four o'clock milking. Victoria was running up and down the aisles. She stopped and pulled this one cow's tail. It began to pee. She goes back to running around and stopped to pull the same cow's tail. This time, she made a cow flop. Some of it had splattered into the aisle. Victoria goes back to her running. All of a sudden she slides, face first in the cow flop. My cousins roared with laughter, they told her that you're not a farmer until you put your face in a cow flop. Aunt Emma wasn't so pleased, she had to clean her up. Aunt Emma used to save jars from instant coffee. She tied twine around it and made a handle. We'd take these jars and go blueberry picking in the pastures. We'd bring the blueberries in and Aunt Emma would make, pancakes, muffins, and pies from them. One day while Aunt Emma was taking her hour nap, my sisters and I decided to set up a stand and sell the blueberries. Well would you believe our first customer was the sheriff. Aunt Emma had to get up from her nap, because she didn't have a permit to sell the blueberries. Needless to say, she wasn't very happy with us. Aunt Emma also made homemade rootbeer. I liked helping her bottle it and put the caps on. Those two weeks went all too fast. Dad would come a couple of days early to visit with my aunt and uncle. My youngest cousin had a black and white cat. One day when Dad was there, Peter was running around the house calling "Sylvester, Sylvester" which was my Dad's name. My Dad was getting upset, thinking that Peter was being disrespectful. He told Peter to call him Uncle Slyvie or Uncle Jim. Peter replied,

"But Uncle Sylvie, I wasn't calling you, I was calling my cat!"

Soon it was time to go home and back to Gram's. I would cry most of the way home. Again Dad would tell me that all good things must come to an end.

Sometimes I went with Dad on Friday nights to spend the weekend at Aunt Emma's Gram would pack the clothes Aunt Emma had bought me to go. My cousins would set my hair and polish my nails. I remember when Elizabeth's boyfriend was in the army. He would call her when he came home for a weekend pass. She'd slide down the banister to answer the phone. We weren't allowed to have any contact with Mom's side of the family. Especially after Aunt Penny gave her baby up for adoption because it was a girl, and her husband wanted a boy. It was drilled into my head, that you can leave your mate, but you don't run out on your kids. Aunt Penny had even named her baby after me. Mostly, Dad didn't want Mom's relatives telling her where we were.

Grandpa was still molesting me every chance he got. It was also the time Carrot top and I began to be curious about our changing bodies. We would touch each other's private parts. We had both got our first training bras. Carrot top wanted me to let Grandpa touch me so that I could tell her how it felt. She said that she would try to stay awake to see if she could hear her parents having sex. Starting in the sixth grade, the girls were shown a film on menstruation and given pamphlets. Some of the boys would try to peek through the black curtain covering the classroom door window. After the class, they would ask us about the film and read the pamphlets. Dad would ask Gram occasionally if I had started my period yet. One day when I was thirteen, I got "the curse" as Gram called it. That evening she invited three of her children and grandchildren to supper. During the meal, Gram announced "that I had become a woman that day." I was so embarrassed. Grandpa stopped molesting me after that.

# CHAPTER NINE

For seventh grade we had to change to another school that only had grades seven and eight. One day out for recess, we were playing softball, the girls against the boys. When it was my turn to bat, most of the boys came infield except the boys from our neighborhood. They tried to tell the other boys that I could hit, but they didn't believe them. I whacked that ball over the fence!

One Saturday afternoon, Carrot top wanted to go roller skating at the YMCA in town, but she wasn't allowed to go alone. Gram made me go with her. All the time I'm thinking, here's three hours of falling on my face. Well we got there, and rented our skates. Carrot top began to skate easily. For the first half hour, I struggled. Then I began to skate! It was wonderful! It was the first sport that I picked up naturally. While I was skating, I was in my own little world. There was no Mom and no Gram. I had no idea at the time on how that afternoon was going to have such an impact on my future.

I had a best friend that lived across the street from the school. She was unpopular like me because she was overweight and big busted. She started her period at nine years old. She'd want me to spend most weekends at her house. Many times I did, but I was scared. Her dad would be sober all week, then began drinking when he got off of work on Friday. Cheryl and I would put our pillows over our heads to try to block out the screaming and her dad beating on her mom. I left for home after church on Sunday to be there for dinner, and wait for Dad to pick us up. He never missed a Sunday. Except one Sunday he called and said that he couldn't make it because of a snowstorm. He wanted to talk to each of us on the phone. I told the girls not to start crying, because maybe he wouldn't call the next time he couldn't make it. He did come to visit for a couple of hours after they cleared the roads. After Sunday dinner, we'd go up on the hill and stand alongside the small hut so that we could see the road. We'd tell each other that the next car would be Dad's until it was. Many times Dad would take us to a fraternal lodge he belonged to. He'd put us in the TV room. Lots of times his friends would buy us sodas and snacks. We'd leave in time for him to feed us supper. Six o'clock would come awful fast. I never got to watch the movie "The Wizard of Oz" until I was fourteen, because they would show it on Sunday evenings at six o'clock. Dad bought me my first "Beatle" album "Meet the Beatles" Dad would be sitting at the kitchen table reading a dirty book. every once in a while he'd go "Yeah, Yeah, Yeah. One afternoon I asked him what the word "rape" meant. He sent me across the street for Aunt Emma to explain it to me. I had to keep the album and the pocket transistor radio Uncle Stan bought me at Dad's. If you had a pocket transistor radio, you belonged to the "in" crowd. I told them I had one but that it was at my Dad's. They didn't believe me.

I had made my First Holy Communion shortly after moving to Gram's Aunt Emma took me to buy my white dress and veil. The dress had a pleated skirt. The boys had to wear white suits. The girls walked down the aisle in single file, and so did the boys. We looked like little brides and grooms. Now it was time to make my Confirmation. I chose Bernadette as my Confirmation name. She was my patron saint, and is how I chose my pen name. When Bernadette entered the convent, they had to change her name because of all the publicity about the grotto. They named her Sister Mary Bernard. I added the name Shay. Well, I had a mad crush on one of our priests. He was too handsome to be a priest. At Mass, I would sit in the front pew, just to look at him. When it became my turn to go up to the bishop and get my tap on the cheek, this priest told the bishop to tap me a little harder, because I needed more help.

We had animals at Gram's. We had a male and female sheep. Billy, the ram would come to the fence and let you pet him all day if you wanted to. The female Mary, you couldn't get near her. And yes Mary had a little lamb. Gram would have the neighbor across the street shear them and she sold the wool and had blankets made. We also had ducks, and for a short time a Shetland pony named Nicky. Gram had to sell him because we were in a residential area. A couple of years earlier Gram had ordered a tan cocker spaniel from Spiegels catalog. We had to go to the train station in Meriden to pick him up. His doghouse and where he was chained was on the hill where we played. Gram never saw the dog because it was up to me to give him his food and water. Gram fed him a lot of table scraps. His name was "Bootsie" also. One day I told Gram that Bootsie's collar was getting too tight and was cutting his neck. She didn't believe me. The collar finally cut open his neck. Gram took him to the vet to get him stitched up. About a year later, Bootsie stopped eating. Gram told me to unhook him and let him roam free. He still didn't eat, but began drinking water like it was going out of style. Gram took him to the vet. The vet said that Bootsie had leukemia. They tried to give him a blood transfusion but it was too late. Bootsie died. Gram hated cats, because a cat she had once killed her bird while she was cleaning the cage. One day a black angora cat strayed into our yard. Gram assuming it was a male, took it in. On one rare occasion when Gram let me have a friend over after school, saw the cat and told me it was pregnant. I told Gram, but again she didn't believe me, until the cat started wanting to sleep on my bed. Gram made a box for her and put in an old blanket. One day the kittens were born. Victoria loved animals, especially horses. We were playing on the hill. Gram called us down and made us watch as she put the kittens in a burlap bag, then drowned them in a tub of water. Victoria was so upset, she went after Gram to hit her. She also told Gram that someday she would have a horse. Gram told her that the only part of the horse she would ever have was the ring underneath the tail. It was always a battle of wills between Gram and Victoria. Gram was a stubborn Irish woman, and Victoria was just as stubborn. Cynthia and I were afraid of Gram. Once Gram made Victoria wear a clothespin on her nose all day, because she said she was nosey. Gram also had a canary whose cage hung from the kitchen window. Gram's son Uncle Willie always wore a red cap. He'd always stand in the corner of the counters near the bird cage. That bird would squawk, until he took his cap off.

That year Grandpa had a stroke. He was paralyzed on right side. Gram set up a hospital bed in the living room for him. Many times I helped Gram wash him and turn him and change his bed. I didn't know it then, but that was early training for my future life's work.

Sometimes during the winter, Gram would call us in from the kitchen to go into the living room to watch TV. We got to watch "The Lucy Show" and half of "Jackie Gleason. "Sometimes on Saturday night, she'd brew tea from tea leaves. After we drank our tea, she would read our fortune. Mine was never any good.

During the summer, the school system set up a summer school at the school playground for the elementary school kids. Once a week they went to the town park for swimming and a picnic. I was too old to go, but Gram made me go anyway. The counselors didn't know what to do, so they let me stay. After summer school was over, Gram made us a lunch and made us go to the park. We would cut through the woods to get to the park because it was shorter. My eyes were always on the ground looking for snakes. We couldn't come home until it was time for supper. Sometimes they closed the park because of a thunderstorm, but we still had to stay. Sometimes the girls would cry because they were tired and thirsty.

The day in my life that I will never forget is the day President Kennedy was assassinated. It was two o'clock in the afternoon. I was in my seventh grade science class. Suddenly the principal came over the loud speaker. He told everyone to go home and turn on their television sets. We watched as Walter Cronkite announced that the President was dead The next thing we knew they had arrested the man who fired the three shots. The Governor of Texas was also wounded. They had been shot by an assassin while driving in a motorcade through Haley Plaza in Dallas. We watched as a young First Lady took off her wedding band and placed it on her dead husband's finger. We watched as the Vice President took the oath of office aboard Air Force One. We watched as thousands of people passed the coffin in The Rotunda to say a last good bye. We watched as the alleged shooter was shot and killed by a nightclub owner as he was being transferred from the Dallas County Jail. We watched the funeral procession and watched as a young three year old boy saluted his father's casket from the Capital steps as it passed by. We watched as he was laid to rest in Arlington Cemetery, an eternal flame marking his grave.

I graduated from eight grade. Aunt Emma and Uncle Bill bought me a wrist watch. They were at the farm the same time we were. Uncle Bill was my favorite uncle. Him and I would have long talks as we walked through the fields. He told me that he and Aunt Emma would take me anywhere I wanted to within reason if I graduated high school. I had my first boyfriend that summer, though Gram didn't know. I had been "teacher's pet" in one of my eighth grade classes. He began calling me "Annie" instead of Ann Marie. Soon my classmates were also calling me Annie. This teacher was also working at the park that summer as a lifeguard. Bill and I could only see each other at the park. It seemed everywhere we went in the park, my teacher would have the habit of showing up. There were a few other boys from my class that began to take a interest in me. I guess that I had become to develop a figure. They only wanted to take me into the woods. That would be the last thing I needed was to get pregnant while we were still living at Gram's. I had been better off dead. There was a good looking boy that road his bike from Meriden to the park, which was at least fifteen miles. He and I became close friends. He came to the park two or three times a week to see me. Also that summer, I was swimming in the pool at the park at the end where the diving board was. I became tired and tried to stand up in the water. I panicked! The water was over my head! The lifeguard jumped in and got me out. Also that summer, a bunch of girls from my eighth grade class, decided to chip in and charter a bus to go to the beach. I had never been to the ocean before. I also had my period the day we were supposed to go. Gram told me not to go in the water because I'd get bad cramps. I was so dark complected that I had never had a sunburn. I fell asleep on the beach. I got such a bad sunburn that I had sunstroke. I blistered and peeled. My first day of high school came and I had to ride the bus. The lifeguard who saved me was on my bus, and he was a senior! I was so embarrassed.

# CHAPTER TEN

Many of the kids from elementary school were in my home room or in some of my classes. I still had to wear Gram's granddaughter's hand me downs to school. The skirts were too long for me. I would have to roll them up at the waist. Aunt Emma had taken me school clothes shopping for clothes that fit, but Gram wouldn't let me wear them. I had to take home economics. One of our assignments was to sew an A-line shift from a pattern. I missed up the neckline. I tried to fix it by hand sewing it. It came out horrible. After that I hated sewing and still do.

I got asked to my first school dance. Gram helped me get ready. Even the dress I wore to the dance was a hand me down. The boy's father picked me up and brought me home. The boy I went with was a redhead. After a couple of minutes into our first slow dance, his face got as red as his hair.

Grandpa died at home that year. It would be the first wake and funeral I had ever been to. When I walked up to the casket, he didn't look dead. I was physically sick for a week. Especially almost everyone came to the house after the cemetery. Some began drinking. I washed up the dishes afterward. I didn't have to be told to do them. If their were cups and saucers in the sink when I got home from school from Gram's Wednesday card parties, I knew better than not do them.

That summer Uncle Stan and Dad were going to bring us to the farm for our two week vacation after the Fourth of July weekend. On the Fourth of July, Dad and Uncle Stan were at the lodge, drinking and shooting pool. Uncle Stan was the youngest of my grandparent's children and used to getting his own way. He was also a sore loser. Dad and Uncle Stan got into an argument over a pool game. Uncle Stan left to go to his girlfriend's house. We had a thunderstorm while he was on his way to her house. My uncle had power brakes on his car. He hydroplaned and skid into a telephone pole. When the police began to investigate the accident, they learned of the argument that Dad and Uncle Stan had before he left the lodge. They wanted to arrest my Dad, accusing him of tapering with my uncle's brakes. While Uncle Stan was in the hospital, Dad asked me to give the apartment a good cleaning for when he came home, which I did. But Uncle Stan didn't come home. Uncle Stan lived a week, and during that week, the only person Uncle Stan wanted to see was my Dad We didn't go to the farm that year. It would be the last summer I would spend there Victoria was born on Uncle Stan's birthday while he was in Korea. Uncle Stan had lived through two wars, only to die in a car. Dad gave us the best news. He was going to bring us home to live with him. home to live with him. I gave my friend (the bike rider) my Dad's phone number.

I was fourteen, Cynthia was ten, and Victoria nine. One day, I spent the whole day cleaning their room. I changed their bed, cleaned their drawers and closet, washed the windows, hung clean curtains, and washed and waxed their floor. They came home, and because I had some of their clothes in the wrong drawers, they dumped the clothes on the floor. They ran out of the house laughing their heads off. I chased them halfway down the street. If I had caught up with them, I would have beat the daylights out of them.

Dad decided that I was old enough to wear lipstick, but no other makeup. He asked Aunt Emma' youngest daughter my cousin Dot to bring me to the drugstore to pick out a good shade. I wore other makeup, but washed my face before Dad came home.

In my sophomore year I began smoking again. One night Dad was home which was unusual. He was at the lodge almost every night. I wanted a cigarette and didn't know how I was going to have one without Dad finding out. Out of the clear blue sky, Dad said,

"You left your cigarettes on your desk this morning." I froze, I remembered the time he had slapped me for smoking in the sixth grade. Then he said,

"Just don't get expelled from school for smoking." I quit after I had permission to smoke in front of him.

I had to take the town bus to school. Dad would buy the tokens. He would wake me up to get ready for school before he left for work at six. I would get up and get ready, and sometimes I'd go back to bed and would wake up after the bus left. It was a mile and a half walk to school, so most of the time I stayed home. The school would call at nine o'clock. I would tell them that I was having bad cramps with my period. One day the principal called me into his office. He suggested that I see a doctor, because I had my period more often than anybody else he knew of. All the years we were at Gram's, each year I got the perfect attendance award. One time the school nurse sent Cynthia home because she was sick. Gram made her go back to school. I made a couple of friends at school. After school, instead of taking the bus home, we'd walk the short distance to the plaza. We began stealing clothes, and 45 RPM records. We'd slide the records inside our notebooks. I had all the popular records. I had so many new clothes, that Dad asked me if I had a "sugar daddy." Cynthia would often go in my closet and wear my clothes. One day my friend and I walked into the drugstore. I was wearing a light blue windbreaker with a zippered pocket that I had stole. My friend decided she wanted a candy bar. She took the candy bar and put in the pocket of my windbreaker. Then we walked out of the store. Once outside, suddenly a man was grabbing both of us by the arms. He reached into my pocket and took out the candy bar. He said that he was going to call the police and our parents. I got hysterical. My Dad would be very upset with me. Finally the man relented, but told us that he never wanted to see us in his store again. Believe me, even as an adult did I ever go back into that drugstore. But can you imagine! With all the merchandise that we stole, to get caught with a ten cent candy bar.

# CHAPTER ELEVEN

Dad gave me a fifteen dollar allowance for cleaning the house and taking care of the girls. I spent my allowance at the roller skating arena. I would go an hour earlier to help the skate boys set up, and a hour later to help them clean up. I went Friday night, Saturday night and Sunday afternoons. I got to dance better on skates than I did on my own two feet. One night it was a moonlight skate, and I was skating without a partner. A skate boy came up to me and told me to get a partner, or I'd have to get off the floor. A boy was skating alone ahead of me. I skated up to him and asked him to skate with me. He was just a little taller than me. He wore a black leather jacket and his hair was greased back into a DA. After the skate I figured he'd skate off, but he didn't. He wanted to skate with me the rest of the evening. I really didn't want him to, but I didn't know how to tell him. He even walked me home. His name was Phil, and when we got to my house, he asked if he could take me out. We gave each other our phone numbers. I felt important because I was going out with an older boy. I was fifteen, and Phil was nineteen. He worked at the movie theater so he could go to the movies free.

There was another boy I met at the skating rink before I met Phil. His name was Bill. We were exactly the same age. We were born on the same day. We would meet at the elementary school playground just up the street from my house. We would talk and neck. I had to bribe my sisters into not telling Dad. Sometimes I would go to the school and Bill wouldn't show up. Sometimes I'd walk to his house. I'd cut through the cemetery because it was shorter. Bill had twin sisters, and a younger brother that was sickly. The apartment was always a pig sty. Bill's father was the only one that did any housework even though he had a job. Sometimes I'd walk all the way to his house, and he wouldn't be home. One time Bill's dad told me that I was too good for his son. I learned a valuable lesson while seeing Bill. The school was having a "Sadie Hawkins" dance where the girls ask the boys. I just took it for granted that Bill was going to take me since we were going steady. Dad bought me a pair of black stretch pants, a white blouse, and a pink cashmere sweater to wear to the dance. I spent all day getting ready. The time came for Bill to pick me up, and he didn't come. An hour went by, and still no Bill. I was crying my eyes out on my bed, when the phone rang. I jumped up assuming it was Bill. Instead it was a boy from one of my classes. who wasn't really popular. He told me that he had a feeling that Bill would stand me up. He said that if I wanted to, he'd be proud to take me to the dance. I went with George and had the best time. I learned that you don't judge a book by its cover Bill and I stopped seeing each other.

Phil and I had a couple of dates. Then one night Alan called and asked me out to the movies. He said that a friend of his was giving him a ride. Dad wanted to meet him before saying that I could go. Dad told Alan to have me home by eleven. That would give us time to go to Mc Donald's after the movie. During the movie, I felt something hit me a few times, and someone was throwing popcorn at us. Dad called from the lodge at eleven to see if I was home on time. I was. The next morning, Dad knocked on my bedroom door. He told me that he liked Alan, only the next time we went out, his friend should bring a date. He said it didn't look good for one girl going out with two boys. I was surprised that Dad liked Alan, because he was Italian. Dad was very prejudiced against Italians and Frenchmen. The next day, Phil and I were supposed to have a date. He didn't call, so I called him. That phone call would turn out to be a big mistake. Phil got on the phone and the first thing he asked me was if I had a good time last night. He was the one throwing things at us at the movies. Alan and I went out again, only this time we double dated.

Dad hated Phil. He said he looked like a hood and was too old for me. One night I was talking to Phil on the phone, when Dad came home from the lodge drunk. He grabbed the phone away from me and told Phil to stay away from me. Before I knew I said it, I told Dad to shut up. He slapped me so hard, that I landed across the room and into the living room chair. We had been taught at an early age to respect our elders. That was the second time Dad slapped me. One day Phil was at my house. The girls were carrying on so bad, that my grandfather came downstairs. I was sitting on Phil's lap in the living room chair. My grandfather put me on the couch, grabbed Phil by the shirt and threw him out the front door, telling him that he didn't want to see him on his property again Grandpa would come downstairs other times and try to molest me. I'm ashamed to admit it but I didn't always didn't try to stop him. Dad warned me about his father just before we moved in with him. Once I came home from school and my grandmother had all my things out of my room. My room had been Uncle Stan's bedroom. She had all the curtains down and was painting the window frames. She said she was cleaning the room for when Stash (Polish for Stan) came home. She didn't speak English so I couldn't explain to her who I was. She had gone senile many years before. She believed that Dad was a priest. He was the farthest thing from a priest you'd ever want to see. When we were small, Dad would bring us upstairs to visit with her. All she'd want to do is feed us. Even though she was senile, she had never forgotten how to cook. My grandmother was a four hundred pound woman. She wasn't flabby fat, but solid.

The next day after Dad slapped me I was so upset with him that I took a half a bottle of aspirin. I slept for three days, and nobody noticed that I hadn't come out of my room all that time. Phil and I continued to see each other. I had to sneak out the back door and meet him at our favorite restaurant. I'd get upset with him sometimes, because he'd sit me in a booth, order our food, then spend most of the time playing pinball.

Phil lived in a three room apartment with his parents and sister-in-law and baby nephew. Phil's brother was in the Navy. Phil slept on a mattress on the floor in his parents' bedroom. His sister-in-law and baby slept in the living room. Phil had a job making minimum wage, yet his parents expected him to pay most of the household expenses, like rent, food, and electricity. Yet both of his parents worked.

One night Phil came to my house because Dad wasn't home. He brought with him a couple of packets. I didn't know what they were, so I just set them on the arm of the couch. The next day, Dad knocked on my door. When I let him in, he was holding the packets. He told me that those packets wouldn't keep me from getting pregnant. Once he saw that I really didn't know what they were for, he called Aunt Emma to tell me. The packets were douche. I guess Phil didn't know what they were for, he just grabbed them from the medicine cabinet in his bathroom. By this time, Phil and I were having sex.

That Christmas, Dad got very drunk. It was a tradition in our family to open our gifts on Christmas Eve. Dad practically threw our gifts at us. I went into my room crying to open my gifts. He had bought me a new pair of roller skates and skate case with a key. I loved them so much, but Dad was in no condition for me to tell him how much I loved him and how I loved my skates. I had thought of roller skating professionally, but I didn't want something I enjoyed so much to become work.

I'll never forget the first time I got drunk. My girlfriend, the one I got caught shoplifting with, told Phil and I to come over to her house after eleven o'clock. Both her parents worked third shift. There was a bar in their rec room. Wendy made me a highball with ginger ale and Four Roses whiskey. Before I was finished with my drink, she took it and poured about four more shots into it. Later I had to go upstairs to the bathroom. I saw two flights of stairs. Phil and I had to walk him which was almost five miles. We stopped in a donut shop and Phil bought us coffee. I saw four cops in the shop, but Phil said there was only two. Phil didn't dare bring me to my house in that condition, so we went to his house. I slept on the living room floor. The next day, Phil's mom made a roasted chicken dinner, about the only thing she could cook. She said she made it for me because it was my favorite meal. The smell of the food turned my stomach, but I ate a little bit anyway. That afternoon, Phil walked me all over town ending up at the skating rink. I finally got sick in the ladies room. Of course some of the girls in there that heard me getting sick, started a rumor around that I was pregnant.

Dad was drunk almost everyday. He would say that his car knew its way home because he always took the back way home and at one spot you needed to go through a tunnel, one car at a time. We began arguing. Sometimes when he was drunk, he'd call me by my mother's name. He especially got mad at me when one day he came home from work and I was washing my hair with his last can of beer. We had a big fight a few days before my sixteenth birthday. He threw me out of the house. I went to stay at Phil's. I slept on a crib mattress on the living room floor. I went home a couple of days after my birthday because I needed some clothes. I went while Dad was at work. I walked into the kitchen and there was a birthday cake on the counter for me. I was so hurt, he throws me out, then expects me to come home for my birthday. I picked up the cake and threw it against the back door. I walked out leaving the mess Dad called me a few days later at Phil's and asked me to come home. We still fought, especially when a friend of mine wanted to give me a kitten. Dad hated cats. He finally gave in on the condition that I keep it in my room so that he'd never have to see it I named her "Missy" She was my first pet. I fed her bologna when I couldn't buy cat food. I used dirt for her cat box. Another time my friend (the one that told me Gram's cat was pregnant) invited me to a slumber party. There was going to be a boy girl party first, then the girls were sleeping over. Her parents were going to be there to chaperone. Dad had to meet her parents before letting me go. Dad called every hour while the boys were there. He was the first parent to pick me up in the morning. The girls were getting more and more out of control, and he was powerless to stop them. Dad took me out of school two days after my sixteenth birthday, thinking I'd go back in a couple of years and graduate. He didn't think that I could take care of the house, the girls, and keep my grades up. I was an average student. I could have gotten better grades if I applied myself more. I had a World History teacher that taught me to love history. I had flunked it in ninth grade. I averaged a B+ in his class. Business math was another story. The teacher always sat me in the front desk. He was a roly-poly man. My business math was counting how many times he rocked back and forth in his elevator shoes.

I took a baby-sitting job taking care of five kids, two girls and three boys aging six to two months. The mother worked next door at the diner Phil and I went to. I babysat from six in the morning until three in the afternoon. The house was a pig sty. The first morning she made the baby's formula. She expected me to clean the house, take care of the kids, wake up her husband at two thirty PM for work if he didn't get up himself for fifteen dollars a week. I was uncomfortable about having to wake up her husband, but most of the time he got himself up. He'd bring me a milkshake from the diner. I also went with the mother to help with the kids when they had an appointment at the well child clinic. The baby didn't wake up until afternoon to get fed. I mentioned this to Phil's mom and she said that wasn't normal, so that worried me.

Things weren't going well with Phil's dad and himself. Phil's mom was very involved with her church, The Salvation Army. Phil and I would go with her sometimes even though I was Catholic. Phil and I began to talk about getting married. I don't know which one of us brought it up first. I think maybe

I did, because all I wanted was for someone to love me and a peaceful home. Phil had been smoking since he was eight years old, but he didn't drink. We began looking up states that you could get married without parental consent. We saw that in Maryland, you could get married at fourteen without parental consent. A friend of ours was going to drive us to the bus station in Hartford to get a bus to Maryland. We were stopped at a traffic light in a three way highway in West Hartford. Tommy was driving, I was in the middle and Phil was asleep with his head on my shoulder. All of a sudden, there was Phil's Dad opening the passenger side door and pulling him out of the car. He shoved him over to his car and pushed him into the back seat. Phil's Mom was in the front seat on the passenger side. The captain of the Salvation Army helped me out of the car and into his. He told Phil that he wanted him to meet him at the parsonage. That's where the captain brought me. When we got there, captain called my Dad to tell him that I was alright. He sat Phil and I down at the dining room table. The first thing he asked was if I was pregnant. I wasn't. I had just had my period. Phil went home. Captain called my Dad to tell him that he was keeping me overnight, and that I'd be home in the morning. My Dad was so angry, that captain didn't want to send me home.

I used to confide in my favorite cousin Elizabeth. She was like an older sister to me. My room at home was always a mess. It would take me two days to clean it. Then I'd have her come over to see it clean. She would praise me. I thought the things I told her would stay just between us. I told her that Phil and I still wanted to get married. She told Aunt Emma and Aunt Emma told my Dad. Dad said that he would sign for me because he'd never hear the end of it if he didn't.

Phil and I began to have second thoughts about getting married. Then a couple of months later, Phil had his dad's car. We were driving down a street Phil was distracted and hit a parked car. His dad was furious and demanded that he pay for the damages. Afterwards his dad brought up the subject any

48

chance he had. It was May, and I missed my period. I thought that it might be because I got shook up during the accident. Phil couldn't take his dad's grief anymore, so we planned to get married in June. I had to call Alan as much as I didn't want to, to tell him that I was getting married. We were going to take over his parent's apartment because Phil's dad was supposed to take a job in another town. His mom was going to spend the summer with Phil's great aunt Rose at her cabin in Vermont. His dad would be busy taking school buses down to North Carolina. Captain David of the Salvation Army was going to marry us. We were planning a June 27th wedding, which was a Sunday afternoon. The morning of our wedding Phil woke me up early to get ready, even though we weren't getting married until one o'clock, then he went back to bed. Phil's dad was sitting at the kitchen table in just a bathrobe drinking coffee. He told me that he wouldn't be able to come to the wedding because he had to leave for North Carolina. I went into Phil's parents' room to wake up Phil. If I wasn't so naive, the red flags should have gone up. Phil was sleeping in the double bed with his mother and she was naked! I asked him about it later, and he told me that his mother wasn't in bed when he went back to sleep. Since Dad signed permission for me to get married, I couldn't live home anymore. So I was staying at Phil's. I had bought a white dress, hat, and white shoes. The cafeteria where Phil worked was going to supply sandwiches, donuts, and punch. A lady he worked with, made our wedding cake. Captain's wife bought my bouquet and Phil's buttoneer. Dad refused to let my sisters come to my wedding. I got married without anyone from my side of the family being there After the wedding, Tommy( the one that tried to drive us to the bus station, drove Phil's red and white 57 Ford Fairlane all decorated through town, blowing the horn. A police car pulled us over for unnecessary noise on Sunday. Phil told him that we had just gotten married and showed him the marriage corticated. The cop took on look at me and said that I should still be in school and what he'd do to me if I was his daughter. Then he let us go. After that, we went to visit Phil's grandma Grace. I loved her. She was such a sweet woman. Then I went grocery shopping for us for the week. I spent five dollars! We'd be getting leftover sandwiches and donuts from the cafeteria.

We spent our wedding night at the apartment. The bottom frame of the bed had been wired because Phil's mother's three hundred and twenty five pound body had broken it. About four o'clock in the morning, the bed broke! Don the neighbor underneath us sat on the front steps most of the day, waiting for Phil to come out so that he could tease him. Finally Phil had to go out because he needed cigarettes and Don was ready for him.

I still had my cat Missy, and Phil had a cat named Tom. I had taken half of a package of hamburger that I had bought, and set it in a bowl on the kitchen table to thaw. Phil came home from work, and I went into the kitchen to fix supper. The bowl of hamburger was empty and licked clean! The two cats went by licking their chops. I didn't know that cats loved raw hamburger. One morning Phil's cat Tom didn't come home. He didn't come back all day. After work, Phil went looking for him. He found him dead in a gutter on Main Street. Soon after I got married, Dad couldn't control the girls anymore. He took them back to Gram's. They called the state on her for child abuse. Dad brought them back home until he could place them somewhere else. He placed them in two different school for girls that were on the same street in Hartford. The day that the social worker came to get Victoria she ran out of the car, while the social worker was stopped at a light. It was a busy intersection. The social worker chased Victoria for blocks in her stocking feet, while at the same time holding up traffic. Victoria kept running away from the school in Hartford. Dad finally placed her in a school for girls in New York.

# CHAPTER TWELVE

Phil was on vacation two weeks after we were married. We got Don downstairs to watch Missy while we went to Aunt Rose's cabin in Vermont. I put the leftover donuts we had on a sheet of wax paper on the shelf of the refrigerator. We left for Vermont. Phil's dad came home while we were gone. He was not the type to fix himself something to eat. His cup and saucer, jar of Sanka, sugar and creamer were also on the table. He drank about twenty cups of coffee a day. He opened the refrigerator and saw the donuts. Well, by now they were as hard as rocks. He told me later that he called me every name in the book.

I began to call Phil's parents Mom and Dad. Dad came up to the cabin while we were there. His new job didn't pan out, so he and Mom would have to live with us until another apartment came open. There was no electricity in the cabin because it was on a mountain. Aunt Rose stored some things in a cold-room just outside the cabin. Aunt Rose was a character. When one dress got dirty, she'd just put another one on top of it. One time some ants had gotten into some watermelon she had stored in the cold room. She cut off the top, saying that the ants hadn't got all the way through it. Some oranges were beginning to go bad. She cut off the blue parts and ate the rest. One Sunday afternoon we all went for a ride. We stopped at a hot dog stand. There was a long line waiting, but Aunt Rose insisted on going to get our hot dogs. We looked and she was at the end of the line. A couple of minutes later, she was second in line. One day there was a jar of pickle spears on the table. There was only one left. I made the mistake of eating it. Afterwards she told everyone that I had eaten all her pickles.

I started getting morning sickness on our "honeymoon." One day I was in the outhouse. There was a green garter snake laying along one of the boards in front of me.

I'm thinking to myself, if I hurry up and get out of here, I'll be alright. Then he turned his head and was looking right at me. I ran out of the outhouse with my pants down and screaming my head off. Everybody came running out of the cabin to see what was wrong. Later after our son was born, he was on the thin side. One day Dad and I were in the living room watching TV. Dad remarked,

"Remember that day you ran out of the outhouse with your pants down, you scared off any fat that kid is ever going to have."

Before we left for home, Aunt Rose's friend had given me a male silver gray angora kitten. He rode in the car well. for the three hour trip home. We named him "Sam. "Shortly after Phil and I went to the dog pound and adopted a puppy we named "Duke." One day my Dad came to visit us. He was drunk. I had newspapers on the kitchen floor because I was housebreaking Duke. My Dad got on my case about the newspapers. My Dad also said that our car looked like a circus wagon because Phil had written all over the white part with black magic marker. Phil's dad asked my Dad to leave, and not come back unless he was sober. Sam was quite a cat. One day I was going to get a towel out of the linen closet in the bathroom, when there was Sam sitting on the side of the toilet seat, doing his business in the toilet! Duke was very spoiled. If we couldn't take him with us, he'd cry and make himself sick.

One weekend Phil decided that he'd like to go to Vermont to the small town where Aunt Rose's cabin was for its fall festival. It was only a three hour ride. Phil's parents took care of the cats, and we brought Duke with us. We got to Aunt Rose's around three o'clock in the morning. Phil said that we'd have to leave

Duke in the car, because he wasn't housebroken and Aunt Rose would be upset if he had an accident. This next morning Phil went out to get him and he had thrown up all over the front seat. Then Aunt Rose said that we could have brought him in as long as he stayed in the kitchen. There was carpet in the other rooms.

The town only had one street, the main street in and out of town. It was a beautiful day. There were sack races, egg races and the fire department played tug-of-war with the fire hoses. In the afternoon there was a barbecue. We brought Duke. One of Phil's friend was petting him when he started laughing. It turned out that our Duke was really a Duchess. He asked Phil whether he was sure he married a female. After the barbecue they had a greased pig contest. They would grease a pig and who ever caught it won a prize. This guy was chasing the pig, when the pig fell off a ledge and broke its neck. I was so upset that I told the guy off. He told me to mind my own business and to go back home. The day ended with fireworks.

Phil's parents were still waiting for the apartment next door to us to get vacant. His parents were still expecting him to pay most of the bills, even though now he had me to support. I had an argument with my father-in-law about this. I actually got along better with my father-in-law than I did with Phil's mother. She had always wanted a girl. It was kind of an obsession with her. She had several miscarriages and only had Phil and his brother. One day while she and I were walking to the Salvation Army, she told me that I was going to have a boy, because their family only had boys. I didn't care as long as I had a healthy baby. When I was about four months pregnant, I bought a mint green crib blanket with puppies on it and a red terry cloth sleeper. Mom said it was too early to start buying things for the baby because I could still have a miscarriage.

Finally, Mom and Dad moved into the apartment next door. I was about five months, when I decided that I wanted to paint the kitchen. I was standing on a chair, when I fell off. The leg of the chair landed across my stomach. I had a woman obstetrician because I was too bashful to have a man have to examine me. Phil brought me to see her, but everything was alright.

A neighbor down stairs complained to the landlord about Duchess peeing on the blacktop in front of the house. The landlord said we had to get rid of the animals. Phil called the dog warden to come and get them. I was on my bed crying. I think Duchess knew because she was laying down beside me looking up at me with her sad brown eyes. We couldn't find Sam anywhere. By the time the dog warden came, we still hadn't found him. Then we checked our bedroom make-shift closet. I had a basket of ironing in there. Sam was all buried up in the clothes. He had never went there before. We called the dog warden back to get Sam. Then the landlord told us that we could have kept the cats because they were good to catch mice.

I was about seven months pregnant around Christmas time. My Dad came to visited. I wasn't very big, and Dad asked me if I was sure that I was pregnant. He said my mother was huge when she carried me. Phil would buy me anything I craved. I especially craved devil's food cake with white frosting and ice cold milk. On my eighth month checkup, my doctor had told me that I had gained too much weight. She told me that if I didn't lose weight, she was going to put me in the hospital. I only had about six weeks to go before my due date.

# CHAPTER THIRTEEN

In January another couple and Phil and I went to the drive-in theater. They had heaters for inside the car then. After the movie, Phil's friend suggested we take a trip to Houlton, Me. because he had relatives there. Of course we agreed, and stopped home to get some things. Just before we hit the Maine state line, it began to snow. We kept going. Then I began to have cramps. By then it was snowing so hard, that they were closing the Maine turnpike. We made it to Augusta. We parked in front of a donut shop for the rest of the night. When we got to Winterport, we began to have car trouble. The owner of the garage said his mechanic wouldn't be in until tomorrow, and we only had money enough to fix the car good enough to make it to Houlton. Bobby would borrow the rest of the money from his aunt. That night the owner of the garage left the ladies room open for me because there was heat. I slept on the ladies room floor. Phil, Bobby, and his wife slept in the car. After the car was fixed we headed north. We had to go through the Hanesville Woods. Back then the road was as treacherous as that trucking song said they were. A little later the car started acting up again. We were near Mars Hill. Bobby had an aunt that lived there. We stopped and Bobby asked his aunt if she could put us up for the night. They were going to go on to Houlton, fix the car, and come back for us. Bobby aunt fixed soup and sandwiches for supper. Phil was just about to bring a spoonful of soup to his mouth, when all of a sudden we hear,

"On the Holy Blood of Jesus!"

Phil's spoon of soup went flying. Apparently she was a Holy Roller. Later that night she showed us where we were going to sleep. She came in with a hot water bottle. She asked me when I was due. We lied and told her April which really was February. Then she told us that she was a midwife, and if anything happened, she'd know what to do. I told Phil that he'd better not let her touch me. Bobby and his wife came the next day. They said that they were going to take us to The Salvation Army in Bangor, and they would get us back home to Connecticut. So at least now, we were heading south.

The Major of The Salvation Army got Phil and I a hotel room with its own bathroom, because I was pregnant and meal tickets to eat at a diner close by. Phil found a can of Colt45 in the room. He opened the window and stuck it in the snow on the ledge to get cold. We found enough change to buy me a soda pop from the machine in the hallway. The waitress at the diner gave us more food than I know was on the meal tickets. She made sure that I drank plenty of milk. The extra food and desserts must have come out of her tips. Finally we were on the bus going home. Phil called his dad to come and pick us up at the bus stop, but he wouldn't, even though it was just down the street. We walked home, though it was all uphill, and, and very hard for me.

Three weeks later, I went into labor. Since we had been home, Phil had me keep a glass of water on the dresser to throw at him to wake him up because he was a very heavy sleeper. He told me to make sure I got out of the way because he woke up swinging. I was a week early. Phil called a cab to take us to the hospital. Our son was born at quarter of three in the afternoon. I had a seizure from high blood pressure just after he was born. I had gotten toxemia. I was getting a shot every four hours. I was so duped up I couldn't read or watch TV because I saw double. The first time I held my son, I made him a promise, that if he never had anything else in this world, he'd have a mother that loved him. My Dad came to the hospital, but he had to be escorted out by the security guard because he was very drunk. Phil bought me a heart of chocolates because Phil Jr. was born the day after Valentine's Day. The nurse made him take them home. One of my nurses would come into to tuck me in every night at eight o'clock. One of them, her husband worked with my Dad. One night I couldn't go right to sleep. I could hear all the other new mothers laughing and talking. When it came time to go home, Phil wanted to dress our son. He wanted to put his diaper on in the shape of a triangle. We brought the red sleeper to bring him home in. We went home by cab. I was very sore from the stitches. Phil brought the baby half way up the stairs and then came back. He didn't want to leave Phil Jr. upstairs alone while he came to help me. I told him to bring the baby upstairs and get his mother to come over to watch him. I really needed Mom's help, because I wasn't supposed to be alone until all the medicine was out of my system. The walls of the apartment were paper thin. She would hear Phil Jr. wake up for his two o'clock feeding. She would come padding across the porch. I'd meet her at the door, and tell her that I would feed him. I felt like she was trying to take my place.

Phil Jr's head was a little out of shape from the forceps. The pediatrician told me what to do to shape his head. We didn't have our own phone, because Phil didn't pay the bill. I'd been home about three days, when Dad came to get me, saying that I had a phone call from Phil Jr's doctor. Dad thought I I was supposed to take the baby to the doctor, and forgotten. The doctor asked me if there was something wrong with Phil Jr's head. I told him no, that he had told me what to do, and that I hadn't called him. The doctor said that he understood that I was only sixteen, but if I had a question, for me to call him, not my mother-in-law. She had called him and told him that she thought Phil Jr. had a brain tumor!. I ran out of their apartment fuming. I met Mom at the door, but just went around her. Phil came home from work and found me crying. He asked me if the baby had given me a hard time. I shouted at him "No your mother!" I told him that if he told her when Phil Jr's six week appointment was, I'd leave him. I also told him that I wanted to move. A few days later, it was a balmy February day, so I decided to put Phil Jr in his carriage, and go to my girlfriend's for the day. It was about a half hour walk. Mom came over and wanted me to take Phil Jr. to the doctor. One day, I went to check on Phil Jr. and the carriage was empty. He was sleeping in a antique carriage we got at the Salvation Army. I thought someone had kidnapped my baby! Mom had come and taken him out of the carriage and over to their apartment without telling me. Whenever I put Phil Jr. in his carriage, I'd cover him up to the shoulders and tuck the blankets in on all three sides. I was so afraid of crib death. When Mom would put him back, she'd just cover him. I'd go right behind him and tuck him in. Later, my Dad bought us a crib.

The day I went to my girlfriend's, I was getting ready to leave so that I'd be home by the time Phil got there. Phil Jr. began crying because he was hungry. I wasn't going to have him crying all the way home, so I fed him before I left. I saw the guys Phil rode with on my way home. They shouted that he was home. I got home, and there was a big hole in the living room wall. Phil had left and walked all the way to my girlfriend's house, instead of waiting for me to get home. We had our first argument. Another time I was invited to my cousin's bridal shower. Phil was supposed to take care of the baby. During the shower, the doorbell rings, and there stood Phil with baby in tow. I was embarrassed and so were my cousins because Phil had to stay in the kitchen by himself. All the other men had left because of the shower.

# CHAPTER FOURTEEN

We moved to a four room third floor apartment close to my in-laws, but so that Mom couldn't come all the time, because she had trouble climbing stairs. Phil had bought us a double oven stove for ten dollars a month. A salesman came and we bought baby furniture that interchangeable. We would bring Phil Jr. over to visit his grandparents at least once a week. Sometimes Mom would want to keep him Saturday night and bring him to church with her in the morning. It was good for us because we could go out and sleep in the morning.

When Phil Jr. was about three months old, Phil wanted to go to a church retreat for the weekend that was being held in the middle of the state. Mom was going to baby-sit at our apartment. Phil Jr. had the sniffles that morning, but he didn't have a fever or anything. We gave Mom the number where we'd be and the doctor's phone number.

After going to a meeting Saturday afternoon, I realized that I hadn't seen Phil for awhile. I went to our cabin, thinking he might have gone there to take a nap. I opened the door, and there was Phil making out with one of the girls from our church group. She buttoned her blouse and ran out of the cabin. I confronted Phil. He said she came on to him, and that he loved me. We had only been married a little over a year, and he was cheating on me. I had never denied him sex. The next day, Sunday, I couldn't wait to get home. My maternal instinct was telling me that something was wrong with my baby! We finally got home. Phil Jr. was burning up with fever and Mom was getting ready to take him to church! She and those old biddies at church thought that it was just a teething fever. We took Phil Jr. to the emergency room. He had a temperature of 104degrees. The doctor wanted to know why we hadn't brought him sooner. We explained that we had been away, and that his grandmother had been baby-sitting. The doctor looked at Phil and remarked,

"She raised you and you're still here." Phil Jr. had a viral infection. The doctor gave us a prescription. I vowed that Mom would never baby-sit again, because her church was more important than her grandson's health. I didn't let her baby-sit again until Phil Jr. was about seven months old.

Phil brought our car to a garage that specialized in transmissions. The transmission on our Ford was acting up. My skate case and skates were locked in the trunk of the car. At the garage, the mechanic told us to junk the car, because it would cost too much to repair. We went to take our personal belongings out of the car. We opened the trunk and my skate case was missing! Someone had stolen my skates. Phil bought another car. It was a gray and white 57 Chevy with light gray interior and whitewall tires. It was a beautiful car. When Phil Jr. was about nine months old, I decided to take my two men to meet my aunt and uncle at the farm. Phil Jr' slept just about all the way in his car bed. He woke up when we stopped for gas. It was late when we got there, but Phil Jr. was wide awake. My uncle was so pleased that he went right to him. My uncle was sitting at the dining room table and there was a plate of cookies in front of him. The next morning Phil couldn't get over how good Aunt Esther's pancakes were. She would dice apples and put them in the batter. Aunt Esther was watching me feed Phil Jr. his breakfast. She told me that my mother used to shove the food in my mouth. She always told me a secret that I've kept even now. It would hurt someone I love if it got out. The next morning we were getting ready to leave and our car wouldn't start. My cousin Paul (the mechanic) adjusted the automatic choke. We were on our way. That was the last time I was on the farm. When I was little, I dreamed of bringing my kids to the farm. We forget that our relatives get older.

One day when Phil Jr. was about nine months old, I can't remember why, but I spanked him hard. All of a sudden, I felt like my mother. I picked him up and rocked him. I was terrified that I had the same illness as my mother. One difference, I loved my son, and I'd would rather die, than have him hate me like I hated my mother.

At nine months, Phil Jr. was getting around in his walker. We took him to see his great grandmother Grace. She lived in a one room studio apartment. She had a lot of knick knacks around. She told Phil Jr. the same thing she had told his dad when he was that age. She told him that she was an old lady and that she couldn't keep getting up to slap his hands if he touched something he wasn't supposed to. Phil Jr. would go up to a knick knack and start slapping his hands.

One Sunday afternoon I walked over to Mom's with Phil Jr. I had to wait on the porch because Mom wasn't home from church yet. Phil Jr. was walking around the porch in his walker. All of a sudden he opened the screen door to our first apartment and went inside. I didn't know the person that was living there now, and how I was going to get my son. Then a skinny young woman came out on the porch. She invited me in for coffee. I accepted. That invitation would change my whole life. Her name was Denise and she was pregnant. She also had a five year old son, Nicky. Her husband was in prison. After I drank my coffee, Mom was home. Denise and I became friends and saw a lot of each other. I also found out that month, that I was pregnant again.

Phil Jr's first birthday. I baked him a cake in the shape of a heart. He was cranky because he hadn't taken a good nap. Shortly after his first birthday, the double oven stove got repossessed. Phil Jr. took his first steps at the Salvation Army chapel, almost in the same spot his dad and I were married. He was walking good at thirteen months.

Denise and I spent a lot of time together. Nicky loved playing with Phil Jr. One day Denise's uncle by marriage had come to visit her while I was there. He had just been divorced and was living in a rooming house close by. His name was Earl and Denise's husband was his nephew. He was in his early forties. There was something about him that made me uncomfortable. I couldn't put my finger on it. I would go sit on the porch or leave to avoid him. If I was on the porch, he'd come out to talk to me.

# CHAPTER FIFTEEN

One night Phil and I and Phil Jr. went out to visit Bobby and his wife, the couple we had taken the joyride to Maine with. We came home and there was a padlock on our door. The landlord had put it there because we were behind in the rent. I needed to get in to get some things for Phil Jr. We went to the police department. An officer came back to the apartment with us and asked the landlord to let us get some things we needed. The landlord let us take some clothes and baby things. We went back to Bobby's because we had nowhere else to go. Bobby said that we could stay with them, but they were moving to Houlton Me. in a week. We had a week to find an apartment which we couldn't do. During that week, Bobby convinced Phil that we should move with them, "and get rich on potatoes". I had no choice but to agree. So we packed up and headed for Maine. It was kind of cramped in the two cars with the four adults and Bobby's three kids, two boys and a girl, and Bobby's younger brother George, and George's American Husky Champ plus our belongings. When we got to Houlton we stayed with Bobby's aunt and uncle while we looked for a place to live. Bobby and Phil found an acre of land with a house and a cabin on it for six hundred dollars in a small town twelve miles outside of Houlton. It only had a town office that was only open two days a week. They were to go half, three hundred a piece. Bobby, Belle, the three kids and George took the house because it was larger. Phil and I got the cabin. Bobby's aunt gave us a wringer washing machine. We set it out in the yard. We had to haul water from a nearby stream. During the winter, we would have to use the Laundromat in Houlton. Our car gave out after the trip, so we were dependent on Bobby for transportation. Bobby and Phil raided gardens at night. I ate so many tomato and mayonnaise sandwiches. They got a job with a local farmer up the road. They siphoned gas at night from the potato trucks that they were going to need for work the next day! We had moved in early summer, and I was due in August. Bobby's aunt babysat the kids so that we could pick potatoes. Phil and I picked a hundred barrels one day at thirty six cents a barrel. Because of my pregnancy, the farmer put me on the harvester.

On August 9th, around midnight, I woke up with really bad cramps. Bobby and Phil took me to the hospital in Houlton. Bobby made the twelve mile drive in fifteen minutes. When we got to the emergency room, they didn't want to treat me because we were from out of state and had no insurance. Phil told them that he wasn't bringing me anywhere else, and that I'd have to have the baby in the lobby. Our daughter was born at three AM. I breast fed her because Bobby and Phil were without jobs. Bobby wouldn't get up one morning and they were late, so the farmer fired them. We got into a hassle over her name. From the time I got pregnant with Phil Jr. Phil said that if it was a girl, he wanted to name her after me. I wasn't crazy about that, because I really didn't like my name. All Bobby had to say that he didn't like the name, that people would call her Annie Jr. All of a sudden, Phil wants to change her name. I was so upset, he wouldn't change it for me her mother, but he would on just his friend's say so. I signed the birth certificate naming her after me, but with a different middle name.

After I was home a couple of weeks, Bobby and Phil got jobs again. I put Annie on the same formula that Phil Jr. had been on. In Maine, it wasn't like Connecticut., if you had a question about your baby you just called the doctor. Here in Maine, without insurance they didn't want to know you, especially if you were from Connecticut. Maine people felt that people from Connecticut were taking jobs away from them. I was feeding

Annie on formula. I didn't notice that she was sleeping more and had a lot of diarrhea. One morning I was feeding her and I thought that her eyes looked like they were sunk in. It was September and the nights were getting chilly. I needed to do some shopping and it was too cool to take a newborn in and out of the stores. I had only one friend that I trusted in Houlton. She was an elderly woman. I asked her to baby-sit the two kids while I went hopping. When I went to pick up the kids, she told me to get Annie to the emergency room right away. She had been a nurse. I think she knew what was wrong with Annie but she didn't tell me. Phil and I went straight to the hospital. The doctor admitted her without even examining her. He said that she was severely dehydrated. I was only eighteen years old. I had never heard of dehydration, only once, my nephew had dehydrated from the heat. The next day I went to visit Annie. I began to take her out of the crib so I could sit in the rocking chair and rock her. The doctor came in just as I was about to pick her up. He said that I couldn't hold her, that she needed all her strength. Her skin was so transparent. I went home. The next morning a state trooper came out to see us. He said we had to get to the hospital immediately. A Catholic priest had baptized Annie and gave her Last Rites. She had another bout of diarrhea during the night. I left the hospital and walked to the nearest Catholic Church to pray for my baby's life. When I got back to the hospital, I swear there was color in her cheeks. After that she continued to improve, and finally we were able to bring her home.

# CHAPTER SIXTEEN

Phil had bought a car identical to Bobby's. Both were black, the same model Ford and the same year. The only difference was that Bobby's was a four door and Phil's was a two door. The sheriff in Houlton had no use for Phil and was just itching to get something to pin on him. Every time something was stolen, he always came out to our place. One time the sheriff asked Phil if he had seen a truck load of Christmas tress that had been stolen. Phil told him yes, that it was upstairs in our bedroom. Also many people in Houlton knew how badly Phil was taking care of me and the kids. If you went to the end of our town road, there was a patch of grass shaped like a triangle. If you went straight, you went to Oakland, but if you veered right, it went to Houlton, The sheriff used to park on the grassy patch hoping to catch Phil going to Houlton. One day both Bobby and Phil were going down the town road at the same time. The sheriff was parked in his usual spot. The guys spotted him. Phil decided to go straight, and and Bobby went towards Houlton. The sheriff decided to follow the car going to Houlton. He was upset when he saw that he had been following Bobby. The next time the sheriff saw Phil in Houlton, he told him that he was going to slip up and that he'd be right there to nab him.

One night Phil and I had a large argument about his not working. Winter was coming and if he didn't get a job, we wouldn't be able to buy heating fuel. We were getting some government surplus food. I stormed out of the cabin and began walking the twelve miles to Houlton. The road was dark and there were strange noises. Then a pickup truck pulled over and asked me if I wanted a ride. I didn't know him, but he knew all about me, the kids, and Phil. He told me that he'd heard how Phil wasn't taking care of us. He told me that he was a selectman, and a widower. He had a dairy farm down state. He offered me a job as his nanny. I would have my own apartment large enough for me and the kids, all the dairy products I needed, and to do some simple chores around the farm, such as gather eggs and feed the chickens plus eighty dollars a week, which was good money then. He told me that if I agreed, he'd come with a tractor trailer for me and the kids and my things. I told him that I would do it. He drove me back home. The next day I had gone across the road to visit a neighbor. I didn't see the truck pull into our dirt driveway. Phil went out to meet him and told him that I changed my mind.

It was December and already had started to snow. On real cold nights we stayed at Bobby's because they had heat, or sometimes just the kids would sleep there. One night Phil and I were arguing. I climbed the stairs to the loft where we slept. I pulled down the bed and there was frost on the sheets! I told Phil that we'd finish the argument in the morning, and to come to bed so that we could keep each other warm. We slept with all our clothes on.

The neighbor that I had gone to visit and thought was my friend, called Child Protective Services and reported me and Phil. A social worker came out to see us. She asked us many questions, mainly what Phil was going to do about finding work. She said she'd be back in a week, and if things hadn't changed, she was going to place the kids. I called my Dad to ask him to borrow the money to go back to Connecticut. I wouldn't have asked him if it was just me, but I thought he'd do it for his grandchildren. My Dad told me that I had made my own bed now lie in it.

The social worker came back. the next week. She had bus tickets for me and the kids. Phil Jr. was two, and Annie four months. Phil didn't want to come, he wanted to stay in Maine. It was just about a week before Christmas. The day we were leaving, at the last minute Phil decided to come with us. I think the social worker knew he would because she had bought a ticket for him too.

Shortly after the bus left Houlton, Annie came down with a croupy cough. If she had been coughing before we left, I wouldn't have left until she was better. Passengers on the bus were whispering about what kind of parents were we, that we'd travel with a sick baby. We stopped in Bangor for supper. Phil Jr. wanted a milk shake so we ordered him one. He threw up on the bus the rest of the way home. I was glad Phil had changed his mind about coming with us or I really would have had my hands full.

We got back home, Phil called a cab from the bus stop to take us to his parents. The cab driver that picked us up was a minister of a small church. When we got to my in-laws, they wouldn't let us stay. They wouldn't even let the kids stay. My mother-in-law had to change Annie before she'd believe she was a girl. The minister took us to his church. In the basement he fixed us something to eat. He set up two carriages so that the babies could sleep. There was a couch. The minister told me to get some rest. He and Phil went to get Phil's job back and some groceries. It was the Christmas holiday weekend. The minister called a landlord that had furnished apartments about letting us stay in one until after Christmas. The landlord agreed. After Christmas the landlord said that as long as we paid the rent which was weekly, we could stay until we found a larger place. The city paid our first two weeks rent, giving Phil a chance to get a paycheck. He went back to work at the cafeteria which was just across the street. My mother-in-law was upset because she wanted to show her granddaughter off at church Christmas Day. She even had bought them new outfits. Christmas Day, Annie was admitted to the hospital with pneumonia. While she was there, the pediatrician told me he thought that she might be blind because her eyes didn't follow the light. He put her on a special formula to build up her immune system. I made an appointment with an eye doctor for her, but it would be four months before he could see her. While we were living in the two room apartment, my mother-in-law called Child Protection saying that there was no heat in our apartment. She had never been to the apartment and didn't know that the heat was included in the rent, but a social worker had to check it out anyway. My mother-in-law was hoping she'd get the kids. The landlord took his furniture out as we purchased second hand furniture for a larger place. We bought a camping cot for Phil Jr. to sleep on. He slept in the kitchen. The minister's church donated a crib for Annie.

We found a large one bedroom apartment next door to the library. Believe it or not, Denise, Nicky and her baby daughter lived next door. Her husband was out of prison, but left her because the baby obviously wasn't his. The apartment house was even closer to Earl's rooming house. He spent a lot of time at Denise's, and after we moved in, spent time visiting us. I still felt uncomfortable around him, but Phil liked him. I thought "he was a dirty old man." I had spent one New Year's Eve alone, because of him when he invited Phil to stay when Phil had given Denise and her husband a ride to Earl's house New Year's Eve party. Earl was still with his wife then. He knew that Phil was married and that I spent the holiday alone. I still blamed him for that.

The doctor put me on birth control pills. They were making me sick. Instead of Phil taking me back to the doctor, he flushed the pills down the toilet. The next month I had my period, but it was very light. Annie was seven months old now, happy and healthy. As far as development, she was only a month behind Phil Jr. which wasn't unusual since she had lost a month when she dehydrated. She was very spoiled though. I felt so guilty for almost losing her that I gave in to her all the time. When I had to leave her with a sitter, she cry, but she'd still be crying when I got back. The next month, I missed my period With three kids we were definitely going to need a three bedroom apartment.

We found one in the suburb of our town. It was a rundown two story house. It had been owned by an old woman that died. There was a family living upstairs. We moved into the first floor. I made a point of not telling Earl where we were moving to I made friends with the woman across the street. She worked at a diner that was open twenty four hours. She worked from eleven at night till three in the morning. She got me a job working the same hours as she. One night I was pouring coffee from the urn, and another waitress brushed up against me spilling the hot coffee all over my hand. The cook stuck my hand in the bucket of ice, and then the owner brought me to the emergency room. The doctor told me that I had third degree burns, and that my hand would be scarred. When I got back to the diner, I wanted to go home, but the dishwasher said that I didn't need to go home. He took me back to the kitchen and had me soak my hand in a bowl of apple cider vinegar for about a half hour. It took the burn out, not only that, it didn't even blister, and I have no scars. One day the owner and I got into an argument. It was Forth of July weekend. I walked out on him and started walking home which was about five miles. He came after me. We talked and I ended up working almost straight through the weekend.

Another time, the owner accused me of eating too much of his desserts. We were allowed a meal and some desserts except for the pies. I had just found out I was pregnant when he hired me, but didn't tell him because I wanted the job. Now that I was starting to show, I had to tell him. A couple of days later, he took me off the counter and put me in the back washing dishes. I quit soon after, I wanted to waitress, not do dishes. Not only that, but I needed the tips. One night a regular came in drunk. He put five dollars in quarters on the counter and told me to keep playing "Spanish Eyes" because he said it reminded him of my eyes. After about the third time he fell asleep at the counter. I kept the rest of the money One day when I was about five months pregnant, Phil's boss came to the house. Phil had an accident at work. A seven hundred pound foundation had collapsed and fallen on him. At first they thought he was dead. They didn't want to tell me until they knew that he was going to be alright. They were afraid I'd have a miscarriage. They brought Phil home from the emergency room. The back of his head was stitched up. He needed cigarettes and couldn't drive. I didn't know how to drive, and I couldn't get anyone to go for me. It would have taken me too long to walk with Phil alone with the kids. I got in our car, started it up and drove to the store. I don't know how I did it. I had to cross two heavily traveled streets twice. But I drove there, got the cigarettes and drove home.

Annie was sixteen months when Amanda was born I was due the day after Christmas. We had spent the whole month buying gifts for Phil Jr. and Annie. Phil and the kids decorated our artificial Christmas tree. One night when they were all asleep, I redecorated it my way. I wanted to be home Christmas morning to watch them open their gifts. I didn't care if I went to the hospital in the afternoon. I went to the hospital in the morning of December 28th. In the meantime my Dad had a new girlfriend, who had grown kids of her own. They were living together. They took care of Phil Jr. and Annie while I was in the hospital. I had no cramps but one terrific backache. They admitted me because I was past due. Come to find out that her head was toward my back. Unless I laid on my back, I had no pain. That night they let Phil in the labor room with me because I was the only one in there. We talked and played cards. After he went home, I could smell the nurses eating fried chicken. Amanda wasn't born until almost midnight on the twenty ninth. She was the spitting image of Phil. Amanda was almost that year's New Year's baby, but a baby boy was born New Year's Day night. I came home from the hospital New Year's Day. Amanda couldn't come home with me because she hadn't been in the hospital seventy-two hours yet. We went to pick up the kids at my Dad's. Annie looked like she was awful sick, so we brought her to the emergency room. The doctor checked her out and could find nothing wrong. I told the doctor that she had a new baby sister upstairs in the maternity ward, and that she had been staying with her grandparents He told me that what was wrong with Annie, that I had been away from her. The next day we all went to the hospital to get Amanda. Phil told me to wait in the car with the kids, while he went in to get her. A few minutes later, Phil came out without the baby. He said that they wanted some money on the bill before they'd discharge her. I started crying. Phil went back in. The next time he came out he had Amanda. He went back in two or three more times, coming out with formula, sweater sets, and crib blankets. I don't know what he told them, but I had my baby. Amanda was a very good baby, except suffered from colic. If she didn't quite finish all her bottle, I'd let Annie finish it. I'd sit right next to Annie on the couch, and help her hold her baby sister. She was never jealous of Amanda. One night after I'd been home a couple of days, there was a knock at the door. I answered it and it was Earl. When you had a new baby, they put your name and address in the newspaper. Amanda was asleep in the carriage in the living room. I never put my babies in a crib until they were three or four months old. I put them in a carriage right next to my side of the bed. I was so afraid of crib death. We showed Earl the baby and he visited for awhile. Then he left. A couple of minutes later, there was a knock on the door. I opened the door, there was Earl. He had been out in the hallway. He asked me if I was missing anything. I looked around, and nothing seemed to be missing. I then checked the carriage. It was empty. Earl had Amanda all wrapped up underneath his coat. I didn't appreciate him scaring me like that. The next week I started getting a diaper service that I hadn't ordered. The company told me that they couldn't tell me who was paying for it.

The doctor had told me when we got back to Connecticut to put cereal in Annie's bottle because she needed the extra iron and I wouldn't have gotten enough cereal in her by spoon. I did it, but didn't like the idea. I thought that it was a lazy way of feeding her. Now she was healthy I knew she didn't need the cereal in her bottle anymore, but didn't know how I was going to break her of it. One morning I gave her her bottle and she just threw it out of the crib. That was the last time I had to put cereal in her bottle. Changing her from baby food to table food was another matter. I had to decrease the baby food a little bit at a time or she wouldn't eat. My daughter wasn't going to do anything she didn't want to do until she was ready. She was stubborn, which was probably what saved her life. Her first birthday cake, she smeared all over her head. By a year old, she was on table food. Amanda on the other hand, loved to eat. I would just put extra on my plate, and sit her on my lap. I got to eat my food hot with the rest of my family Phil Jr. was four. We had bought him a pair of black cowboy boots. They looked cute on him because he had small feet. When he outgrew them, I gave them away after he was asleep. We bought Phil Jr. another pair of cowboy boots, but to him they weren't the same.

Earl was still coming to visit. One day Earl came to visit. He asked me to come outside to see his new car. There was a 61 navy blue Cadillac with long fins parked in front of the house. It shone in the sun, because he had just waxed it. Somehow it didn't fit in front of a house that had no paint on it. There was a fourteen year old girl that lived across the street. She sometimes baby sat for me. There was also one colored family on the street. Their daughter would also baby-sit sometimes. She had a little brother the same age as Phil Jr. They played together often. One day Phil Jr. told me that Patrick had told him that he couldn't play with him anymore until he got as black as him. Phil Jr. informed me that he wasn't going to take anymore baths until he was as black as Patrick.

We had some friends that lived in a low income housing project that we would visit. One day my girlfriend's five year old son told me that they were going to Maine to visit "his broken grandma". My girlfriend explained that her mother was in a nursing home in Maine and had lost a leg up to the knee from diabetes. She asked if Phil and I could find a baby-sitter for a weekend and go with them. The girl across the street was going to baby-sit at our house and her mother was going to help her. So we went to Maine for the weekend, and believe it or not, nothing went wrong until we got home. We got home about five in the morning. Phil told me to wait in the car, while he went in to wake up Tess, the baby-sitter. He said he didn't want to scare her. I waited and waited but Phil never came out to help me with our things. I finally went in the house. Phil had Tess pinned up against the bathroom wall and he was all over her. She broke away and ran home crying. Later she came and begged me not to tell her mother. I knew it was wrong, but she was so upset, I agreed. We had to move again, because Phil wasn't paying the rent. He was working, but went through money like it was water.

He always worked for these fly by night contractors doing aluminum siding. Phil loved it and was good at it. They were always supposed to pay him when the job was done, but never did. When he complained, they would give him some money, but not the amount they owed him.

# CHAPTER SEVENTEEN

We moved to a housing project that had once been army barracks. It was the same project that my first steady boyfriend Bill had lived in. Earl helped us move. We didn't have our bottled gas hooked up yet. That weekend was my twenty first birthday. Earl came with a pizza and put twenty one candles on it. Every time Phil went out to bring some things in, Earl would pull me into a corner and kiss me. He would come over sometimes when Phil was at work. He continued to make passes at me. Most of the time I could handle someone making passes at me, but it was to the point that Earl wouldn't stop. One night I told Phil about it, thinking Phil would talk to Earl and that would be the end of it. Instead, Phil told me why not give in to him, that he was a nice guy. Earl came over one afternoon. The kids were napping, so I had the shades drawn. Earl was kissing me, and I was getting aroused. I figured that I'd go with Earl to get back at Phil. I was too naive to know that he'd been cheating on me every chance he got. With my cheating, he'd have nothing to feel guilty about. I had cheated on Phil once before, but it was only the one time. I felt too guilty afterward. I went in the bathroom and came out with my pants off. We made love on my couch and it was beautiful. I actually saw fireworks. Earl and I began our affair. Earl would take afternoons off from work to see me.

One day, Phil and I had put the kids in their strollers and walked downtown shopping. It was a cool day and Amanda sat facing the outside of the stroller. Later that day, Amanda rolled off the couch and unto the floor. I didn't see any bump and she hadn't fallen that far. The couch was low. She kept crying and I couldn't calm her down. The neighbors on the other side of us heard her crying and threatened to call Child Protection on us. We brought her to the emergency room. The doctor checked her out, and said that she had a severe bout of colic. She must have swallowed air when we went shopping. He gave her some medicine to relieve the colic. When Amanda was seven months old, we had to move again for the same reason non payment of rent. With a boy and two girls, we needed three bedrooms. Earl helped Phil rent a truck and we moved to a third floor five room apartment in Terryville. Earl worked at a plastics factory in Terryville. I must have been about a month pregnant when we moved there. I purposely helped carry heavy boxes up three flights of stairs, hoping to cause a miscarriage. it worked. There was sixteen months between Annie and Amanda, and there would be sixteen months between Amanda and this one. Earl was still working on aluminum siding all over the state. He'd leave early in the morning and get back late at night. Sometimes he didn't see the kids for a couple of days at a time. Earl would come often after work, but otherwise I was alone day in and day out with three small children. I didn't have any friends I could go and see. or to go for coffee. The landlord lived on the first floor, and I really wasn't friendly with the tenants on the second floor. To top it off, we had brought roaches with us from the housing project. Earl and I continued our affair. By this time, he kept his room at the rooming house, but was living with Denise. He also had an elderly lady as a companion, and me. I don't know where my self esteem was, but by now I was in love with Earl, and he said he loved me also. The landlord and the tenants on the second floor knew that I was having an affair. I also think that they thought that Earl was related to Phil or I because of his age.

Even so, our affair continued. He had told me how bad his first marriage was and how he had lost everything. He had four daughters that he was supporting, but had no contact with. I was so naive. I believed that if I could give him a son, I could make all the hurt go away. One night after we finished making love, I knew that I was pregnant. I can't explain it, but I knew. I was right. I was pregnant. I began to feel guilty because I wasn't sure whether it was Phil's or Earl's. I told Phil that the baby might not be his, His response was that the baby was half mine, so that made it his. But the guilt was eating away at me, though I didn't realize it. Phil Jr. was getting hurt and I wouldn't be able to remember how it happened. Earl told me much later, that he didn't know what he'd find when he got to the top of the stairs.

The people on the second floor began banging on the ceiling, even when Earl and I weren't in bed. Once Annie was outside on the swings when Earl was there. The landlady came upstairs and said that I'd better get my daughter because she had a messy diaper, which she didn't. I think that she was hoping to catch Earl and I in bed. On one wall of the kid's bedroom I drew Snow White and the seven dwarfs in pencil and then colored it in with crayon. On the other wall, I drew Donald Duck, Mickey Mouse and Goofy. The drawings came out perfect. I craved strawberries, fried egg sandwiches with cheese on white bread, orange juice, and I drank a lot of black iced coffee. Earl was taking me to my doctor's appointments. On my sixth month visit, the doctor thought that I was carrying twins. Earl was excited, because twins ran in his family.

The landlady had reported me to Child Protection. A social worker came to see me. He suggested that I'd try to get a baby-sitter to get out of the house, even if it was just for a walk. Once in awhile I'd ask the lady downstairs to watch the kids for about an hour. I'd walk downtown to the dairy bar where Earl had lunch. He'd buy me lunch, then give me a ride home. A couple of times I went to meet him for lunch, Denise was with him. It was getting to a point that I was afraid to be alone with my own kids. I called Aunt Esther at the farm and asked her if just I could come and stay with her for awhile. She explained to me that her health was real bad, and she was almost an invalid from arthritis. About three weeks before I was due, we got an eviction notice for non payment of rent. One day my mother-in-law was baby-sitting the kids while I did some packing. Her mother was also living there with her and Dad. Dad and his mother-in-law didn't get along. Mainly because she would keep snacks in her room, and eat them in the living room without offering any to anybody. For a seventy something year old lady, she had a figure to die for. Mom called me later in the day, and said that Annie was giving her a hard time and that she couldn't handle her. I tried to get a hold of Phil and Earl to give me a ride to go get her, but I couldn't reach either of them. So nine months pregnant, I decided to walk. It was a five mile walk.

Someone stopped when I got to the center of Terryville and offered me a ride. I know it was because I was so pregnant, but I didn't know him so I refused. I was almost at Mom's and I stopped to take my shoes off because my feet hurt. I stayed at Mom's until Phil came to get me and the kids. My feet were so swollen I couldn't wear shoes for two days. After we were moved out, We stayed at Mom's, but her apartment was for adults only. She told her landlord that she was just watching the kids until I had the baby. One night, a day before my due date I went into labor. Earl was there visiting. Every time I had a pain, I went into the kitchen. I was hoping that Earl would leave so that Phil could call the doctor. I didn't want to create problems between him and Denise. I think she suspected that he was involved with me and her. Finally, Earl left. Phil called the doctor and he told me to go to the hospital. We had to go by cab, because again we didn't have a car. My son was born at quarter after four in the morning. I didn't feel like I had just had a baby, but rather like a monkey had been sitting on my back for so long, and finally gotten off. I called Earl at the factory on his morning break to tell him that I had the baby. He said he knew. He told me that night he had the worst stomach ache and it didn't go away until about four in the morning. I named the baby Paul Anthony. While I was in the hospital, I had to make arrangements for my three other babies to be temporarily placed in foster homes. I didn't even have a home to bring my new baby to. The doctor knew of my situation and only charged me half of his fee.

Phil's grandmother was awfully strict with kids. One day Phil Jr had asked her for some milk. She gave him milk and cookies. He drank the milk, but didn't want the cookies. She made him stay at the table until he finished the cookies. She also wanted me to take Annie's bottle away from her because she was three years old. I told Gram that now wasn't the time to take her bottle. It was her security, and she was going to a new home with strangers. Paul Anthony slept in a laundry basket while we were at Mom's. The day came when the social worker was there for me to sign the temporary custody papers and take my three babies. I resented and blamed Phil for having to place my babies. They were crying and begging me to let them go with this strange lady.

Phil and I and Paul moved into a furnished two and a half room apartment. Soon after, Things were so bad between Phil and I that we agreed to a trial separation. Earl and I were still seeing each other. One day Earl was at the apartment. My Dad and his girlfriend were living together now. Dad had gotten special permission from the church to divorce my mother. One day my step brother came to the apartment looking for Phil. His mother needed help putting a stove pipe together in their new apartment. Phil wasn't there of course, so Earl volunteered to go help her. Later, my stepmother told my Dad that Earl had made a pass at her. My Dad was a very jealous man and believed her.

After that Dad had no use for Earl.

Annie and Amanda were placed in the same foster home. Phil Jr. was in a separate one. On my first visiting day, I immediately took a dislike to Phil Jr's foster mother. She reminded me too much of Gram. I asked my landlord if I could bring him to live with me. He agreed, and even set up a twin bed for him. The social worker agreed, so Earl and I went to bring my son home. Paul was three months old, and already pulling himself on his stomach to get around.

One day Phil came by to visit the boys. One thing led to another and we made love. I also got pregnant again. Paul was only three months, and I didn't even have a home for Annie and Amanda. I didn't want this baby at all. When I was about two and a half months, I got bad stomach cramps. Phil called my doctor, and he said that I didn't need another baby, and to let nature take its course. At the same time, Earl had walking pneumonia. he gave me a half of a pain pill he was taking. The cramps stopped. I was determined that if I had this baby, I was going to give it up for adoption.

The government was renovating the apartments in the low income housing project. A two bedroom apartment was finished. Phil and I and the two boys moved in. We were going to give the kids the two bedrooms. We bought a sofa that opened up into a bed. I cleaned the apartment until it was spotless. The social worker came to inspect the apartment and said that we could bring Annie and Amanda home. Denise was also living in the housing project now, and Earl was still living with her.

The new baby was due on Halloween, two weeks after Paul's first birthday. The night before Paul's birthday, Earl took me grocery shopping to get things for the birthday party. Earl also took me for a ride because he said that I wouldn't be able to go out for awhile. I was going to have my tubes cut and tied while I was in the hospital. I hadn't changed my mind about giving the baby up. As I was unpacking my groceries, the bottom of the paper bag ripped open. A jar of spaghetti sauce broke, and there was sauce everywhere. It took Phil and I until three in the morning to get it cleaned up. When we finally went to bed, Phil wanted to make love. That morning Phil and the kids were in the living room watching cartoons. I was trying to feed Paul his cereal. I had bad gas pains, like I had to go to the bathroom.

Phil was watching me and the clock. Finally he said to me that he'd never seen gas pains come on time before. I wanted to be home for Paul's first birthday party. Finally around noon, Phil called the police to take me to the hospital. I had been trying to wait until Earl arrived for the party. He was upset with me when I hadn't let him take me to the hospital for Paul. While they were having a birthday party at home, I was having a baby. While I was in labor I knew that I wouldn't be able to have the baby and not see him or her. I told myself, that if you can take care of four, you can take care of five. Also I knew that I was going to have an operation, so that I couldn't have anymore. Earl came to the hospital while I was in the recovery room He had an artificial plant with him. The nurse was just bringing my baby boy to the nursery. She took the plant and handed Earl the baby. She told him that if he wanted to see his wife, that I was in recovery. He told her that he wasn't my husband. She took the baby away from him. When they brought me to my room, the plant was on the nightstand. I thought they were putting me in the wrong bed. The nurse described the man who brought the plant. She told me to be surprised, that he was acting like Santa Claus. I read the card and recognized Earl's handwriting. I named the baby Peter Joseph. We called him PJ for short I was nervous about the operation. I had never been operated on before. Phil said that I could change my mind, but I knew I couldn't. After I got home, I saw the pictures from the birthday party. You would have to be blind not to see that Paul belonged to Earl. He was a carbon copy of him.

When Paul was about nine months old, he developed a high fever and he was crying constantly which was unusual for him, plus he had a rash. I took him to the pediatrician. He told me that the rash was baby measles. He told me to give him baby aspirin and oatmeal baths. I did as he told me, but the next day he was worse. His fever was higher. I took him back to the doctor. The doctor was upset with me for bringing him back in, saying that he had told me what to do. The next day Paul was still crying and still had the fever. I called his doctor and told him that I was bringing Paul to the emergency room. I also told him that if it was more than baby measles, I'd have his license He told me that he was going to admit Paul. It turned out that Paul had a severe viral infection. The nurse asked me what his favorite food was and I told her egg salad. It probably was all the fried egg sandwiches I ate while I was pregnant with him. I used to give him some in a bowl, because he'd just pull the sandwich apart and leave the bread. One day when I went to visit him they had him in a playpen. I told the nurse that he knew how to climb out. That afternoon he stood on a rubber ball in the playpen and out he went. They found him crawling around in Maxi Care. I also told them that they needed to put a guard on his crib, because he'd climb out of that too. My mother-in-law had gone to visit him. When she left, she left the chair next to the crib. They saw him crawling past the nurse's station. The next time I went to visit, he was in a high chair. There was bread and saltines on the tray and floor, but no egg salad. There was also a guard on his crib. They put Paul on a meat formula, and I had to make it with spring water, in case it was the chemicals in the city water that caused his infection.

Earl would stay overnight sometimes. He'd hear PJ wake up for his two o'clock feeding He'd tell me to stay in bed that he'd feed him. Sometimes in the morning I'd find the two of them asleep in the chair. I was still punishing Phil Jr. too severely. This is one thing that I still have a hard time forgiving myself for. Now I know that I suffered from post partum depression and PMS. At that time, doctors didn't believe that there was such a thing as PMS. They thought that it was all in a woman's head. That still doesn't make what I did anymore right. PJ was very sensitive to my moods. If I was upset, he wouldn't take his bottle for me. Then I'd have to ask a neighbor to feed him.

When PJ was about seven months old, Earl was going to Maine on vacation. I tried to talk him into bringing me with him, but he said that he couldn't. His family would never accept me or our relationship because they were strict Catholic. I convinced him to take me as far as Farmington. I was going to spend the weekend with my girlfriend's family and visit her mother at the nursing home. I was going to take the bus home. We made love on the way in several places on the turnpike. He brought me to my friend's house. I didn't get to go to the nursing home because by Saturday afternoon, I was feeling real sick. While I was there, I was drinking coke like it was going out of style. I caught the Blue Line bus in Farmington. Later at one of the stops, an elderly gentleman got on and sat down next to me. He was talking to me nonstop about people I didn't even know. I was so sick, that I just wanted to be home. Finally, the gentleman said, that we could go to dinner and see a movie in Boston. This way we wouldn't have a six hour layover in Hartford. The bus depot in Hartford was in a very bad section of the city. I agreed because I didn't want to be alone in Hartford for six hours. When we got to Boston, I changed clothes in the ladies room, and we left for the restaurant. We had a nice meal. He paid for it. After dinner, we went looking for a movie theater. We walked past this building that had showgirls on a billboard. The gentleman said to me that I wouldn't have nerve to go into a place like that. I didn't understand what he meant so I told I would. We went back to the building and got in line. The doorman turned a couple of guys ahead of us away., but let us in. A waitress showed us to a table. I looked up at the stage and there was about twenty strippers! The gentleman saw the look on my face and said we could leave if I wanted to. I said no, I'd already seen them. The waitress came to take our drink order. The gentleman told her that he did not partake in any alcoholic beverages, but I could have a drink. I ordered a screwdriver and he a ginger ale. It cost him as much for his ginger ale than it did my drink. I hadn't slept in like thirty six hours. The gentleman offered to pay for separate hotel rooms, but I just wanted to get home. When we got off the bus in Hartford, a couple of black men were hanging around the terminal. One started to come up to me, but once he saw that I was with someone he walked away. The gentleman took me to breakfast, then we were back on the bus. I was going to Bristol, and he was going on to Bridgeport.

I got home and took a couple of over the counter sleeping pills. and went to bed. Later I got up to go to the bathroom, and everything was spinning. Phil checked up on me and said that I was burning up. Phil got a neighbor to watch the kids and brought me to the emergency room. The doctor gave me a prescription for antibiotics. The next day I wasn't any better, in fact my fever was higher. That day I had blocked off the living room so that I could watch the kids. I was trying to get Paul to get me a pamper so that I could change him when there was a knock at the door. It was the visiting nurse. This nurse was noted for taking kids away from unfit mothers. She called Phil and told him to come right home. Phil brought me back to the emergency room. This time the doctor told Phil to get someone to help me take care of the kids. Phil went to get his mother. She wasn't much help. I had to keep getting up and getting things for her. I was drinking grapefruit Tang. I couldn't get enough to drink. The next day, Mom called the emergency room because I was as red as a lobster. The doctor on call told her to get me to the emergency room, but not to let anyone examine me until he got there. The police brought me to the hospital. By now my temperature was 104 degrees. I remember seeing my social worker there. The doctor asked me if I could be pregnant. I remember telling him that I'd had my tubes cut and tied but forgot to tell him that I missed my period that month. He admitted me. He was treating me for a kidney infection. They packed me in ice. That night the doctor came to my room and asked me if I wanted to see my kids, that he'd arrange it. They couldn't get my fever down. Phil had to place the kids while I was in the hospital because he had to work. My fever started coming down a little bit. One day an orderly came into my room and began touching me all over. My doctor arranged for an obstetrician to examine me. He came while I was at an appointment in another part of the hospital. He didn't come back. I was in the hospital nine days. The doctor wouldn't let me bring the kids home because my temperature was still 101. He said that I needed at least a month to get my strength back. The next month I was talking on the phone, when all of a sudden a gush of blood was all over the floor. There was some spongy tissue mixed in it. I called the ER and they asked me if I could bring itto the emergency room. They did some tests. Apparently I had been pregnant in the scar tissue of one of my tubes. Slowly I got better, and we brought the kids home. Earl was upset that no one had called him in Maine to tell him how sick I was.

One day Phil and I had a big fight and he locked me out of the house. I had to get back in the house because my kids were inside. I kept knocking on the glass paned storm door, thinking that he'd get tired of hearing me knock and let me in. My arm went throgh one of the panes of glass and cut my left wrist. One of the neighbors applied a tourniquet until the police got there to take me to the ER. At the emergency room the doctor thought that I was lying on how I cut my wrist. He thought that I tried to commit suicide. Also the tourniquet had been applied wrong.

My next door neighbor and I became good friends. She had four kids around my kids age. Her baby was only two months older than PJ. One day we'd clean my house, the next day her house, and the third day we'd do something with the nine kids. Her husband worked at a store, so Thursday nights he'd have to work till nine. We'd hunt around for enough change to buy a quart of beer to go along with our cheese and crackers. She was from Wisconsin. Her and her husband had met at Bible college.

# CHAPTER EIGHTEEN

After Dad put Victoria in the girls school in New York, he brought Cynthia home to live with him and his girlfriend. My Dad was now too sick to work. His girlfriend was in charge of all the bills. She and my Dad moved every couple of months, because she didn't pay the rent. One time she applied at The Salvation Army for a food basket. I had been to their house a couple of days before, and her cupboards were full. Mom even asked me why she needed a food basket. My Dad never lived like that. He drank yes, but we kids always had everything we needed. I would take the kids to visit Dad sometimes, but we'd always end up in a fight. Eventually I stopped going. The only time I could visit my Dad was when he was in the VA hospital because he'd be sober. My Dad and Ruby decided to get married. One stormy Friday night in November, there was a knock at the door. Dad answered the door, and there stood Victoria looking like a drowned puppy. She was wearing only her clothes, a sweater and sneakers. She had hopped a freight train in New York, and hitchhiked from the train station in Meridan to Dad's house. She wanted to see her long time boyfriend. My Dad called the school to tell them she was there, and that he was keeping her for the weekend. He never sent her back. One time Ruby beat Victoria so bad that that she was black and blue. She told my Dad that Victoria and her daughter had gotten into a fight. Cynthia and one of my step brothers were becoming involved. They both moved out but at different times and found an apartment together.

Ruby knew that they were living together and kept it from Dad. Nobody told me that Dad didn't know they were living together.

My Dad went into the hospital. I went to visit him. My Dad had a sneaky way of finding out what he wanted to know, without you knowing it

He started asking me about my sister and step brother. He got out of me that they were living together. By his reaction, I realized that he didn't know. I left the hospital and drove to Cynthia and Dave's apartment to warn her that Dad knew they were living together and that I was sorry for telling him. When I got there, they weren't home. Ruby had gone to pick them up so that they wouldn't be there when I arrived.

The last apartment that Ruby and Dad had was only two rooms. The beds were for Ruby's kids and grand son. One of my step sisters had a baby out of wedlock. Victoria was married by this time, and Cynthia and Dave got married. My Dad was furious about Cynthia and Dave getting married even though they weren't related by blood. My Dad was in a coma at the kitchen chair in his underwear for three days before Ruby called an ambulance to take him to the hospital. My Dad was in intensive care, and the doctor said that it didn't look good. Ruby tried to get the doctor to agree with her that I shouldn't see my Dad. The doctor talked to Dad and Dad told him that he wanted to see me. We were in the waiting room. Ruby had her best friend there with us. Only one person at a time could go in for five minutes at a time. Ruby and her friend were taking bets on what time my Dad would die. Ruby told her friend that she had picked out Dad's casket shortly after they got married. My Dad did die. Aunt Esther and Uncle Harold came down from New Hampshire for the funeral. Dad had a military funeral. I don't know why, but I couldn't cry. My Dad was at peace and nobody could hurt him anymore. Aunt Esther really lit into me after the funeral. She said that I wasn't a very good daughter to him. I tried to tell her how very much I loved him, but she wouldn't listen. My Dad had been her favorite brother. Phil's dad had died when Phil Jr. was five years old. I didn't take him to the funeral. We just told him that grandpa was in heaven with Jesus. Annie was five years old, when my Dad died.

# CHAPTER NINETEEN

The Housing Authority gave us a three bedroom apartment across the courtyard from the two bedroom. The kids that lived on our end all played together in the courtyard. They were a mixed blend of white, black, and Puerto Rican. One day I had the kids outside with me while I hung out clothes. Suddenly I felt a ping in the middle of my forehead. Then I felt blood trickling down my face. One of my neighbors who was black, followed me into the house. Apparently her son had thrown a rock and it hit me. I was just thankful that it didn't hit one of my kids. She took me to the emergency room and paid my doctor bill. The doctor said that I shouldn't be alone with the kids at least for that day. Phil was driving a truck for a car parts company. He had a girlfriend that lived in the southern part of the state. I knew that he wanted to go and see his girlfriend. After the kids were in bed, I told him to just go. His girlfriend later on, got her car fixed using Phil's company credit card and took off to Arizona. He had to pay the repair bills, plus he lost his job.

I had a terrible fear of a dentist. I wouldn't go unless they put me to sleep. Over the weekend I had gotten a terrible toothache. I was holding whiskey in my mouth to try to numb it. Earl got a hold of my dentist and got him to prescribe some pain medication. It was strong and made me sleep. The dentist told Earl to give me one each time I woke up until he could see me on Monday morning. He and Phil looked after the kids. On Monday, Earl took me to the dentist and he pulled the tooth. The next day Phil and I got into an argument and he hit me in the mouth. I was still in a lot of pain. I didn't realize it, but I held my arm straight out and swung. I hit Phil just below the temple.

A tiny bit higher and I could have killed him. He hit the wall and slid down on the floor. Later I saw him taking some aspirin for a headache. That was the first and last time he ever hit me.

It was a stormy New Year's Eve. It was freezing rain and everything was nothing but a sheet of ice. At midnight, I had two men in my living room fast asleep, Earl and Phil. I weighed about two hundred and thirty pounds then. I said to myself, that I didn't like the way I looked, and nobody was going to do anything about it but me. My New Year's resolution was to lose the excess weight. I put myself on a diet, mostly of meat and vegetables but fixed differently, no frying, only baking or roasting. I didn't add anything to my vegetables. In two and a half months, I had lost twenty five pounds. My girlfriend was a good support system.

My girlfriend came across the courtyard one day for coffee. She had even taught me how to drink my coffee black. We talked, and then she broke the news. Her family was moving to Vermont. Her husband had got offered a better job as a traveling salesman. They were going to buy a trailer in Vermont because the sales tax was so low. I was heartbroken, though I understood. The day they were supposed to leave, I packed up the kids and went away for the day so that I wouldn't have to say good bye. I came home a couple of hours after they said they were leaving, but their plans changed and she was still there. They were leaving the next day. I couldn't get out of not saying good bye. She said we'd see each other when she came to visit her in-laws.

One night, this young woman who had a two year old daughter, wanted to go out bar hopping. I offered to keep her daughter overnight. I had five, what was one more. She turned me down and got a fourteen year old male baby-sitter. Her electricity had been shut off for non payment. About two in the morning I was waken up by red flashing lights. Phil and I got up and looked out the door. The young woman's apartment was on fire. The baby-sitter had lit candles for light. It was summer and the windows were open. A breeze blew the curtains over the candles and caught fire. The firemen found the baby-sitter's body in the closet, and the little girl was dead in her crib. Everyone in the project donated money, food, and flowers for the young woman. Phil and I went to the funerals. We went to the young woman's mom's house after the cemetery. The young woman changed into jeans and went out to a bar.

It was now time to enroll Annie in kindergarten. After a couple of months, I got a call from the principal asking me to come in and see him. He asked me to keep Annie home for awhile until they could get her tested by a psychologist and to save the teacher's sanity. Apparently there were only two girls in the class, and only one doll, It wasn't Annie's day to have the doll, so she literally destroyed the classrom. She tested borderline retarded. They put her in a special class for the trainable retarded students. After six months, the teacher called me to come in for a conference. She said that this class wasn't the right class for Annie. She could read, do math, and spell. So they tested her again. This time she tested a little higher. She had to go to a different school that had a behavior modification class. They said that she was socially maladjusted. Phil and I had taken her to doctors who ran different brain wave tests, but none gave us a direct answer as to what was wrong with her. She would have bad temper tantrums over something minor. If something did happen that should have upset her, she'd handle it with a grain of salt. The pediatrician put her on Ritalin. It helped, but when it wore off, she'd have crying spells, so he weaned her off it. She had been wearing glasses since she was three years old for a stigmatism. When she had a tantrum, the first thing she'd throw was her glasses.

I wanted to go to work. I wanted to be a nurse's aide. I applied at the local nursing home. There was no position open for a nurse's aide, so they gave me a job in housekeeping. The head of housekeeping I think took a immediate dislike to me. He gave me the two dining rooms, the staff dining room and the recreation room to clean and mop. These were large rooms that should have been mopped by a man. I did my best and managed to have everything done by three o'clock. One day he gave me a pink slip. his reason was I worked too slow. A few months later a position for a nurse's aide opened up, and I got the job. After a few months, the nurse's went on strike, and I was one of the strikers. The only thing I gained was that I lost my job.

The next Christmas Eve, I had gone to a church service. Phil was baby-sitting the kids. Just as I got home, one of Phil's black friends was there dressed up as Santa Claus. He was passing out gifts to kids in the project. Annie was looking at him and looking at him, then she said to Phil, "Guess what Daddy. The black kids have their own Santa Claus!" Greg, Phil's friend laughed so hard he peed his pants!

A couple of days after Christmas, I had gone to a neighbor's for coffee. Phil was watching the kids. The kids were upstairs and Phil noticed that they were awful quiet. He went upstairs to check on them. He found Phil Jr. and Paul in their bedroom closet with the door closed. Phil opened the door. Phil Jr. had pieces of wrapping paper and matches. He was lighting the paper for Paul to blow out. He grabbed both boys out of the closet. He spanked Phil Jr., something he had never done. He was crying when he called me to come home. He said all he could see was those two boys starting a fire and being trapped in the closet.

It had been about two years since my best friend moved to Vermont. We had kept in touch. One weekend I decided to take the three hour bus ride to visit her. She was going to meet at the bus stop and bring me to her house. I know weighed one hundred and thirty three pounds, When I got off the bus, she hardly recognized me. On the way to her house we past a drive-in theater. A Walt Disney movie was playing. Her husband wasn't able to make it home that weekend, so she gave me their bed. We spent the evening talking and drinking. When I went upstairs to get ready for bed, I looked out the window. You could see a blurred image of the movie playing at the drive-in. I called down to Cheryl and told her that a dirty movie was playing at the drive-in. She came running up the stairs asking, where, where. You have to remember that she had gone to bible college to become a minister. The weekend passed all too quickly. She put her kids in their car and gave me a ride home. She was going to visit her in-laws.

One day Cynthia called me. She had found our mother in Florida. Cynthia had kept in touch with our mother's side of the family after Dad died. She gave me our mother's address. She told me that it was up to me to do what I wanted to with it. I wrote my mother a letter. She wrote back. It had been twenty years since I last saw her or heard from her. We corresponded a couple of more times. I asked her the questions that I desperately wanted the answers to, mainly why did she abuse me. I never got any direct answers from her. She always found ways to get out of telling me what I needed to know

The project was getting more and more dangerous. Before it was just the upper end where the drugs and rapes, and gang fights were that was dangerous. Now it was moving toward the middle and soon would be down the bottom of the project where we lived. Phil and I decided that it was time to move. We moved back up to the old army barracks where we had lived before, until we could find a three bedroom apartment

# CHAPTER TWENTY

The only apartment available was next door to a Puerto Rican family. The manager asked me if we still wanted it, because Puerto Ricans usually have cockroaches and don't kill them. We took the apartment. The woman had seven kids and you could eat off her floor. Her husband was only home on weekends. One of her sons became my baby-sitter. His youngest brother was four years old, and still had a pacifier.

Paul was now about four years old. Earl had bought him a small bicycle at a tag sale. Earl took the training wheels off Phil Jr's bike to put on Paul's, but it made the bike lopsided. Paul tried to ride the bike with the training wheels on. He was getting really upset about the bike being lopsided and that he couldn't ride it. Earl took the training wheels off and leaned the bike against the house. Earl said that if Paul wanted to ride the bike bad enough he would. About an hour later, we heard Paul yelling for Earl and I to come outside. He was riding the bike.

I had a guinea pig. My baby-sitter fell in love with it. We named him Henry. I also adopted a medium sized female dog from the animal shelter. Every time she got the chance to get out she'd run, and not come back. I don't know how many times Phil Jr. was late for school chasing her and bringing her home. She only ate table food. The only time she ate dog chow was if I mixed it with homemade soup. She also only rode on the floor of the passenger side in the car. She only slept under my bed, never on top of it. She'd had to have been someone's companion. I think when she ran off, I think she was trying to find her master. I ended up giving her back to the shelter

One day Aunt Emma came to see me. She had a check for thirty two hundred plus for me. It was part of the ten thousand dollars from my father's estate It was Dad's share of my grandparents money. Dad's share was split between us three girls. Aunt Emma said that my Dad would have like to see me buy my own home with that money. Phil had never seen that much money all at once. We contacted a couple of realtors and looked at houses, condos, and even a trailer. We were always short about fifteen hundred for the down payment. With the money in the bank, it wouldn't be too long before the interest on the money would give us enough. Phil even asked Earl to go halves with us, but Earl was fully aware of how Phil paid his bills. Phil kept wanting to take money out of the bank for things we didn't need. It was in a joint account so he did make a couple of withdrawals. We had a huge fight when I found out. The kids were in the car, and Phil started going down the road at about ninety miles an hour. I called the bank because I wanted his name off the account. They told me that I would have to withdraw it, then redeposit it. I didn't sleep all night. I was at the bank at nine o'clock the next morning. I put the money all in my name. When I saw that I wasn't going to get my house, I decided to spend it on me and the kids. I bought a floor model color TV, stove, dishwasher. I took the kids on day trips. We went to Santa's Land in Vermont in July. When they say that money is the root of all evil, they sure are right! I had never been so unhappy while I had that money. My stepmother was upset because she wasn't entitled to any of that money. Cynthia told me that Ruby had forged our names and cashed in our insurance policies that my Dad had paid on since we were little. We could have cashed them in when we were twenty one. By the time I paid attorney and proved it in court, it would have cost more than the insurance policy was worth. So you see, I didn't do well in the stepmother department either.

We found a three bedroom apartment in the center on the west end of town. The good thing was Phil Jr. and Amanda didn't have to change schools. Earl said that it was a bad move because there was only a parking lot, and no back yard, plus it was on a busy intersection., but we took the apartment anyway. Again Earl helped us move. We gave Henry the guinea pig to our baby-sitter. He had a hard time talking his mother into letting him have it, because he shared a room with his youngest brother, and his brother was afraid of it. So Pedro took Henry to school. Then the teachers went on strike. Henry turned out to be Henrietta. He not only had to bring her home, but her babies too! He told me that his mother was talking so fast in Spanish that even he didn't understand her!

Paul went to afternoon kindergarten and PJ went to pre-school in the morning. For his birthday, the preschool sent PJ a birthday card. Paul was with me when I got the mail. He was so upset that there wasn't a birthday card for him. He went in their room and tore all the sheets and blankets off PJ's bed, crying that he even had to share his birthday with the little creep. I couldn't go to the drugstore and buy him a card and put a stamp on it. He was smart enough to know that there was no cancel sticker on it. I had to have two separate birthday parties because they both had different friends, I had Paul's birthday on the fifteenth, and PJ's on the sixteenth. I had a talk with my mother-in-law because she always sent Phil Jr. a birthday card, and also the other kids except Annie. She told me that she forgot Annie's birthday because it was in August. I told her that if she couldn't do for all the kids, I wouldn't allow her to do for any of them.

Phil was working second shift at a factory. One night I was giving Annie a bath. As I was drying her off, she told me that daddy had touched her peepee.

I called the police and told them what Annie had said. They told me to call Phil at work and tell him that he needed to come home because there was an emergency. The police brought Annie and I to the emergency room to get her examined. There wasn't a gynecologist on call to examine her and they couldn't get one in time to gather evidence. On the way home, the officer told me that what he was going to suggest, made him sick to his stomach. He told me that if I pressed charges and it went to court, they would rake my daughter over the coals. and most likely he'd walk anyway. Of course I believed her having caught him with my underage baby-sitter once. I started keeping a closer watch when Phil was around the girls. I tried not to leave him alone with them. One time I came home and Phil was in our bedroom with the girls. They were only dressed in their underwear. I didn't see anything that I could prove. The girls were laughing and jumping on our bed.

# CHAPTER TWENTY-ONE

One day there was a knock at my front door. I answered it, but didn't recognize the gentleman standing there. Then he called me "Button" then I knew that he had to know me. It was my Uncle David, my mother's brother. I hadn't seen him since I was about six years old. It was the only brother that Dad had liked. I invited him in. We talked about my mother. I was hoping that he'd have some answers to explain what she did to me. He told me that he had nothing to do with mother after she left us. He told me again, you can leave your husband or your better half, but you don't run out on your kids.

Earl was no longer living with Denise, and wasn't seeing the elderly companion anymore either. He was staying back at the rooming house.

Cynthia now lived only a block away from me. She had a baby daughter now. She called me to tell me that she had paid for our mother's plane ticket to come to Connecticut. I didn't know how I felt about seeing my mother again after twenty years. I was glad that Cynthia hadn't found her while Dad was alive. Our mother would be staying with the superintendent of Cynthia's apartment building. I went to Cynthia's to see her. We talked. I asked her questions that I wanted answers to, but she kept avoiding them. She tried to blame everything on my Dad. I told her that we maybe couldn't be mother and daughter, but maybe we could be friends. She bought each of us a initial pin from a jewelry company. Victoria couldn't seem to care that she was back.

We had a pool table in the basement that belonged to the tenant on the third floor. Earl got a set of lights at a tag sale for over the pool table. Sometimes our landlord and his son would come to shoot pool. I was getting better at learning how to shoot and get the balls in the pocket. One day while I was out, Phil and Earl were downstairs shooting pool. Suddenly they heard Paul screaming. They ran upstairs. Paul was bleeding profusely from his left arm. He had been outside, when some neighborhood kids started chasing him. He was running to get in the house when his arm went through the glass storm door. Earl wrapped Paul's arm in a towel, and both men jumped in the car to get him to the emergency room. In the center of town, a police cruiser put on his siren and was after them for speeding. Earl and Phil got to the hospital before the police. He needed over thirty stitches in his arm, both inside the arm and outside. Thank God he only had minor scratches on his face. After Earl replaced the glass with plexi glass. For a long time after, Paul wouldn't wear a short sleeve shirt.

One day I invited my mother to come for supper to meet my kids. Earl and Phil were shooting pool. My mother and I talked while I was fixing supper. After supper, Phil had to leave for work. Earl offered to give my mother a ride to Cynthia's. Earl must of stayed for awhile. About one o'clock in the morning, he let himself into my apartment and came rushing to my bedroom. His face was beet red and I had never seen him so angry. He told me that Phil had told my mother that he was going to divorce me and slap a paternity suit against Earl for Paul and PJ. Earl thought that I had told my mother that Paul was his, which I hadn't. Earl left as fast as he came in. After that I didn't see much of my mother.

One day at school, Phil Jr. had supposedly told one of his friends that I was sleeping with him. His friend told his mother, who called Child Protection. The next day, an older woman from the state came to see me. She told me what the complaint was. I told her that if I was that hard up, I'd pick someone up from the bar across the street. I gave her permission to talk to Phil

Jr. alone. He denied ever saying that to his friend From then on Child Protection would be in and out of my life.

Earl started spending more time at Cynthia's. He told me that they spent most of the time playing cards. A couple of times, Cynthia, Erica, the superintendent, Earl and my mother went out together. One time Earl brought her to see my Uncle Ray, her other brother.

I was still losing weight. I joined the fitness center at the mall. One day Earl was so sick, that he drove himself to the hospital, but didn't remember getting there. He wasn't admitted until four days later. He was bleeding internally from bleeding ulcers. The doctor told him that the medication he had been on when he had his elbow operated on, probably caused his ulcers to start bleeding He received eighteen pints of blood. He almost died. The doctor operated on him and made him a new passage way to the stomach. When he began to feel a little bit better, he called my mother to ask her to drive his car to Cynthia's I didn't drive at the time. My mother called me to tell me that Earl was in the hospital. She took me with her to see him. We had to wait in the hall while the nurses tended to Earl. While we were in the hall, my mother told me that Earl must care for her more than me because he called her first. The weight loss had given me more self confidence. I told her that if she could break up what Earl and I had for six years, than she was more woman than I was, but that I wasn't going to hand him over to her on a silver platter. I wasn't jealous of her, but I was jealous of her age. She was only five years younger than Earl, and I was twenty five years younger. When Earl was able to sit up in a chair, he'd often invite my mother to have supper with him. I'd be down in the waiting room until I could see him after she left because it had gotten to the point that we couldn't be in the same room together. One night Earl asked me if I would go to my mother's and pick up his mail, and car keys. and bring them to him the next time I visited. The next afternoon, I went to Cynthia's.

The only one home was Erica. My mother and sister were out. She asked me how Earl was doing, and told her that he was almost ready to come home. When I went to visit him, my mother had just left. Earl lit into me big time. He told me that he couldn't even ask me to do him a favor without getting into a fight with my mother. I told him that the only one that was there was Erica. I told him that I hadn't even seen my mother. I told him that this was no soap opera where you get mother and daughter both, then turned to leave. He called me back. My sister had been helping my mother break up Earl and I by lying for her. I understood why she did it. She finally had her biological mother back. She didn't need to look for mother substitutes any more, but I still couldn't forgive her. The next night, Earl invited my mother to supper again, only this time would be different. He asked her why she lied about arguing with me.

My mother told Earl that if he would promise not to have anything to do with me or my children, he could have her and anything she had. Earl told her that she didn't have a pot to piss in and that he had helped my Dad take care of her girls. He told her that she was no longer welcome at my home. He told me later, that he couldn't believe that a mother could hate her own child so much.

My mother moved out of Erica's after that and took a studio apartment in New Britian. One day I got a phone call from the city clerk of New Britian. Apparently my mother had applied for city welfare. She had put my name on the application as her dependent. The woman told me that if I was working, I'd have to send her my last thirteen check stubs. She also said that legally I was responsible for my mother's support. She also said that because of my large family, I probably wouldn't have to help support her. I told that woman that I would go to jail than to give that woman a dime. I told her that my mother didn't take care of me when I needed her, and I wasn't going to take care of her. She couldn't get Social Security because she wasn't sixty two yet.

Phil moved out. He had found a girlfriend. He brought me to the welfare office to apply for welfare. He waited in the car. I was able to receive welfare. The kids could see Phil whenever they wanted to because he was only a couple of streets away. His girlfriend was a para legal and had three teenage daughters. Phil and I decided to get a divorce. We were still friends, and just agreed that we had gotten married to young. We had been married eleven years. The kids were out of school for summer vacation. Phil called me and asked me if Phil Jr. and Annie could live with him and his girlfriend for the summer. I agreed. At the end of summer, he sent Annie home, but said that Phil Jr. wanted to live with him. Our court date was coming up for temporary custody of the kids. I had a lawyer from legal aid. The night before we were to appear in court, Phil called me and said that the hearing had been postponed because his lawyer couldn't be there. I called my lawyer and she told me there was no need to go to court if the hearing was postponed. Phil had lied to me. He went to the hearing and got temporary custody of Phil Jr. because I failed to appear. I called my lawyer, and told her what Phil had pulled. She advised me to do everything in my power to get Phil Jr. living back with me. She said the parent that had temporary custody usually got permanent custody. I called Phil and asked him to pick me up, that we needed to talk. He picked me up and we drove to the park so that we could talk in private. I told him that I wanted Phil Jr. back home with me when he got out of school. I told him that if he didn't, I would pack up the other four and deliver them at his doorstep. I told him that the kids weren't going to grow up separated. I was gambling that his girlfriend didn't want to raise eight kids and work too. Phil told me that he'd have to talk it over with his girlfriend first. I told him that they were our kids, not hers and I wasn't getting out of the car until I had his decision. He took Phil Jr. out of school early and brought him home. When we went to court, I got custody of all five kids. Phil had to pay ten thousand dollars in back child support or go to jail. He never paid it and never went to jail. He also had to pay me a dollar a year until I remarried. Sometimes Phil and his girlfriend took the kids for a weekend. They would go to New Jersey to visit her relatives. The boys had a male friend that sometimes took them to Vermont fishing.

# CHAPTER TWENTY-TWO

After a few months, Earl said that I didn't have anybody and that he didn't have anybody. If it was alright with me, we'd live together. He also told me that if there ever came a time when I wanted to make a life for me and the kids, he wouldn't stand in my way. He told me that he'd never get married again, but if he did, it would be me. So Earl moved in, but still kept his room at the rooming house. He also rented a garage there. He would have one or two tag sales a year.

One night Earl and I were coming home from the club. About half way home, he blacked out at the wheel. I guess adrenalin took over because I took the steering wheel and got his foot off the gas pedal and put mine on. The road had a long curve and bordered a river. I don't know how, but I got us home safe. I even parked his town and country station wagon right. The next morning Earl couldn't remember how we got home. I told him I drove us home and also parked the car.

One day I asked Earl to teach me how to drive. He said he couldn't but would pay for me to go to a driving school. I began driving lessons in February. One lesson we had to end early because it had begun to snow. I even got my first accident during a driving lesson. A town truck didn't stop at a four way stop sign. One lesson I did real bad, because I was sick. On my next lesson, I did much better. The instructor told me that after my last lesson, he didn't think I'd ever get my license. I told him I was sick. He said that I should have rescheduled. I got my license. I bought my first car. I was so proud of myself that I had found a car for a hundred dollars. It was a 68 Chevy Camaro. What the guy that sold it to me didn't tell me was that the car was impounded at the police station. It had been in an accident. The guy put the date on the bill of sale to be before the accident. I had to prove that I didn't own the car at the time of the accident.

Earl told me not to drive the car until he could get a chance to get it repaired. The damage was the fender on the passenger side. The fender was dented and was rubbing against the tire. The fender needed to be replaced. My best friend's boyfriend was a whiz with cars. He and Earl had a hard time finding a 68 passenger side fender at the junk yard. There were some for the driver's side. They ended up having to buy a 67 passenger side fender. Buddy was able to work on my car right away. The fender had to be made to fit. I was anxious to drive my car. I wanted to go to bingo just down the street. I easily could have walked. I took the car. I had gone too far under a red light. Without looking if anyone was behind me. I put the car in reverse and bumped the grill of the car behind me. Of course we exchanged insurances, and I just got a warning. I drove the car back home and parked it in the parking lot. Finally my car was fixed. I was nervous about driving it, even to the gas station down the street. I didn't put the kids in the car. I was afraid of an accident. Eventually I got over that. One day the kids and I were going down the road. Suddenly, Phil Jr. says,

"Mom! we're going as fast as everybody else!"

I took the kids to the drive-in movies and up to West Peak Tower. It had a castle tower at the top. It was the highest peak on the east coast. On a clear day you could see three towns. Then my radiator began to leak one day on the road to the tower. I used the melted water in the ice chest to get me down the mountain to a pond where I could get more water. Until Buddy could fix it, I kept jugs of water in the car.

I began to notice that Earl was drinking quite a bit. Sometimes the first thing in the morning, he'd mix a drink. One day he was drunk and we had an argument. He made the remark that his taxes were paying my welfare check. I decided the next day I was going to look for a job. My girlfriend and I walked or took the bus putting in applications everywhere. I had heard that there was a nursing home that was so short of help, they were literally hiring off the street. It was the first time I had ever hitchhiked. Luckily the guy that gave us a ride was someone my girlfriend knew. We both got jobs. After I washed my hair, I set it. Earl asked me where I was going. I told him that I had a job, that I was going to start the next day. I told him that his taxes weren't going to be supporting me anymore. He tried to talk me out of it, but I would have had to look for work anyway once PJ went to school all day. The state paid so much for a baby-sitter. My first day of work, there was an aide working only a half of day to train me. In the afternoon I was on my own. I'm surprised that I never dropped a patient. My first week I worked fifty six hours. I loved my job. It made me feel good that I was making someone clean, dry, and comfortable. On the the days that I had extra time, I would set a woman's hair and apply makeup. There was a nurse that didn't like me. Sometimes if Annie's behavior was out of control at school, I'd have to leave work, sometimes leaving my assignment for the other aides to pick up. When Annie was that out of control, a baby-sitter wouldn't be able to handle her. The Director of Nurses went on vacation. One Thursday before leaving work, I read my schedule. It was written in pencil. I thought I had Friday off. I went to Buddy and Sam's for the day. The nursing home called, but they called the wrong house. Now that Phil and his girlfriend were married, we both had the same last name. My brother-in-law answered the phone and said that I left for work, thinking that they were calling for Phil's wife. The nursing home called again later. This time Phil's wife's daughter answered the phone. She told them that her mother had left for work. They let me work that weekend. On Monday, this nurse told me I was fired for failure to call in. She didn't have the authority to fire me. The nurses and some of the patients went to see the administrator on my behalf. He called me and offered me my job back. I told him that I had another job, making more money. Eventually, sometime later, I went back to work there. The Director of Nurses asked me what happened the last time I worked there. I told her. She asked me why I didn't wait until she got back from vacation to talk to her.

The family that moved in upstairs over us had been burned out of their last apartment. It was quite a coincidence that no one was home at the time. Both husband and wife had been arrested for collecting fire insurance from two companies. When they moved in, they redid the whole apartment, bought all new furniture, and he bought a new pick up truck for his aluminum siding business, plus two vehicles for two of his five kids. This meant that they had three vehicles. It was a six apartment house with one parking place per tenant. One time when I pulled into my parking place I accidentally touched the fender of his truck. There was mo dent or scratch, just a small line of red paint that an SOS soap pad would have removed. My car insurance had elapsed the day before. He had a brand new fender put on his truck and charged me a hundred and twenty three dollars. One morning I was driving to work, when a lady in the next lane shouted to me that I was leaking gas. I was closer to work, than home, so I continued on to work. Luckily no one threw a lit cigarette out their car window. I told them about the gas leak at work. They called the fire department to clean up the spilt gas. I called my girlfriend's boyfriend Buddy. They lived about two minutes from work. He came and picked up my car, and brought it to his house. He looked at the gas tank. It was a clean puncture as if made by an ice pick. I couldn't prove it, but I'm sure someone upstairs punctured my gas tank. They thought that I'd junk the car, and they'd have an extra parking place. Earl bought another gas tank from the junk yard, and Buddy put it on. It was Buddy who kept my car on the road. I paid him, but not what a garage would have charged me

One Christmas Eve, they were predicting a severe snowstorm. I had to work second shift at a nursing home about fifteen miles from home. I asked Earl to take me to work and pick me up. He had a Town&country Chrysler wagon. He told me no, to take the main roads all the way home. When I got out of work, the snow was half way up the back door. I cleaned off the car, and I couldn't even tell if I was out of the parking lot it was snowing so hard. I couldn't even see the road, the plow hadn't been by yet. I drove about twenty miles an hour. Once in awhile I was able to follow someone's tail lights in front of me. The plow was plowing the opposite side of the road. I get to town and I had to climb a hill. Half way up the hill, I slid off the road. I didn't hit anything and I wasn't hurt. I had a cross pendant that I always wore. I took the cross in my hand and prayed to God to get me home safely so that I could spend Christmas with my kids. I took a deep breath and put the car in low gear. Slowly I got back unto the road. I knew that I'd never make the next hill, so I took a main road that was flat. This road was plowed almost clear as was the rest of the roads I needed to take to get home. What would normally take me twenty five minutes to get home, took me an hour and a half. I parked the car on the side of the road because I couldn't get in the parking lot. I went in the house, thinking Earl must be worried sick about me. Instead he was asleep in the recliner. I woke him up and told him to never tell me I couldn't drive!

One night I went to a party at Phil and his wife's apartment. I was drinking, but I didn't think I was drunk. It hit me when I went out into the cold air. I only had to go down the street to get home. I started down their street. The road had a curve. I didn't make the curve. I ran into the snow bank. It took me awhile to get myself out. I made it home. The next day, I go to get in the car to go to work, and noticed that the front tire on the passenger side was leaning on its side. I had bent the tie rod when I went into the snow bank. My landlord gave me a ride to work, and I rode home with one of the girls I worked with. I had to junk the Camaro. The next car Earl helped me buy was a green Chrysler. We bought it from a private owner.

# CHAPTER TWENTY-THREE

When Paul was six years old, he had his own customers that he shoveled snow for. He'd be out all day, using some of his money to buy lunch. One day the owner of the shoe store told Paul that he'd pay him to shovel the front of his store. There was a bridge next to the shoe store. Paul shoveled the brige. He went into the store to get paid. Paul told him that he owed him for the front of the store and the bridge. Dom told him that the bridge belonged to the city. He told Paul that the city would have to pay him, with no idea what my son was going to do. Paul walked the block to city hall and went to the city clerk's window. He told her that the city owed him for shoveling the bridge. I think the woman paid him out of her own pocket. Dom at the shoe store would give me a break. I was on welfare and it seemed like all five kids needed sneakers or shoes all at the same time. I'd walk into the store with the kids, and Dom would tell me there was an instant sale. He'd take a couple of dollars off each pair. Paul would even offer to take his sisters' turn at dishes if the paid him. He didn't waste his money, actually he was pretty tight with it. Sometimes when Earl got home from work, he would empty his pockets of change all over the floor. The kids would scramble for the change because whatever they got was theirs. Once when Paul was about eight, Earl played a game of penny ante poker with him, letting him win on purpose. Paul was so excited that he had won all those pennies. The next game, Earl played for real and Paul lost most of his pennies. He was very upset. Earl explained to him that he wanted to show him that it was easy to win money, and just as easy to lose it. When Paul was eight years old, he won second prize at McDonald's for drawing the starship Enterprise. Earl was so proud of him. He took Paul to the toy store to pick out his prize.

I made a friend that lived a couple of streets away. She had a brand new baby. She had just come out of the state mental hospital because she would forget to feed the baby. This baby was diagnosed as a failure to survive baby. She seemed better now. I spent a lot of time at her apartment. I confided in her about the problems I was having with Earl because of his drinking. One night Earl and I got into a big argument, we were both drunk. I was drinking Scotch, which my system doesn't tolerate whiskey very well. There was a knock at the door. It was a police officer saying that he got a call that someone needed to go to the hospital. We told him that nobody here had made the call so he left. The next morning, I woke up around noon, still feeling drunk. Buddy's girlfriend had come to visit me. She saw that I wasn't up which was unusual for me. She got PJ ready for pre-kindergarten and put him on the bus. I walked into the kitchen and my social worker was sitting at the kitchen table. She told me that she'd gotten a call saying that I had taken an overdose of pills. I only had two prescriptions, both from my gynecologist. One was Empirin with codeine, because I had severe pain in my legs during my period, and the other was an anti depressant. Apparently my friend up the street flushed one of my prescriptions down the toilet and called the state and told them I overdosed. I checked my prescriptions, and the anti depressant bottle was empty. If I had wanted to kill myself, I would have taken the Empirin with codeine. The social worker told me that I was signing temporary custody papers for the kids to go to foster homes, and I was going to the state mental hospital. She had called the Red Cross to drive me there. I was to sign myself in when I got there. I was sober by the time we got there. They took me up to the locked ward. What saved me was the blood test they take when you're admitted. There was no medication in my system just a heck of a lot of alcohol. I told the doctor that I absolutely refused to take the drug Thorazine. That drug fries your brain, and you have no chance of getting better. He put me on a low dosage of Elavil instead. Earl and my landlord came to visit me on locked ward. I thought my landlord came just for the rent. I told him that Earl was paying my bills while I was there. He said that he just wanted to make sure that I was alright. On the second day, one of the staff took us to cooking class. One of the patients snuck out a can opener, and another a can of cherry pie filling. I was in a room with three other patients right across from the nurse's station. That night, we took one of the sheets off one of the beds and spread it on the floor. We had the goodies our visitors brought us, plus our can of cherry pie filling. What I saw on that ward was hell on earth. I saw orderlies purposely agitate a patient so that they could put them in a straight jacket. Patients were zonked out on the hallway floor and in the restrooms. You were supposed to stay on locked ward for five days. After two days the doctor put me on open ward. You had more privileges. I was smoking again and they let me keep my cigarettes. Most of the other patients could only have one an hour and had to go to the nurse's station for it. One night I got up and went into the dayroom. You weren't supposed to smoke in there or the restrooms. I lit a cigarette. Even being a smoker I could smell it. I hurriedly put it out and went back to bed before I got caught. They checked your mouth thoroughly to make sure you swallowed your meds. They wrote down everything you said or did and how much you ate. You could go outside and make phone calls. I called and talked to my kids. I made a leather bracelet in occupational therapy. The person in charge of my ward on the second shift and I became friends. She was a colored woman they called "Pepsi" She got permission to take me to an indoor carnival in town. I stayed up later than the other patients so that her and I could play cards. She taught me a couple of versions of the card game "Setback".

You had to sign yourself in for ten days, but the doctor could keep you an extra five days if he wanted to. My doctor decided to keep me the extra five days, because Easter was coming, and the kids wouldn't be home. The night before I was supposed to be discharged, Pepsi and I were playing cards. I was coughing because I was coming down with a cold. Pepsi said that she was going to tell my doctor that I was sick so that I would have to stay. She was joking of course.

While I was in the hospital, the woman with the baby had called a storage place saying that she was my sister, and needed my furniture stored. She also called the light and phone companies and tried to get my services disconnected. If it wasn't for Earl, she would have gotten away with it. If I didn't have an address, I wouldn't have been able to come home. One day she came with her baby in the stroller to my apartment. Earl was cleaning the kitchen floor. He had everything but the stove and refrigerator out on the back porch. He let her walk into the kitchen. Once she was inside, he gave it to her with both barrows. He also told her that he was going to tell her husband what she had done.

The doctor wouldn't let me bring my kids home for a month. I'll never forget the feeling of being able to take a walk and not worry about going off the grounds. The first visit was about two weeks after I came home. The girls and my boys were in separate foster homes again. We went to visit the girls first. Then we went to see the boys. When Phil Jr. answered the door, the three boys were standing there. Phil Jr. and Paul gave us a big hug and kiss. PJ had this strange look on his face. Phil Jr. told him that I was mommy. PJ was five and even though I talked to him on the phone from the hospital, he had this idea that when you went to the hospital you died. The foster family had a full-blooded chocolate-faced Siamese cat named Chee Chee. They were looking for a home for her, because she was going after the litter of kittens she had. The cat had taken a liking to Paul. She slept with him every night. They asked us if we wanted to take her. They had her spayed and she was declawed. The foster mother said that she'd be good company for me until the boys came home. On the way home Earl mentioned that we had forgotten the cat, and wanted to know if I wanted to go back for her. I didn't trust her because she was Siamese, so I said no, that she was okay where she was. The state didn't want to give me back my kids. I was so upset one night that my neighbor and a woman that was visiting her came downstairs to my place for coffee. The woman suggested that I contact her lawyer, and that he wouldn't charge me for the consultation. I made the call. He told me to go to the state office and tell them I wanted my children home. He said that they still could take me to court, but it would take them awhile. He said to tell them I wanted the kids until then. Well, he must have called our state office before I got there. The supervisor called me into her office. There was a sign "No smoking" and she offered me a cigarette. She asked me when I wanted to pick up my kids. It was the middle of the school week, so I told her I'd bring them home on Saturday. The next visit we were bring the kids home. We went and got the girls first. When we went for the boys, the foster mother mentioned that we had forgotten the cat. She said that if we didn't want her, they were going to have her put to sleep. I didn't feel right about that, so we took the kids and the cat home. It was a long ride, but the cat was good. I scratched her under the chin. She seemed to like that. I was thinking where she was full-blooded I wouldn't have any trouble giving her away. When we got home, the cat went straight underneath our bed. I had to feed her and put a litter box under there. Slowly each day she come out for short periods at a time. By two weeks she was used to the house, and we were used to her. She went to the door like a dog when she needed to go out. She slept with the boys until Earl went to bed. Then she'd sleep in the crook of his arm under the blankets. If I went to bed later than Earl, she'd meow when I got into bed.

She was even good with a guinea pig I had bought as a baby. Rusty was very tame. I tamed her by picking her up a little bit each day. When Earl would come in the door from work, she'd squeal. He'd take her out of the cage. She'd crawl into his shirt pocket and go to sleep. I mated her once with one of the guinea pigs the woman upstairs was raising. I had to take her babies away from her because she was biting them. Rusty lived to be ten years old, which is three times their average life span. I think her heart just gave out. Earl was so hurt when she died. He had a special knack with animals.

# CHAPTER TWENTY-FOUR

The family that charged me for a new fender for his truck, had moved to Maine. He was from Earl's hometown. He opened a nightclub there but he went under. They moved back to Connecticut, and got their old apartment back because it was vacant. We became friends and their oldest daughter babysat for me. I even had an eighteenth birthday keg party for her brother. I charged two dollars a head and checked ID's It was also the first time I tried pot. I had weird dreams from it. I saw walking trees. It was enough that I never tried it again.

The six month waiting period for Phil's and my divorce was finally over. I couldn't help thinking of the good times we had, and the good things about him. I wasn't sorry we were divorced, but it was like a death of an eleven and a half year marriage. You do go through some of the stages of grief.

Call me crazy, but I wanted to give Earl another child that he could claim as his. The gynecologist that I saw for my painful periods, was experimenting with inserting plastic tubes for women that wanted to get pregnant after they had their tubes cut and tied. He examined me and took X-rays and said that I'd need a complete hysterectomy. I had tumors and cysts. One cyst was the size of a grapefruit. I wasn't sure that this is what I wanted. I was afraid that it would make me less of a woman. The doctor told me that the pain in my legs when I had my period, would get worse. He said that I wouldn't be able to get out of bed until the pain medication kicked in. He was right. A couple of months later, the pain was so bad, that I couldn't get out of bed until I took my pain medicine. Nothing scared me more than not being able to walk. I called and made the appointment to have the operation. I weighed one hundred and twenty two pounds when I was admitted. I had also gotten my period. I thought that they might have to postpone the operation, but no, I was good to go. He wanted the state to approve another surgeon who could remove some of the excess skin from all the weight I lost. He could have done it while I was open for the hysterectomy. The state wouldn't approve it because they considered it cosmetic surgery. I didn't wake up until the next morning. I had complications. My blood pressure instead of going up and stabilizing was dropping. I know the doctor asked me when I was in his office if they had taken my appendix out when they cut my tubes. He said that it didn't show up in the X-rays. I told him I didn't know. Nobody had told me. Because I never had medical insurance when I was with Phil, they only did what absolutely had after the birth of my babies. I never even had a D&C. When I woke up the next morning, my doctor was asleep in a chair at the bottom of my bed. His head was on the bottom of my bed. He had been there all night. The other bed was empty. My doctor told Earl that he could stay as long as he wanted to, and if he got tired, to lie on the other bed. The doctor woke up when he felt me stir. He asked me if I was going to stay with him or not. I told him only the good die young He explained to me that I had lost a lot of blood, and my appendix wasn't where it was supposed to be. He had to go looking for it when he had me open. Somehow it was behind my liver. I had more pain on my side than I did on my bikini line. For the first couple of days I was on a liquid diet. When I could eat, we bickered over my diet. I wanted a low calorie diet, but all he'd agree to was low fat milk. I would save my supper for Earl to eat when he came. I was also on hormone pills. I had a fear of gaining all my weight back. I was to have no visitors except for Earl and no phone calls unless it was an emergency. Somehow, my social worker got through the hospital switch board. She accused me of having a nervous breakdown and going to a hospital in New Britian so that she wouldn't find out. When I told her that I was operated on and almost died, she apologized. When my doctor found out she called, he was livid. He told her supervisor that he didn't care if she was the President of the United States, that when one of his patients needed complete rest, that's what he meant. The next day my social worker sent me a dozen of roses She couldn't do anything because my baby-sitter was eighteen years old. She took care of them during the day, and while Earl was visiting me at the hospital. She probably charged the state for them. I finally got a roommate. We both liked watching TV. The television was supposed to be shut off at eleven o'clock. We would bribe this plump third shift nurse with goodies to let us leave the TV on. We were out of luck on her nights off. The doctor kept me in the hospital nine days because I had five small children at home. When I got home and was situated I washed my large kitchen floor, which was something I wasn't supposed to do yet. Phil Jr. was a big help. He was ten. He kept the house presentable. I sent Earl to the store for easy things to eat, like sandwich meat, and chips and paper plates and cups. It was summer time. Earl paid for the boys to go to summer day camp at the Boys Club which was just around the block. So I just had Annie and Amanda who were eight and nine at home during the day. My social worker came to visit and offered to get me a homemaker. I told her we were doing just fine without one. Two good things came out of my hysterectomy, I already had my family, and no more PMS. I was a much better mother.

# CHAPTER TWENTY-FIVE

I was obsessed about gaining back the weight. Two weeks I had put on ten pounds without going off my diet. I called my doctor and he lowered the dosage of my hormone pills. Earl was getting upset with me, because when we went out to eat, I'd order a low cal meal and salad. He said that he wasn't going to take me out to eat anymore. He said that I could eat salad at home. So I began to order regular meals. When he wasn't around or if he was, I'd go outside and make myself vomit by sticking my finger down my throat.

I also started dating. Earl had made it clear that we would never get married. I began dating Buddy's girlfriend's older brother. Her and I were best friends. She set up a blind date for me and her brother. It was the first blind date I ever had. The woman who had called the state about my sleeping with Phil Jr. and I were friends. She didn't know me when she made the call. She was a single mom with five kids, three boys and two girls, like me. Our kids were all about the same age. We'd exchange baby-sitting. If I had a date, She'd have all ten kids overnight, and if she had a date, I'd have the ten kids. Sam's brother was much better looking than her and stood six foot three. The girls upstairs helped me get ready for my date. They did my hair and make up and helped me chose what I was going to wear. I even borrowed a pair of platform shoes so that I'd be taller. I was only five three. We hit it off. Come to find out we were both Aries, I was in the beginning and he at the end. We went out to eat and then to a movie. The Disco Age was in full swing, so we often went to our favorite disco club. Aries is the ram, and usually two Aries will lock horns. Dennis and I knew each other well enough that if one was talking about an unpleasant topic to back off and change the topic of conversation. He was divorced with three kids. He still loved his ex wife but couldn't go back to her because she was living with a black man, and that he couldn't stand. One day I invited Dennis over for dinner, thinking he might enjoy a home cooked meal. I told the kids to be on their best behavior. The three older kids sat at the table with Dennis and I. Paul and PJ had their own little table. The kids were good, using their manners. Dennis remarked about how well behaved they were. Then leave it to Annie, she told Dennis that if they didn't behave, I was going to kill them. Dennis just laughed. His middle name was Herbert. The kids started calling him "Herbie the Love Bug." Earl babysat sometimes for me when Dennis and I went out. The trouble was, Earl liked him. I think that he thought if Dennis was a jerk, I'd find out my own way, and that would be the end of the relationship. We began arguing about my going out with Dennis. I told Earl that I loved him, but wasn't going to waste my life on a man who wasn't going to marry me.

That New Year's Eve Earl and I went supposed to go to the party at the VFW club which we did just about every year. Earl had been drinking all day, and by supper time he was in no shape to go out, he'd already had too much. We ended up in an argument. He said that he wasn't going to take a whore like me out for New Years. I called Dennis to see if he had a date. He said no, so I asked him if he would take me out. I asked my friend to keep the kids overnight, because she wasn't going out. He picked me up and we went to the disco club. Our picture and that of other couples came up on a big screen. When the evening was over, I spent the night at Dennis' There was no commitment between us, just good friends, but we did have an intimate relationship. I got home around noon New Years Day. Earl had picked up the kids from Bree's. He had a turkey in the oven and was doing my laundry. He didn't ask me any questions, and I didn't volunteer any information. After Dennis and I stopped dating, I began dating someone else. At first he

118

was nice. He brought me and the kids to the ocean. Annie got upset because the new sun hat I bought her fell in the water. To Mark, two of the kids had misbehaved. We stopped for lunch, and he wouldn't buy the two kids lunch. I stopped seeing him after that. But he began stalking me, like parking across the street from my apartment, and following me everywhere I went. At that time stalking wasn't against the law. The police said that until he threatened me, there was nothing they could do.

# CHAPTER TWENTY-SIX

Earl was at the club one night. The kids and I were watching TV. Phil Jr. who was ten asked me a question. He wanted to know what was normal between a man and a woman. I'm thinking okay, "facts of life" time. He told me that his dad had put his penis up his rear end and that it hurt. When Phil Jr. started talking, so did Annie and Amanda. They told me that their dad wanted to teach them how to have sex with each other and watch. I couldn't believe what I was hearing, but I knew the kids were telling the truth. I called the police and they came and talked to the kids. They also believed them. They asked me for a recent photo of Phil. After they left to pick Phil up, he called me before they got there. He had a police scanner and knew the police were looking for him. He threatened to kill me and the kids if I didn't drop the charges. I called my friend Bree and told her what had happened. I asked her if she could watch the kids until Phil was in custody. Bree lived about four houses down on the opposite street. Phil didn't know her. I told Phil Jr. to make sure that they all held hands and go through the back yards to Bree's. I called Earl at the club and asked him to come home. One good thing about Earl. He would never have the bartender lie for him and tell me he wasn't there. He knew that if I called him, it was important. Earl came straight home. I also called the police back and told them that Phil had threatened me and the kids. They didn't have him in custody yet, even though he only lived two streets away. He wasn't home when the police got there. The police asked Earl if he could stay with me. They said it was none of their business where he slept. We kept looking out the bedroom window every so often. There was a cruiser parked in the parking lot across the street from my house. It was there until three in the morning. I also got my mother's telephone number from Cynthia. I called her and told her what happened. I knew that she couldn't change it, but I just wanted to feel like a little girl again and have her tell me that it was going to be alright. She was my mother, she owed me that. She told me that I made my bed, so lie in it. I told her that I'd never ask her for anything ever again. That was the last time I ever spoke to her.

My social worker came the next day. She suggested that I go to the emergency room and tell them that I wanted to kill myself. She said this way I'd be safe until Phil went to court. I agreed and this was going to bite me in the butt some time later. She paid Bree as a temporary foster mother for my kids.

Phil went to court. He had a woman judge who set his bail at ten thousand dollars, thinking that he wouldn't be able to post bail. His girlfriend got her parents to put up their house as collateral. He was out of jail until he went to trial. I tried to warn my friends that had kids about Phil, but they didn't believe me. They thought that I was just trying to get even with Phil for divorcing me, when actually I divorced him. Phil was the kind of guy you'd like as soon as you met him. Kids liked him because he'd play and horse around with them. He was the last person you would expect to be a child molester.

It took two years with continuances for Phil to finally go to trial. By this time, there were thirteen kids involved. The kids of the friends I tried to warn. His defense was that he didn't remember doing these horrific things to these kids. He served a year and a half. I couldn't help but hope someone would do him in in the prison. Child molesters are the lowest next to cop killers on the prison totem pole. They kept him out of general population. He was out three months, and got caught again with one of his new girlfriend's girls. This time he served seven and a half years, then the last two and a half years at a halfway house. He moved in with Amanda. He lived with her even after she got married, even though Amanda's husband and Phil hated each other. Amanda took care of Phil until he died. He had a much better daughter than he deserved. He had to register as a sex offender. He wasn't supposed to be anywhere around children, but he was. He never stopped molesting children, he just didn't get caught again.

I didn't want the kids to hate their father. I kept my feelings about him to myself. I told them that their father had a sickness, and that he couldn't help what he had done to them. Earl and I took the kids to counseling at a children's clinic.

# CHAPTER TWENTY-SEVEN

I was working second shift. A girl across the street was baby-sitting for me. The state was paying her thirty dollars a week. I paid her twenty dollars more, because she was baby-sitting for five kids forty five hours a week. I would make their supper, all she'd have to do is heat it up. Phil Jr. was giving her a hard time. He wouldn't come in the house until about a quarter of eleven. He made sure that he was home before I was. Debbie was so upset, that she was threatening to quit. One night I asked my nurse if I could do my ten o'clock rounds a little early, so that I could leave early. I told her that I had a problem at home that needed to be taken care of. I got home around ten thirty. From the chair in the living room you could see the back door clearly. I sat there in the dark waiting for Phil Jr. to come in. He came in around ten of eleven. I let him come in and head for his bedroom, that he shared with Paul and PJ. Just as he was to enter his bedroom, I switched on the light. He saw me standing there and just froze. I told him that I needed to work, and I wasn't going to lose my job because of him. I told him that I'd call every night that I needed to work, and that he'd better be home. Debbie agreed to try it again. It worked for awhile by my calling, but it was getting to the point that he wasn't home when I got home. Many times he was drunk or high or both. Debbie finally quit. I had to quit my job until I found a new baby-sitter.

Sometimes Phil Jr, would stay away from home for two or three weeks at a time. I pretty much knew where he was staying, with his male friend that used to take the boys fishing in Vermont. I couldn't ground him because he'd go out his bedroom window. He knew that I couldn't leave four kids in the house alone and chase him. One time a police officer brought him home. He was picked up shoplifting in a grocery store. He wouldn't go to school either. I'd give him a ride, watch him go in the door. As soon as I got home, the school would call reporting him absent.

I changed jobs. I went to work for a two wing rehabilitation center. The nurse on one wing was an old Army nurse and was very strict. You couldn't have one tiny wrinkle in your made bed. She would bounce a quarter on your bed, and if it didn't bounce she stripped your bed. She only wanted the same aides which included me to work her wing. One weekend when she was off, the other nurse scheduled me for her wing. This upset the Army nurse. I also had to be certified now. Since the certification class was over. they had me do a task and have a nurse sign it off. Then I took a book test. I passed. Mrs. Smith told me that they had one certification pin left. She handed it to me. I didn't know that she expected to pin it on me. Finally, she asked if she could put it on me. I didn't know how to handle someone especially a female doing something nice for me. Sometimes I had to change jobs often because of baby-sitter problems.

I had one male baby-sitter. He was good with the kids and they liked him. Sometimes if he was going to the park, he'd stop and ask if he could take the kids. One night I couldn't get Steve, so I found another baby-sitter. The kids were supposed to go to bed at nine o'clock. The kids changed all the clocks back an hour, so they could stay up later. Sunday morning we're getting ready for church, mine and Earl's watch said one time and the clocks another. I had Steve as a baby-sitter until he found a girlfriend.

One day I brought the kids to the park to go swimming. I never went swimming while they were in the water. I would sit on the beach and count heads. I was checking on the kids in the water. One minute all five were there, and the next time I turned around I didn't see Annie. I went in the water, looking everywhere and still didn't see her. I told the lifeguard. He got

124

everyone out of the pool. They made a chain, walking from one end of the water to the other. They didn't find her. People began checking the grounds of the park. They searched for a couple of hours. Then Suddenly Annie was standing beside me. She had fallen asleep on the grass. The people searching must have stepped over her at least a couple of times. One day our Siamese cat was missing. When she went outdoors, she was very territorial. The farthest she'd go is to the next door neighbor's garden. A couple of times she brought home dead garden snakes. One she left at the doorstep. I had to get my neighbor to move it so that I could get in the house. The other one, she managed to sneak inside the house. She put it behind Earl's favorite chair She had been gone a couple of weeks. I decided to take the kids to the park, to get their minds off her. I decided to go another way than we usually went. We went by this house. There was a Siamese cat on the porch. The kids got all excited calling Chee-Chee. I told the kids that it might not be her. Chee-Chee had a habit of jumping up on your shoulder. I called her and she came and jumped on my shoulder. I checked to see if she was spayed and declawed. She was. A woman came out on the porch and tried to say it was her cat. There was a police car on the corner. I told her that I'd get the officer to settle this. She not only gave me the cat, but two weeks worth of food. Instead of going to the park, we brought Chee-Chee home. At first I thought that maybe a kid had picked her up and brought her that far. A couple of days later, I noticed that the woman who had her, worked just across the street. She probably picked her up looking for a reward. One time Annie had snuck in a pregnant female calico angora cat She had it in her bedroom for two weeks, before I found out about it. I thought Chee-Chee's food was going down faster, but just thought the kids were feeding her more. One day Amanda went out the back door and came right back in screaming that there was a mouse on the mat just outside the door. Well it wasn't a mouse but a newborn kitten. I brought the kitten in and fixed a box for the mother cat in my closet. I'd check on her once in awhile. She had three more. When I had to let the mother cat outside, I had to put Chee-Chee in the bathroom. One thing she couldn't stand was another cat. I would have liked to keep one of the kittens. When the kittens were old enough to move around inside the closet, she'd perch outside the closet door. I was lucky enough to give the mother and kittens away to a farmer who wanted them to kill mice.

# CHAPTER TWENTY-EIGHT

Earl and I and the kids spent a lot of time going to family outings from his work, from the VFW, DAV and the American Legion. We would bring our baby-sitter to his shop picnic, because it was held at a large amusement park. Earl would pay for her ride tickets. It was held in the same spot that Phil had brought me to teach me how to drive. I almost crashed into an apple tree. Earl also tended bar at the VFW. Elections for the new commander of the VFW were coming up. Not too many members wanted the job because it was a lot of responsibility. One night around three o'clock in the morning, we got a call that someone broke into the club and stole beer, cigarettes and the juke box,. It had to be more than one person. We got the call because our phone number was in the alarm system.

Earl got elected for commander. It was something he had always wanted. He got about four bottles of scotch as gifts. It was quite a party. This was in May. That night when we were in bed, Earl asked me to marry him. I don't know why, but I started laughing. I couldn't stop. I told him that if he asked me to marry him in the morning, I would. marry him. Earl told me that sister who was an old maid had some choice names for me when he told her that we were getting married. She had been his beneficiary, now of course I would be. I really thought that he'd had a little too much scotch. About a year before while the kids were in foster care, and the state wanted to keep them, I went to see a palm reader. I felt she couldn't tell me anything worse than what I was going through then. She told me that I was going to marry a man that had been married before and had children. She didn't know if I would be helping him raise his children, and that I would go north. I really didn't believe her, because at that time there was not even a hint that Earl and I would ever get married. The next morning, Earl purposed again and I said that I'd have to ask the kids about how they felt about Earl and I getting married. They all agreed. They already called him "Daddy Earl." I told Earl yes, that I would marry him. I had waited eleven years to hear those words. We had been living together for a little over four years, but it had been eleven years since we began our relationship. We set a date for July 28th. A couple of days later, Earl wanted to postpone the wedding. I told him that I'd postpone it for two weeks and no longer or I wouldn't marry him. About a week before the wedding, Earl told me that he was bringing me to Sam's because he had a date. I din't want to go because I had set my hair and it wasn't dry yet. Not only that, but that he had a date. Eventually he talked me into going. Sam was going to be my maid of honor. Sam was waiting for me at the door. Then all the girls came out of hiding shouting "surprise!" Sam had planned a wedding shower for me. I got some nice gifts. Earl knew about the shower, he didn't have a date, he had to get me mad enough at him to go. Earl got my rings at a tag sale. No, I'm not kidding. The girl next door had broken her engagement so all she wanted was the money she had put on the rings which was a hundred dollars. I wanted Earl to be romantic when he put my engagement ring on my finger. There were neighbors sitting on the porch with us. He put my ring on, then told me to let him finish watching the ball game. He doesn't like to show affection in front of other people.

I bought my wedding gown from the basement of a bridal salon. There was a white gown there in my size that had a pink sash and pink centers on the daisies in the skirt. I tried it on and it fit me to a tee. It was only ten dollars! I bought a pink net with a comb in it for three dollars! My gown and veil only cost me thirteen dollars! I bought my shoes with the money I got from my shower, eleven dollars. Sam and I were looking around the thrift store a couple of days later. We found a long mint green dress with a daisy print and pink for their centers.

Before we decided to get married, I was seeing a therapist about Earl's and my relationship, mainly his drinking and how his personality changed when he was drunk. Our relationship seemed always to be an emotional rollercoaster. I didn't feel like I was getting the right kind of help with the issues I was dealing with, including issues I had with my mother. One psychologist suggested that I give my kids up for adoption. She tried to tell me that an adoptive family could give them advantages that I couldn't. I knew that if I gave up my kids, that would be the end of me. We arranged a family meeting. They made the mistake of telling the kids that someone was observing them behind a one way mirror. Well, I'll tell you, I didn't have five kids in that room, I had five animals. They were throwing magazines at each other, spitting and making funny faces in the mirror. It's a good thing that we had to walk home from the hospital, because I was fuming. It was only a fifteen minute walk. When we got home I sent them to bed. Even Phil Jr. knew that I had been pushed to the limit. He didn't try to go out his bedroom window. I fixed their supper and let them come out one at a time from the youngest to the oldest. After they had all eaten, I called them out and told them to sit at the table. I got up on the counter. I told them that the state wanted to take them and they had just given them all the ammunition they needed by their behavior at our appointment. I told them that there was one of me and five of them. and if we were going to make it as a family, I was the boss. I told them that if they wanted to go to the state, I'd sign the papers and go on to lead a merry life. I told them to think about what I said. I sent them back to bed. A little while later there was a knock on my bedroom door. They all said that they needed to talk to me. They said they wanted us to be a family. For about three months I had almost the perfect kids. If they started to get out of line, I'd tell them that it was time for a family conference. I changed therapists after that session because the psychologist refused to take me as a patient anymore because I went against medical advice. I and was doing better. At one point my mother agreed to go with me. We were still talking then. The session before the one I was supposed to have with my mother, my therapist told me that he was turning my case over to someone else because he was changing jobs. I stopped going to therapy, it had taken me awhile to trust this one.

The time of the sugar embargo on Cuba, the cost of cereal had sky rocketed. I was buying four or five boxes each time I went shopping. The kids were starting to leave half bowls of cereal. I decided to stop buying cold cereal. They ate pancakes, french toast, oatmeal everything but cold cereal. I did this for about three months. Then one day that I went shopping, I bought one box of cold cereal. The kids ate it like it was the last box they were ever going to see.

Now that Earl and I were getting married, I really wanted to get it right this time. I wasn't that impulsive sixteen year old kid anymore. I also had the kids to think about now. The one thing I really wanted was finally going to happen. I was going to be Earl's wife! I totally blocked out his drinking problem. Maybe I just didn't want to see it.

Earl asked his best friend to be his best man. The justice of the peace was a good friend of mine, almost like a second dad. He had owned the diner where Phil and I used to hang out. It seemed like a lifetime ago. The outgoing commander was going to give us the VFW hall rent free as a wedding present. One of the tenants in our building was going to baby-sit the kids so that we could have a honeymoon. We were buying the liquor and non alcoholic beverages. I found a woman to make our wedding cake just the way I wanted it for twenty five dollars after I returned her cake parts. I chose two doves instead of the traditional bride and groom. We also bought plastic toast glasses. Phil Jr. was going to be the DJ using my stereo and albums. Our wedding day was the day before Annie's birthday. I had her party a day earlier. The day before our wedding I cooked nine pounds of spaghetti, made sauce and meatballs and sausage. The ladies of the auxiliary were going to heat it up in the kitchen for the reception. They also decorated the hall. I made Earl sleep in his room at the rooming house the night before we got married. The day of the wedding I went to the grocery store and bought Italian bread, stuff for salad, and different salad dressings. Plus I still had to go to the beauty salon to get my hair done. My hair was long, so I had to sit under the dryer for an hour or more. Earl bought my bouquet, white roses with baby's breath, and the buttoneers for him and the best man. He bought me a cedar jewelry box with a string of pearls inside for a wedding gift. We were going to get married in the ski chalet at our local park. It had been a very hot August. We had bad thunderstorms all day Friday. We couldn't get married in the chalet because tree branches blocked the road leading to it. We got married in the pavilion by the pool. I was nervous on the drive there. I was afraid that Earl might get cold feet and leave me standing at the altar. I was so happy to see him standing there waiting for me. It was still raining. The wedding went off without any problems. Our friends didn't give our marriage six months because of the age difference. Again I got married without anyone from my family being there. At the reception, the ladies began to serve the spaghetti. The neighbor that was going to baby-sit for us came up to me and said that some of the spaghetti had soured from the heat, but enough was saved to feed everybody. We even went downstairs to the bar to invite anyone who wanted to eat were welcome. PJ was seven, when he danced with Earl, he asked Earl if we could have another brother baby. He thought that when you got married, you automatically had a baby. Earl asked him what he'd do if it was a sister baby. Pj replied,

"We'll give it back. We have enough girls!

PJ also caught the garter. I pulled my gown up just to the knee and let him put just below my knee. After the reception, we went home to change clothes. We were going to go to Maine for two weeks, so that I could meet Earl's family. It was the time of the big gas shortage. Earl was afraid that we'd run out of gas in one of the small towns. We went to a steak house for supper. Half the people from my wedding were there. After we ate, we drove ten miles and got a motel room. A drive-in theater was next door. It was still raining. Earl slept through most of the second movie. After the movies we went to our motel room. I went into the bathroom to change into the white nightgown and matching robe that I had bought at the thrift store. Earl went into the bathroom next. It seemed like he was in there for about an hour. When he came out, he climbed into bed. He gave me a kiss goodnight and told me that I could watch what I wanted to on TV. The movie that was playing was "Whose Been Sleeping In My Bed" starring Dean Martin. The next morning he told me that he hadn't felt good at the wedding. We went out for breakfast. I wrote just married on a napkin. I left my cigarettes behind when we left. The waitress caught up to me with them. It was still raining hard. We were trying to think of a place to go. It was raining too hard to go to the amusement park. So we went home and got the kids and started married life. Later that day, he was going through his wallet and found the money we got at the wedding. He had forgotten about it. We could have gone to Maine if he had remembered.

As the new commander, we had to go to the VFW Convention in Hartford. Earl had been drinking scotch that he had gotten when he became commander. We were late leaving for Hartford. We got to the outskirts of Hartford, when all of a sudden we're going the wrong direction on the interstate. Cars were blowing their horns at us, and weaving around us to avoid an accident. Finally Earl turned onto a break in the median, and we were going in the right direction. When we got to the hotel, they had rented out our room which had all the booze in it. Earl gave them this sob story that we were on our honeymoon, and needed a room. They gave us a single room for the night. The next day, Earl gave me his Mastercard to get something to eat while he attended the meetings at the convention. I could have gone on a shopping spree, but I didn't. That night going from room to room, I got pretty drunk on Bloody Marys. I had one heck of a hangover the next day. In the afternoon, we hooked up with another couple we met in the lounge. We decided to go eat at a Chinese restaurant. We found a Chinese restaurant just down the street. We all had been drinking. We ordered our food. The woman who was with us, told us that her son worked at a popular Japanese restaurant in the mall. We took off from the Chinese restaurant before we got our food. The owner chased us half way down the street. At the Japanese restaurant, the waitress would sometimes look my way. I'm loud when I'm drunk. I told her that Earl and I had just got married. I asked her if I could have the pair of facecloths they give you as a souvenir. The food was excellent, they cooked it on a hot table right in front of you. When your food was done, they put in front of you, and you ate off the hot table. I ordered a drink, and they still served me even though I probably had too much already. That night we went to the disco at the hotel. I had taught Earl how to do the "Hustle." On the last day, I just couldn't drink anymore. I walked around with a glass of plain tomato juice with a stalk of celery in it, so that I had an excuse if someone asked me if I wanted a drink. I ran out of tomato juice, so I called room service. They charged Earl five dollars plus a tip for a quart of tomato juice. When we were packing to leave, I put the pitcher in my suitcase. I figured that Earl had more than paid for it. For awhile our friends were teasing me about my expensive tomato juice. They teased me about making a quick five bucks by selling me a glass of tomato juice,

That April PJ needed a minor operation. He had some polyps his vocal chords which made it hard for him to say certain sounds. He had a teenager for a roommate. They got along great. During that week, I had a strange dream. In my dream, my Dad was dressed in a pin-striped suit. I had never seen my Dad in a suit like that. We were at a funeral. Before I could see who was in the casket, I woke up. The next morning I told Earl that someone I was close to has died. I told Earl about my dream. He told me that it was just a dream. In August I ran into Cynthia at a local amusement park. She asked me if I knew that Uncle Bill died. She told me when he died. It was the week that I had my dream. He was in the hospital the same time as PJ. If I had known, I probably could have went to see him, maybe for the last time. My Aunt Emma and him had such a special marriage, that she didn't put any announcements in the newspapers. I hadn't kept in close contact with my relatives. I wanted too, but just didn't make the time. My aunt couldn't accept my uncle's death, and I don't think she ever did. The last time I saw her, she talked about him as if he was still alive.

When Paul was in the fifth grade, he had the same male teacher as Phil Jr. The teacher had it in for Paul because Phil Jr. had been a trouble maker. I got his class changed and his grades improved. Then another problem arose with Paul. He was trading his lunch for other students' desserts He was also eating the sugar in packets at school and McDonalds Phil's mother was a severe diabetic I made an appointment with a doctor to have him checked for Junior Diabetes. Paul was petrified of needles. I had to promise to let him spend the weekend at his grandmother's, even though it wasn't his turn. The kids used to take turns spending the weekend with Phil's mother. She was losing her eyesight due to her diabetes. The kids would help her cook. It turned out that Paul didn't have diabetes. He was getting high on the sugar.

Also, when Paul was eight, Earl did something that was completely out of character for him. He told Paul that he was his real father. I thought that I would be the one to tell him when he was old enough to understand about the birds and the bees. Also when Paul was eight, he won second prize at McDonalds for drawing the starship "Enterprise" Earl was so proud. He had to be the one to take Paul to the toy store to pick out his prize.

# CHAPTER TWENTY-NINE

Our first year of marriage was unlike Phil's and mine, which had been the easiest. Earl gave up his room at the rooming house naturally. His landlady told him that he had married beneath his class. When Earl and I had an argument before we got married, he'd go to his room and sulk for a couple of days. Now he had to stay and work it out. There is a difference between just living together and making it legal. Our friends didn't give our marriage six months because of the age difference. I didn't feel like I had married my father. I had a good father and nobody could take his place.

Earl hadn't been home to Maine for more than six years, because he had a disagreement with his Dad. His dad was ninety one years old. Earl always felt guilty that he didn't make it home in time when his mother died. She lived to see the roses he sent her. He had borrowed money which luckily this time Phil and I had to go see her. We even let him take our car because it was newer than his. He didn't think his car would make it up and back. The trip was almost six hundred miles. He drove straight through without stopping except for gas. He was going seventy five eighty miles an hour most of the way. He made it there in nine hours, but his mother had just passed away about an hour before he got there. I spent a lot of time trying to convince him to go see his dad before it was too late. He finally agreed.

We went the second summer we were married. We split up the kids with two of our friends and paid them each a hundred dollars to watch the kids for two weeks. We took our time, traveling during the night. Earl was thankful that I was able

136

to stay awake and talk to him while he was driving. We were able to talk about many different things. Things we never found the time to discuss at home. He was one of those that wasn't comfortable unless he was behind the wheel. It took us about thirteen hours. When we got there, Earl said that we wouldn't take our bags out of the car, because being strict Catholic they might not let us sleep together. We went in the house and he introduced me to his brother and sister. His dad was in the front room. Earl talked French to him, telling him who I was, and that I didn't speak French. His dad gave me a hug. There they called him Anthony. He told Earl that he was lucky down in Connecticut, and that he could leave me up here with him and go find himself another one. Earl told me that his dad liked me and we could stay there. Earl told me that his dad refused to go to his first wedding because he knew Earl was making a huge mistake. He went and got our bags out of the car. In those two weeks, I got introduced to the Adadian culture, that was such a big part of northern Maine, such as their music, clogging, and food. My sister-in-law played the violin. A friend of hers would bring her keyboard and Earl would play the guitar and they'd play music. Sometimes I'd dance with Earl's dad. When I got up in the morning, Dad would be at the foot of the stairs. He'd ask me if I had a good sleep. My sister-in-law didn't want me to tell Dad that I was divorced. She wanted me to lie to him. One morning I was out in the garden with Dad. He asked me about my kids. His mind was still sharp, and I wasn't going to lie to him. I explained to him that I got married very young and had the kids at a young age. I told him that Earl and I fell in love, and that he was willing to help me raise my family. One day Dad asked Earl to take him to his bank in Canada. I was excited. I had never been out of the country before. Earl's home town was right on the U. S. /Canadian border. Dad withdrew five hundred dollars and gave it to us as a wedding present. The second time I went across was with Earl and one of his cousins who lived across, but had a camp on Long Lake in the states. We went to a bar. I ordered a glass of beer. Earl told me to slow down on drinking beer. I told him that I had only one glass. It was Moosehead beer. I didn't know that Canadian beer was much stronger than ours. I got a little drunk on that one glass. After we left the bar, we went to his cousin's camp, for a barbecue and more drinking. On the way home, I was sitting in the middle of the front seat. Earl was driving. His cousin thought that I was too drunk to know that he was feeling up my leg. I told Earl about it later. Another day, Earl and I and my sister-in-law went to Fort Kent. We went to the historical blockhouse there. My sister-in-law bought me a small stuffed teddy bear at the gift store. I also bought a baseball hat and tee shirt with the blockhouse on it. The proceeds went to helping the Boy Scout troop that helped out at the blockhouse. We also stopped at a restaurant to eat. The waitress that waited on us made a remark that Earl had brought his wife and his daughter out to eat. The two weeks flew by. The day we were to leave for home, Dad called me into his room. He gave me five black combs. That's how many times he had been in the hospital. He told me to give the combs to his grandchildren. Also, at 93, he was down cellar chopping wood and stacking it. That would be the last time I'd see him. We left with Dad and Earl being father and son again. Dad died two years later in a local nursing home. Earl couldn't get the time off from work to go to the funeral, without losing his job. He would have had to have at least a week off. On the way home I knew that this was where I was going to live someday. Earl said that he'd never move back to Maine and starve again. Everything the palm reader told me had come true. Earl had four grown daughters, (his oldest just a year younger than me), we did get married and I went north.

# CHAPTER THIRTY

A new family moved in upstairs. Amy had three children, a teenage daughter who had a boyfriend, and another boy and girl close to Annie and Amanda's age. This was Amy's third marriage. Her husband was from Maine, just twenty miles farther than Earl's hometown. PJ had natural curly hair just like Shirley Temple. One night he went upstairs to play with Amy's kids. When he came downstairs he was bald! Amy's older daughter and her boyfriend decided to cut PJ's hair. They messed it up, so they shaved his head. PJ wouldn't take off his baseball cap. He even slept with it. He made the front page of our local paper. The photo and article was taken at the Boy's Club day camp as the most original way to stay cool.

It would be two years before we went to Maine again. We agreed to go to Maine with Amy and Reno in one car and split expenses. We were each going to take turns driving. We got two baby-sitters for my kids. One of my friends who she and I had had been friends since my roller skating days. Her and I looked enough alike to be taken for sisters. She was going to take the boys. She had a dog grooming business in her home and my boys often helped her out with the dogs. Another friend across the street had the girls. We couldn't bring our kids because it would have made Earl's sister too nervous. Amy and her husband Reno were bringing her two younger children. Another couple upstairs were also going to Maine the same time we were. This was going to leave the apartment building empty for two weeks. Earl locked and nailed the windows in our apartment.

I hadn't driven in awhile. Amy was going to take me out driving. Earl and I had been out the night before, and I had a wicked hangover. I came close to having an accident at a intersection. After that Amy took over the wheel.

Amy's husband couldn't help out with the driving because he didn't have a license. He didn't know how to read and write. Later on Amy would teach him to read and write. He got to take an oral driving test and passed. We were all packed up and ready to go. Amy's kids were excited because they had never been to Maine before. It was the first time they were going to meet their step father's family. Earl drove first because driving through Hartford in the daytime made Amy nervous. There was one dangerous bottleneck where we would have to change routes. If you were unfortunate enough to get in the wrong lane, nobody was going to let you cut in. Amy took over and drove through Massachusetts. We stopped at Burger King to eat and go to the bathroom. I drove when we hit the New Hampshire border. You were only in New Hampshire for thirty miles. As I was driving I was thinking that this was the first time Earl had rode in a car with me behind the wheel. I mentioned this to Earl. He laughed and told me to pull over so that he could get out. Finally, a welcome site. A large bridge that was the border between New Hampshire and Maine. Earl took over the wheel at the first Burger King in Maine because now the traffic would start to get heavy. We also gassed up there. Earl bought me a whoopie pie. You can't buy them in Connecticut. They are two halves of devil's food cake with cream in the middle. They also make them in other flavors and different cream centers. We still had seven more hours of driving. We finally got to my sister-in-law's house. Amy and Reno continued on to Fort Kent. The house seemed so empty without Dad. Earl's brother Abel and I would walk the short distance to a large department store that had a dining area. We'd order coffee and talk. Abel also tried to teach me French. My sister-in-law was a good cook. She cooked mostly on a wood stove, but had a small apartment size electric stove for baking. Her refrigerator was older than me and still running good. She made French pancakes called ploes on the wood stove. I couldn't get enough of them. They are like a crepe. The two weeks soon were over. Amy and Reno came to pick us up. I didn't want to leave.

We decided to take our time going home. Reno's family had given the kids a tiny bred dog. They named her "Princess". We took Route One going home which is the coastal route. Reno would walk the dog when we stopped. People would remark on how tiny and cute she was. After that Reno claimed the dog, even though it was supposed to be for the kids. We stopped at a lighthouse on Pemequit Point. I love lighthouses. Earl bought me a jewelry box at the gift shop. The scenery was breathtaking. We stopped to eat in Booth Bay Harbor. The restaurant looked like just an old fishing shack but I had the best fried clams I ever ate there. We stopped at Old Orchard Beach. We spent the day there. We got to spend the night there because Reno had an uncle who lived there and put us up for the night. Earl left some money under his place mat the next morning, because Reno's uncle would never have accepted it. We stopped at this small fishing village on the way to visit Amy's aunt in South Bristol. It was so quaint and beautiful. I want to find it again someday. Then came the bridge. Halfway across, we'd be out of Maine. Our next stop was at Hampton Beach in New Hampshire. I collected seashells and put my feet in the water. The rest of the trip was uneventful. I had taken a strong dislike for Reno. There's not many people that affect me this way. If Amy and the kids were watching a show on TV he'd purposely change the channel. If one of the kids were sick, and if Princess would want to lay down with them, he'd make them close their door. He'd go to McDonald's just to get the dog a cheeseburger. He's eat steak and potatoes while Amy and the kids ate macaroni and cheese. Nobody could be in the kitchen while he was cooking. Amy and the kids had to stay in a bedroom or the living room. One day I went upstairs to visit Amy and Reno was cooking.

He tried to rush me into the living room. As I went by the stove I let out a big fake sneeze! He ate out a lot. I told him that he'd be surprised what they did with his food in the kitchen. His reply was that he always sat near the kitchen so that he could watch them prepare his food. He'd call Amy five or six times a day from work. Sometimes we'd go to his sister's for coffee. As soon as we got there, he'd be on the phone. Finally, after several warnings, they told him that if he couldn't trust his wife for eight hours, then he might as well stay home with her. They fired him. Sometimes he'd make a pass at me. Finally I told him that I hated his guts and to stay out of my face.

# CHAPTER THIRTY-ONE

The real shock came when we got home. Our apartment was trashed. There was ground in instant coffee all over the kitchen floor. Chee-Chee hadn't been taken care of properly. I found a pair of panties in my bed that weren't mine. I was really beginning to think that the state of Maine had it in for me. The neighbor across the street said that Annie and Amanda told her that Earl had molested them. I talked to the girls and told them that I would believe them again like I did last time, but they denied saying anything like that. I also talked to Earl, and he denied it, saying that Phil had really messed with their heads. Another time I was the only female that went to the horse races at a fair in Massachusetts with a few of the guys from the club. Earl bought me a beautiful watch. We had a great day until I got back. My dog groomer friend said that the girls told her that Earl was molesting them. I talked to Earl and begged him to tell me the truth. To get the truth from him, I promised not to press charges. all he'd have to do was move out and stay away from us. He denied ever touching them. I spoke to the girls, and Amanda told me that she had seen Earl in his under-shorts once, but he had never touched her or Annie. Annie and Amanda were very close even though they were close in age. They told each other everything. If I needed to know something, especially concerning Annie, I'd have to eavesdrop. Annie was the lady, and Amanda was my tomboy. I think that's why they got along so well because the were complete opposites I found out that Phil Jr. had been the one that broke into our apartment and the apartment of the older couple upstairs. The older couple had an elderly lady living with them. She had seven children who were estranged from her. The only one that wasn't was her only son who was killed in Vietnam. She had received a gold star from the government for being a Gold Star mother. A Gold Star mother was one that lost her only son in a war. Phil Jr. stole this star and sold it for drugs. I wouldn't have been so upset if he was little and didn't know what that gold star meant, but he was almost fourteen. Nothing he could do or say could take away the pain that woman suffered. To this day, I haven't forgiven him in my heart for hurting her that way. She moved out a couple of months later.

One night I got a call from an unknown caller telling me that my girls were at a keg party in the park. I called the police. They asked me how old my daughters were. I told them 12, and 14 They told me that there wasn't much they could do that I'd have to handle it myself. I then explained to them that my fourteen year old was mentally challenged. They told me that they would check into it. Someone must have tipped them off, because when the police got there, the party had broken up. A few months later, something set Annie off. She came at me with a sharp knife, than ran into her bedroom. The girls had iron bunk beds and she literally tipped them over and trashed the room. Earl was across the street at the bar. I called him to come home. Usually if anyone could calm Annie down, it was Earl. I was dog-sitting a friend's Irish Setter. He laid down by her bedroom door, and wouldn't let anyone in the room. Earl told me to call the police. They came and even they were afraid to go past the dog and into her room. They called the paramedics. Earl finally got the dog to move so they could treat her. They brought her to the hospital. By the time she got up to the mental health ward, she was a little angel. After she was released, my social worker arranged for her to go to this special school for girls in the Berkshires. The state of Connecticut was paying Massachusetts a lot of money for her to go there. She was doing well there. She was becoming a lady. After she turned sixteen, she got her father to sign her out of the school.

One Christmas, they were having a craft fair at the mall. Paul and PJ wanted these leather wallets on a chain like the truckers wore. I was working for the visiting nurses in the morning and second shift at a nursing home. It was snowing and slippery, but in between jobs, I walked to the mall and bought them the wallets for Christmas.

For Phil Jr.'s fifteenth birthday party, I let him have a sleep over. I put his two brothers in the girl's room for the night. I made three trips to the store for english muffins to make small pizzas. I also had cake, ice cream, and other snacks. I didn't know that teenage boys could eat so much. One of his friends kept me up to four in the morning just talking to me. In the morning they asked if for Phil Jr.'s next birthday could he invite girls.

One night I was driving home from working second shift. A car followed me almost all the way home with no headlights. I got to the traffic light in front of my house. I was waiting for the light to change, when suddenly I felt something hit the back of my car. It was the car that had been following me. I panicked. I took my left turn when the light changed and pulled into my parking place. It told Earl what happened and he read me the riot act for not calling the police and reporting the accident. He called the police. Come to find out the guy that hit me lived just up the street. His front end was pushed in and the covers were still over his headlights. I got five hundred dollars from his insurance company. My car was still drivable I just had to tie down my trunk. Earl scared me so bad that I was afraid to drive again. Instead of making me get back behind the wheel, he took me everywhere I needed to go, or someone else would. I didn't drive again for five years. I used some of the money to enroll in the EMT course I went all the way through, up till the last two weeks. My partner that I had all through the course dropped out. They were going to put me with a partner from another hospital. I couldn't pass the part of the test where you had to demonstrate your skills with a complete stranger. I didn't do well in those kind of tests. Give me a written test any day of the week and I'd pass it.

A few months later, Phil Jr. and Annie moved with my neighbor across the street. Phil Jr. was best friends with her two boys. He wanted to move with them and go to Job Corp with her oldest son. She also had a daughter Annie's age, and when Phil Jr. wanted to go, so did she. Judy brought Annie home after six months because she had caught Annie in a couple of compromising situations with her boys. About a year later, Phil Jr. came to visit me. Earl was at the club. When he came home he took a quick look in the living room then went to bed. The next morning he asked Amanda who the man was that was visiting me. Amanda smiled and told him that that was no man, that it was her brother.

The three remaining tenants in our building thought that it was odd that the landlord wasn't trying to rent the three vacant apartments. One day he came to tell us why. He was retiring. He had wanted his son to take over his welding business and the apartment house, but his son had other plans for his life. The landlord told us that the building was up for sale. The man that bought the apartment building served us last three tenants with eviction notices. He wanted to remodel the apartments and have them for adults only. The older couple moved out and went back to Maine. Amy and Reno were in the same position Earl and I were, We needed a three bedroom apartment that we could afford. I'd had several different dogs in the ten years I lived there. The dog I had now I had raised from a pup. He was part Springer Spaniel and part English setter. He was the size of the spaniel and the markings of the setter. We'd had him for four and a half years. The new landlord told me that I had to get rid of him, and for me not to try to hide him. He also told me to clean up my apartment, even though it wasn't dirty. He was looking for excuses to get us out sooner. I had a friend bring Harley to the Humane Society because I just couldn't do it. My friend said he tried to bite the attendant that took him from her. He had never tried to bite anyone before. I promised my self then, that I'd never own a another dog until I owned my own home. It seemed like anyone or anything I cared for, had a way of getting out of my life. I began to suffer from severe separation anxiety though I didn't know it then.

The landlord was raising the rent thirty dollars every month, and Earl paid it and kept the receipts. Amy and Reno looked for a five bedroom apartment but couldn't find one they could afford. Since Reno lost his job, they were living on Amy's welfare check. They eventually moved to Maine, leaving Earl and I the only tenants still living there. Earl kept looking for apartments. One landlord told me he'd take me with four babies than four teenagers. He said that teenagers had their friends and boom boxes. I even went to a town meeting held by our state representative and told her about my situation. She told me she'd do what she could to help. There was also a woman who worked in the police department that was an advocate for people like us. She tried to get us into one of the housing projects, to no avail.

This went on for about six months. The rent hikes and Earl paying them. One day the shreiff came with papers, giving us seven days to vacate the premises. We had to put our belongings except for our clothes in storage. On the last day, the sheriff came back to make sure the apartment was empty. He told us that we could sleep on the floor for that night. The kids were at Bree's for the night. The kids had given Chee-Chee away, but she booked. We kept checking around the apartment, thinking if she went anywhere it would be there. She was eleven years old now. Earl said that she must have gone off somewhere to die. Earl drank heavily during this week. We had to stay at the homeless shelter. You could only stay from eight o'clock in the evening until nine in the morning. We slept on army cots. The men and boys slept downstairs and the women and girls upstairs. Both Earl and I were both working, yet we were homeless. When the woman was on duty, she'd do our laundry for us. I made a friend there. Eventually she found an apartment. Me and the kids spent most days at her apartment. We fed the kids and ourselves at McDonalds or in the food court at the mall. PJ was now thirteen, and he could eat two Big Macs without even trying. We did our laundry at a laundromat. It cost us more to live on the street than it did in an apartment.

Earl was a janitor at the mall in the center of town. I had a summer position working for the state in a school for the mentally retarded. The position had the possibility of becoming permanent in September. The only thing was I had to work all three shifts. They would let me out of the shelter if I was working the eleven to six thirty shift. When I had to work the third shift, Earl would park the car in the back of the mall, so that I could lay down in the back seat and try to get some sleep. He'd unlock the employees restroom so that I could wash up and change. It was a forty five minute drive. A few mornings I almost fell asleep at the wheel. I loved the job. It was a good feeling when a resident completed a task that you set up for them. For supper, lots of times we ate outside. We took some of them on field trips.

One night, I had to find a place for Paul to sleep, because he couldn't stay at the shelter because he had been sniffing glue and was high. I asked the woman I met at the shelter if he could sleep at her apartment. She agreed.

One night I was the only woman upstairs at the shelter. It was the man's night to work. He wasn't supposed to go upstairs unless there was an emergency. He came upstairs while I was in the shower and tried to rape me. I fought him off. I reported him to the woman when she came on duty in the morning. She told me that she would take care of it. I also told Earl that I couldn't stay at the shelter anymore. I went to see my girlfriend who lived in the low income housing project. She and I had been friends since high school. I asked her if the kids and I could stay with her until we found an apartment. I agreed to help out with food and household supplies. Because I was only summer help, I got paid minimum wage and every two weeks.

148

Earl came to see me every night and sometimes he was very drunk. Sometimes he stayed in a room at the rooming house when he'd been drinking. The woman on the police force that tried to help us before, came to see my at my girlfriend's to file a complaint against the man at the shelter. They fired him. It was working out okay at my friend's except she was a filthy housekeeper. Earl began staying at my girlfriend's father and stepmother's apartment, also in the project. I was jealous of her. I felt that she was going to go after Earl because she was young and her husband was a lot older than she. She was known to run around, because she was in a sexless marriage. One night I stayed overnight there with Earl, because I could only stay with my girlfriend so many days as a guest. As long as I wasn't there for one night, the time started over again. Earl and I slept on the floor in one of her kids' room. The place was infested with cockroaches. Earl had been drinking and wanted to make love. We did. My girlfriend's stepmother told us the next morning that she had heard us, and we couldn't stay there anymore. I went back to my girlfriend's apartment.

One day I went to a store in the plaza. I picked out my purchases and went to the checkout to pay for them. I opened my wallet and the compartment where I kept my money was empty. I went back to my girlfriend's and told her about my missing money. She denied taking it, but she was the only one that knew where I hid my wallet. I called my social worker and asked her if she could help me get into the project. They were supposed to keep a couple of apartments open in case of emergency cases like mine. She came with me and we sat in the housing authority office all morning waiting for the director to come out of his office in the back. His secretary kept telling us he'd be right with us. Finally, my social worker couldn't wait any longer, and had to leave. I still waited. He came out of his office after my social worker left. He told me that with my and Earl's income we were over qualified. I offered to take the apartment for myself and the kids. He couldn't stop Earl from visiting and spending the night sometimes. He told me that they had a three bedroom apartment but it needed to be cleaned and painted. He said that it would be ready in a week and a half. I told him that I'd clean and paint the apartment myself, but he wouldn't let me. I went back to see him a week later. He told me that he couldn't give me the apartment because a Puerto Rican family was next on the waiting list, and that he had to give it to them. He told me that they would claim that there was prejudice against them. I went back to my girlfriends. The kids were starting to stay with some of their friends. The boys often stayed with my friend the dog groomer. and Annie and Amanda with their friends. I was losing control of my family. They were teenagers now, I couldn't say "now hold mommy's hand now all day long." They would meet me at McDonald's in the morning.

One day I noticed a sore on my face. I put medication on it but it wasn't going away. I went to the doctor. He told me that I had a staph infection. I got hysterical shouting at him to get this off my face. If he just said that I had impetigo, I wouldn't have panicked. I must have got it from one of the residents at work. The doctor put my on antibiotics, but I needed to be out of work for a week. Then near the end of summer, I got tonsillitis and had to be out of work for two weeks. the state was very strict about working sick with the residents. It would bring me to the end of my summer position. I wasn't able to take the permanent position.

One night Earl picked me up from work at eleven o'clock. We went to my girlfriend's house. She told us that we couldn't stay there anymore. We asked her to just let us spend the night, we'd leave at six o'clock in the morning. She refused, saying that she was going to New Britian early in the morning. I couldn't believe her. I was about the only friend she had in high school because she was in special education. Earl and I left. We spent the night in the car parked in back of a coffee and donut shop. Neither one of us slept much. Earl would go in the shop to buy us coffee. I called my social worker the next morning and told her that I was all out of options. We were still looking for apartments but so far nothing. It was getting to be September and the kids needed an address so that they could go to school. The social worker placed Annie and Amanda at a group home near by. I could visit anytime as long as I called first. She placed Paul and PJ with my friend the dog groomer and paid her as a temporary foster mother. Earl and I took a room at the same motel where we spent our wedding night. We were paying one hundred forty seven dollars a week., or twenty one dollars a night. Earl still called about apartments every night after work. I did my own cleaning of our room. The owner would bring me the clean linens. Earl left me money to buy lunch at the hot dog stand next door. During the day, I crotched, did crossword puzzles, or watched TV. After work, Earl and I would go for supper. One day I got a call from my social worker. Annie had picked up a STD while in the group home. She had to be isolated from the other girls until it was gone. I had Earl bring me to town when he went to work. I went to visit the boys. They were doing good at Emily's. I couldn't take being homeless anymore. I went to the emergency room, and told them that if someone didn't help me, I was going to do something to myself.

I always felt that if our five year marriage could survive being homeless, it could survive anything. Earl could have run out on us, but he didn't After all four of the kids weren't his.

Earl found us a one bedroom apartment from the same landlord that had helped that Christmas holiday that seemed like a lifetime ago. We got some of our stuff out of storage, but a lot of it was damaged. Especially my floor model color TV set. One of our friends let us borrow a thirteen inch TV. I called my social worker to tell her we rented a one bedroom apartment for the time being. She told me to meet her for lunch at the mall. After lunch she came to see the apartment. She made a remark that now I had an apartment, I didn't care about the kids anymore. I told her how much it was costing us to stay at the motel. I also told her that this apartment wasn't permanent. It was in walking distance for me to see the boys, and I'd bring the girls here with Earl and I. The group home didn't want to take the responsibility for Annie anymore. They'd keep Amanda, but I didn't want the girls split up. The social worker brought the girls to me. I made a makeshift bed for them in the living room with some heavy quilts. My social worker wanted to know why I didn't give them the bed. Earl would not have been able to sleep on the floor with his back. He'd had a spinal fusion done on his back several years ago. Shortly after, Annie met a boyfriend and moved in with him. Amanda did the same thing a couple of months later. I had met Annie's boyfriend and knew that he was bum. A couple of days before her eighteenth birthday, her boyfriend and her came to see me. Annie wanted me to sign for her to get married. I refused, knowing full well that she'd marry him after her birthday, which she did. He just wanted to marry her because he thought that she'd be getting a large disability check. I felt cheated out of being mother of the bride. The first of my children to get married.

Phil Jr. and his girlfriend moved into an apartment in the next building. I knew his girlfriend and didn't like her. Neither did the cat I had at the time. I had a sign on my living room wall that read "Beware of Cat" She had come to do some cleaning for me and he left a claw in her hand. She threw their ferret across the room for no reason. She worked at the same nursing home I did, and got fired for eating a patient's food and striking another. I was hoping and praying that Phil Jr. wouldn't marry her He didn't. They broke up a short time later One night Paul was trying to get PJ home to me because he was drunk, but decided to take him next door to Phil Jr.'s. Phil Jr's first thought was to put PJ in a cold shower. Its a good thing he didn't, because the shock of the cold water to his system could have killed him. Soon Phil Jr. was dating someone else. One day they picked up a stray kitten. They kept her. Then they had to move and there was no pets allowed in their new apartment. By now, the cat "Dusty" was almost a year old. One day Phil Jr. asked me if I would take her until they found an apartment where they could have her. Of course she wasn't spayed, and I couldn't afford to get her spayed. She was used to going outside, and she became pregnant. My neighbor downstairs had a beautiful orange angora cat. He would get in your lap and you could pet him for hours. I used to bring a towel with me when I went to visit her. Dusty had her kittens. They were born the day after Christmas. She had two males and two females. One of the males looked exactly like the cat downstairs. I was going to keep him. Amanda and her boyfriend came to visit. She fell in love with the kitten I wanted to keep. Though he was only five weeks old, I gave him to her. I kept the other male and Earl brought the other two to the pet shop in the mall. This kitten wasn't cute like baby kittens are. He didn't have that cute kitten face, He looked like a baby tiger cub. I had my picture taken at the mall holding a baby tiger cub, and that's what he reminded me of. I named him "Tigger" I began holding him when he was two days old, so that he'd recognize my scent. We still had Dusty. She took a liking to Earl. If him or I were in the coffee shop, the laundry mat, or the drugstore in the little plaza next door, she come to the door and yowl. We'd end up having to bring her home. When Earl would walk to the grocery store around the corner, she'd follow behind him meowing like crazy. She was a good cat, but each time I gave a litter of kittens away, she'd be pregnant again. Tigger would get in the box with the kittens.

# CHAPTER THIRTY-TWO

One day Paul flipped out on drugs or alcohol at my girlfriend's where he was staying. We took him to the emergency room They treated him and put him on the mental health ward, until the state could find a place where he would get treatment. At the hospital they were treating him with Valium. By the time we got him to the treatment center, they tried to ask Paul some questions. They were so upset with his treatment at the hospital. Paul couldn't answer their questions coherently because he was given so much Valium. It was supposed to be a place where it was impossible for him to leave on his own. Paul managed to escape by climbing over a fence at the end of the property. He hitchhiked back to Bristol. He went to stay with a minister and his family. It didn't work out. The minister was concerned about Paul's addiction around his children. The minister brought him back to my girlfriend's because that's where he said he wanted to go. She didn't know it, but he was stealing drugs from her, which the state or I didn't know that she was selling. She took him back to the minister's. I didn't know where he was until almost a year later. The minister had taken him out of state without my permission and put him in a youth center in Pennsylvania, after asking him whether he wanted to live or die. My girlfriend knew where he was all that time. I had met an elderly lady. I would go to these gospel meetings with her where the woman spoke in tongues. She had people helping her catch people as they fell to the floor. One time I felt a strange power, but fought it and didn't pass out. I'd pray for God to help me find Paul. My prayers were answered. My girlfriend gave me the address and phone number where he was. The first time I called him was Christmas Eve. I wanted to wish him a very Merry Christmas and tell him I loved him. They wouldn't let me talk to him because he had broken a rule. He had to stay there until he was twenty one, which he did. He liked it there and he was off drugs and alcohol. Six years later, Paul came to visit me and he had someone with him. He introduced me to his wife. I liked her immediately. She was someone you felt like you've known all your life. We had a nice visit. Earl gave them a recliner and a TV to take with them.

One Sunday afternoon, I decided to visit Amanda without telling her I was coming. I was surprised, her small apartment was clean. She had been a slob at home. She had lost the cat I gave her. It went out an open window and didn't come back.

My troubles weren't over yet. PJ was not quite fourteen and wouldn't go to school I'd threaten him that the state would place him, but it didn't seem to sink in. I'd send him and sometimes brought him, but he absent quite frequently. Finally, the truant officer referred him to Juvenile Court. The court ordered him to go to school and put him on probation. He broke probation, so the court placed him in a school for boys. There were no guards or gates You stayed there on your honor. He worked on the farm half a day and went to class the other half. He got his tractor's license there. He also adopted a parrot that was almost dead and nursed it back to health. The boys taught the bird to swear. They weren't supposed to listen to this sex doctor on the radio. The bird would go "time for Dr. Smith, time for Dr. Smith." It came a day when the benefactors were vesting the school. The bird started swearing like a trooper. The staff made him give up the bird. PJ was allowed to come home for weekend visits. He was doing well until he was almost sixteen. He knew that they couldn't make him stay after he was sixteen. He began acting out and refusing to abide by the rules. They told him that he had to leave. He didn't want to live with me, because he'd have to obey our rules. He went to live with a friend. Eventually PJ went to Job Corp for meat cutting. Paul got his license to drive tractor trailer.

# CHAPTER THIRTY-THREE

The Hair Dressing Academy was just up the street. At the time, you didn't need a high school diploma. You had to go to school for 1500 hours. Victoria had gone into hair dressing when she dropped out of school. Here, I was doing it at thirty six. I got the loans I needed. I wouldn't have to start paying them back until I'd been out of school six months and working. I wanted to start the first day of hairdressing school, looking like a hair dresser. A couple of days before I was supposed to start, I gave myself a home perm. My first day at the Academy, the instructors told me that my hair was fried. I needed to have a very short haircut, so that my hair would grow back healthy. I did well with the written part of the course, I loved studying. I was old enough now to appreciate that you needed an education. When it came to working on customers, I didn't get as much attention as the younger students, perms, and the instructors checking my haircuts. I was very good with roller sets, because I had been setting my own hair on rollers since I was a teenager. Blow drying and curling irons were just becoming popular. We also did each others hair. It got to the point that Earl didn't know what color hair or style I was going to come home with.

One day while I was in school, working on the floor. The girl that Amanda was living with now came to see me. Amanda had been burned in the face from the steam of a pressure cooker. She had been to the emergency room, where they gave her a prescription for a cream especially for burns. Her friend said that she was going to be okay. I was in the middle of cutting this woman's hair. I wanted to go home, but the instructor talked to me, saying that I couldn't do anything for her at home, that I needed to stay in school and try to keep my mind on hairdressing. The instructor asked the woman if she wanted me to finish cutting her hair, because obviously the woman knew that I was upset. The woman said yes. I finished her haircut and it was probably one of my best haircuts

I went to work at a local nursing home about a ten minute walk from school. I got out of school at four, then worked five to eleven at the nursing home. I was going to hairdressing school because I felt that I had been doing nurse's aide work for almost fifteen years and was getting burnt out. I still liked working with the residents, but I began to notice that I always didn't have the patience that I used to.

I was almost through my hours. I got a job at a salon, in the morning, and going to shool in the afternoon. I was still working at the nursing home. The woman had the shop in her home. A hallway separated the shop from her living quarters. She had a cat. The cat would go from the salon to the apartment at will. She also had a young son who stayed in a playpen in the shop while she was working. Back then, you didn't think about what breathing in the fumes from perms, colors, and hairspray could do to your lungs. One day the cat was on the window sill in the salon. I petted the cat for a few minutes, then turned to go back to work. The cat grabbed me by the wrist with his mouth. He left a clean puncture wound on the inside of my wrist. It didn't even bleed. That night at work, I couldn't unzip a patient's dress. My arm was swelling up toward my shoulder. I showed it to my charge nurse, and she didn't know what it was. The next morning I went to work at the salon. The owner took a look at my wrist. She called her appointments for that morning and cancelled. She brought me to a walk-in medical center. The doctor looked at my wrist I told him about the cat bite. The doctor told me that I had cat scratch fever. He called the other doctors in to observe my arm, because cat scratch fever in adults was rare. A cat bite can be more dangerous than a dog bite because of the different microorganisms. I'm allergic to penicillin so that doctor had to find another antibiotic to treat me. The cat had all its shots. I had to go back everyday for a week. On the seventh day the doctor lanced it. I lost a week's work, both at the salon and the nursing home. Naturally the owner paid all my medical expenses, and took me to my appointments. I think she was afraid that I might sue her. By law, the cat shouldn't have been in the salon.

The day of my graduation was finally here. I had to put in about two more hours to put in. We also had a party complete with gifts when someone graduated. When I got to school, nobody was on the main floor. Everyone was downstairs. I was thinking that I was going to graduate without a party. I had always contributed to the other parties. My time was up and I was packing my stuff up to leave. Then a student came upstairs and said that the dean wanted to see me to give me my diploma. I went downstairs. All of a sudden everyone came out of hiding shouting "Surprise!" I had a great party and beautiful gifts. On my cake was a small plastic brush, mirror, curling iron, and blow dryer.

I rode to Hartford with my best friend at school to take our state test. She was so nervous about the test, that she was physically sick for two days. We both passed. When I got my licence and my grade through the mail, I practically ran to the mall to tell Earl. I was hurt because he kind of brushed me off. I had gotten a ninety two on my test. Later, he bought me a necklace with a blow dryer on it. Its very hard for Earl to express his feelings. I was just supposed to know that he was proud of me.

I checked the classifieds for a salon who was looking for a hairdresser. I called one salon owner and had a short interview on the phone. She set up a time to meet her at her shop. She was only open from Wednesday afternoon to Saturday. On

Wednesday when I and the other hairdresser weren't busy, we cleaned the shop. It was hard to get established being fresh out of school and with no clientele. A couple of customers from school came a few times, but the academy was cheaper. Some of my friends came for me to do their hair. One day Cynthia showed up at the salon with my two nieces, thirteen and five. They barely knew me. Cynthia wanted me to cut their hair while she ran some errands. I didn't even see these girls grow up. At one point Cynthia's mother-in-law who was also our stepmother lived only across the street from me and she didn't even stop to see how me and the kids were when she went there to visit. After I got done with their hair, the younger one said to her sister that I was nice and how come they didn't know me. After Cynthia left with the girls, my boss aked me where my sister lived, because she had heard my niece's comment. I told her that she lived in town. One thing though I felt uncomfortable cutting men's hair. I hadn't had much experience cutting men's hair in school. I got this male customer who worked for ESPN so he couldn't always book an appointment. He'd always take the last appointment when he was in town. I got him, because my boss would give the walk-ins and new customers to me. He had everything a woman could want., good looks, nice hair, single and a good job. The first time he sat in my chair, I asked him how he wanted his hair cut. He just told me to give him a man's haircut, then proceeded to bury himself in a magazine while I was cutting his hair. This made me less nervous. When I was done, he made a comment that I had cut off his sideburns. I felt so bad. He laughed and told me to relax, that they would grow back. I did him all the time while I worked there. The other girls would tease me about having a crush on him. We bought our next car from one of the girls I worked with. We paid $150 dollars for it, because she had just bought a new Park Avenue. We had to put in $150 for an exhaust system, and we didn't put anymore money in it for three years. It made it back and forth from Maine four times. It was also a very comfortable car to ride in. Earl liked it because it was a big car. I was also working part time at McDonald's. I quit because they knew I had another job, but they wanted my life. I then went to work at Burger King which was right across the street from the salon.

# CHAPTER THIRTY-FOUR

One afternoon I had gone to the mall to wait for Earl to get off work so that we could go for supper. I was sitting at a table in the food court, when Earl surprised me with a stuffed "Alf" doll. Alf was one of my favorite TV shows. My stepsister walked up to my table. She said that she was sorry to hear about what happened to Annie. She saw the look of surprise on my face. She said, "My God! You don't know! Annie died, she took an overdose."

I don't remember much after that. Earl said I passed out, and he caught me before I hit the cement floor. I asked my stepsister where she heard this. She answered that Annie's husband had called at her mother's with the news. I called the Waterbury police department where Annie lived to ask them if they had a report of any suicides or drug overdoses in the last forty eight hours. The officer said he'd check, but came up empty. He told me to come in on the day shift, that they might be able to help me more. Annie visited a resident at the local nursing home. They were close. She loved my daughter. I went and spoke to the charge nurse, and told her what I had heard, but didn't have any proof yet. I was afraid that Annie's husband would go visit her, and tell her of Annie's death. I didn't want her to hear anything, unless it was true.

The next morning, I called Sam, my best friend, and she picked me up and we went to Waterbury. We went to the police department and spoke to the officer in charge. I gave him Annie's address. She didn't have a phone. I told him that my son-in-law had called my family and told them that my daughter had died of an overdose. He checked the records, and told me that there

162

had been no calls to that address. He gave us the directions to Annie's address. Sam and I found the adress. It was an old movie theater that had been converted into apartments. It also had a security door. A few minutes later, a Spanish woman came to get into the building. Thank God I remembered enough of my high school Spanish to get her to understand that we needed to get in because my daughter lived there. Sam and I climbed the three flights of stairs and knocked on Annie's door, afraid of what we might find. Annie answered the door after the third knock and my calling her name. She was fine. She told me that her and her husband had split up, because she wasn't going to get the large disability check that he married her for. He needed it to support his drug habit. He thought that if he could get her family to believe she was dead, he could file a fake death report and claim her check. Sam, Annie, and I spend the rest of the day going out to eat and shopping. We also stopped back at the police department to tell them that she was alive and well. Annie wanted to press charges against her husband, but the officer said that until he actually did it, there was nothing they could do. I also went to the nursing home and told them to tell Nina that Annie was fine.

# CHAPTER THIRTY-FIVE

I left the salon I was working at for a full time job at a chain owned hair salon. There the customers were mostly walk-ins. Sometimes you worked eight hours or split shifts. I took the city bus to work. The academy where I graduated from didn't have a good reputation as far as how well they taught the students. I was never broke, the tips were good. Then one day, a couple of teenagers from "the drive" which was the nickname of the low cost housing project came in. I was given both of them. They both gave me a hard time as to how they wanted their haircut. The manager took over and finished cutting their hair The next lady in line observed what these boys were putting me through, and that I was visibly upset. She came up to my chair, and told me to do her hair. A couple of days later, both managers called me into the back office. They pulled the curtain closed on the window. They had a mannequin of a head with a wig on it like we had in school. They told me that it wasn't my fault, that my haircuts weren't blended. They said that I wasn't taught properly. They took the time to show me on the wig how to blend a haircut and check it to make sure that it was all even. I appreciated them doing this for me. They did this around closing time when it wasn't so busy and would cause me less embarrassment. I eventually left there, and got hired at another chain salon. I did alright there, but anyone who has ever worked with the public knows how hard it is to please everyone. I wanted to work in a regular salon, where I could build up a clientele. I went to work in a salon that had two stores, one in Bristol, the other in West Hartford. I had to work three days in the Bristol store and two days in West Hartford. Phil Jr. and his fiancée would give me a ride to and from work when I worked in West Hartford. I think the way the chairs were set up, many people thought it was a school. It was right in the heart of the Jewish community. One day, this middle aged lady was sitting in the lobby waiting for her name to be called. She was dressed in a turtle neck shirt, blue jeans, and sneakers She wearing a cross necklace. I had a nun listed in my book for a perm at nine AM. I didn't see a nun in the lobby. Finally, the woman in the turtleneck shirt came up to the desk. She said that she had nine o'clock appointment for a perm and had been waiting for fifteen minutes. I asked her name and she told me that she was Sister Josephine. I tried to cover my surprise. The nuns I grew up wore habits. I did her perm. Another time, this elderly lady wanted the manager to give her her perm, but the manager didn't do customers. She gave her to me. I wrapped her perm, and when the time to get rinsed came, the manager came and checked to make sure it was ready, just to make the lady more comfortable. Well, I hadn't used all the perm solution. I left the half empty bottle on my table. Instead of picking up the neutralizer, I picked up the rest of the perm solution. I didn't realize it until I rinsed her hair and it was straight. We had to give her a couple of good shampoos and a set. She came back the next week for her perm, and she let me do it.

One day when Phil Jr. picked me from work, he told me that we had to go to this major department store to pick up Katie's engagement ring. We go to the jewelry counter and Phil Jr. gives the clerk the slip. The clerk came back with the ring. She took my hand and said that she wanted to make sure it fit. Phil Jr. face got as red as a beet. He told the clerk that I wasn't his fiancée, but his mother. The woman recovered her embarrassment by telling him how good he was going to look in twenty years.

One day in the Bristol shop, this teenager sat in my chair and told me he wanted a military cut. About half way through the haircut, he changed his mind, but it was already too short for what he wanted now. He gave me a rough time, and said that I screwed up his hair. He demanded his money back. I was very upset. The next Monday morning before anyone came in, the manager asked me what happened Saturday afternoon when the teenager came in. The customers that were in the shop at the time told her that the boy had given me trouble. She asked me why I got so upset. I told her it was because I didn't like messing up someone's hair. I had ordered a weight loss product and wanted it delivered to the shop. A girl signed for the package when it came in, but we couldn't find the package anywhere in the shop. I couldn't prove it, but someone had apparently stolen it. I left that shop shortly after. I went to work in another salon chain store. I wasn't comfortable always doing different people. I wanted my own clientele. I was very lacking in self confidence.

# CHAPTER THIRTY-SIX

I went to work at the beauty salon in the mall. It was nice because sometimes Earl and I were able to have lunch together. Phil Jr. and Katie were planning their wedding. Katie was also five months pregnant. The wedding was going to be at her parent's house. They were going to be married by a Justice of the Peace. I was still small enough to get my dress at a clothing store in the mall. It was mint green with a pleated skirt and a dressy bodice. The day of the wedding was beautiful so we had the wedding and reception in the backyard. When I saw the chance to speak to Phil Sr. alone, I grabbed it. I told him that if I ever heard or saw him molesting our grandchild, I'd kill him. Truthfully I think I could of.

The salon in the mall was nice. One night a gentleman came in for a haircut and a perm. I was alone in the shop because it was my night to close the shop. PJ was with me. The gentleman sent him to get cold drinks. I did his hair, and when I was done, he gave me a fifty dollar tip! I also had to deal with the mall rats that liked to give you a hard time over their haircuts. All the new girls ran into that problem at one time, and I also had my turn. I saw an ad in the paper that the salon across the street was looking for a hairdresser. I called and we set up an interview at her home. I did my own hair. I got the job. When I told the owner at the salon in the mall, she wished me luck and told me that I had the potential to be a good hairdresser. She wasn't one to give compliments freely, so I knew she meant it. I was in luck. The girl that I was replacing had a following. She had left to go into the insurance business. Some of her following went to another hairdresser, but not all. I started the next Monday. I expected Betty to stay and observe my work, but she didn't. I had a booking for a perm. She introduced me to the customer and left. There was another hairdresser, Jane that worked Mondays. In Connecticut most barbershops and salons were closed on Mondays if they belonged to the Chamber of Commerce. It was a nice homey salon. There was a table set up by the dryers with coffee, tea, and munchies. Betty gave a good senior discount on Mondays, Tuesdays, and Wednesdays. Jane worked to eight on Thursday evenings. Finally, I had a following, and it was only a five minute walk. Sometimes I would go home. If a walk-in came in, Betty would call me. On our birthdays, Betty would buy a cake and the rest of us would chip in on the other goodies. We also went to hair shows. At Christmas Betty took us out to a dinner theater. The worst holiday for me was Halloween. We all had to dress up. I wasn't good at creating a costume, and it brought back memories of the Halloweens in the foster home. Jane would always dress up as Charlie Chaplin. She was German, and I think she always wished she had been born a boy. Even when we went out to the dinner theaters, she always wore a mannish style suit. Sometimes a good friend of Betty's would work in the salon. We were the same age, and her birthday was the day after mine.

It was my eleventh wedding anniversary, and Betty had chartered a bus to take us to Gloucester, Mass. to go on a whale watch. Earl said it was fine that I go, but I still felt guilty leaving him alone on our anniversary. The trip was awesome. I saw the Good Year blimp being launched from Logan's Airport. When we got there we took pictures of each other and asked a tourist to take a picture of us at the seamen at the helm statue. We ate dinner at the Crow's Nest. We all had lobster. Then we went out on the boat. I was glad that I had bought a hat at a gift shop. I had a habit of buying a hat or a tee shirt or both when I went on a trip. We were on the ocean five hours. They took us to where the whales feed. The staff would tell us were to look. Some came so close to the boat, and looked like they were going to go underneath it. It was breathtaking to watch them come up and dive into the water so gracefully. They didn't guarantee that we'd see dolphins but we did, a whole school of them. We had time before we had to go back to the bus, so we toured Groton's fish cannery. The day was perfect. I recommend anyone who loves animals to go on a whale watch. It's an experience you'll never forget. A movie came out a few years later called "The Perfect Storm" I watch it every time its shown, because it takes place in Gloucester. We ate, at the restaurant in the movie, visited the museum, and saw the statue of the seaman. and passed the lighthouse in the channel leading you out to sea.

I joined a bowling league made up of our friends from the Moose Lodge. We bowled on Sunday afternoons. After a few weeks, Earl also joined. After bowling we'd go to the bar, and a couple of guys who had good jobs would keep buying rounds of drinks. Earl had a way of putting me down in front of our friends when he was feeling good or drunk. Sometimes we'd go out to eat, and one or the other guy would pick up the tab which was for ten people. We'd finish the day off at the Lodge. It wasn't so good for me Monday morning. It seemed every time I had a hangover, I'd have a nine o'clock appointment. I f I wasn't hung over, there wouldn't be anybody for nine o'clock. I wasn't very good at bowling, but I liked it. The highest score I got was a 203. That was because the night before I had gone out with my friend and her daughter who was getting married to see some male strippers, and boy was I hung over on Sunday. I had also became a grandmother a few days before, so we were also celebrating that.

Earl's sixty fifth birthday was coming up. He's a very hard man to pull a surprise party for, but I did it with the help of my girlfriend. I ordered the cake. We were going to have his party at the Moose Lodge. I also ordered four extra large pizzas, from Paul's. After bowling, all the teams went back to the lodge. My girlfriend made up an excuse that she had forgotten something at home and asked me if I wanted to go for a ride with her. We picked up the cake, pizzas, and paper plates, and plastic silverware, and headed back to the lodge. We went in through the side door which led to the kitchen. When everything was set, we got everyone together. I brought the cake out from the kitchen. For once, I managed to pull something over on Earl. He had no idea, that he was going to have a birthday party.

That Christmas both Paul and PJ wanted the nite glow race track. I went to the toy store in the mall and put it on lay away. It was fifty dollars. It would be one gift for the both of them. When I got it out of lay away, I brought it to one of my friends on the bowling league. She wrapped it and kept it at her house because we were going to spend Christmas with them. I can not wrap gifts so that they look nice. I think the boys played with it about three times, then were tired of it. I ended up selling it. That year Earl bought me one of the microwaves that were just coming out. I had that microwave for more than twenty years. Earl also like buying small sized gifts and wrapping them from a big box down to the right size box. He enjoyed watching me work for my gift. Sometimes he even put a couple of bricks at the bottom of the box.

Early one morning, Phil Jr. called me to tell me that I was a grandmother. They had a baby girl. My girlfriend brought me to the hospital because she was a good friend, and she also wanted to see the baby. The first time I laid eyes on Kristen, it was like seeing Phil Jr. twenty five years earlier. They had bought her almost the exact same red sleeper, that we had bought for Phil Jr. I expected to see a lot of my new grand daughter and her parents, but they spent most of the time at Katie's parents. I rarely got asked to baby-sit, and when they did come to visit, they never stayed very long. Katie would complain that our apartment was too hot. Heat was included in the rent, so we had no way of controlling it. Betty bought a beautiful dress for Kristen. She bought an eighteen months size so that she'd be walking when it fit her. I bought her outfits also, but I never seen her wear them. She would be dressed in clothes her other grandmother got her even if they came from the thrift store. One day Phil Jr. came into the shop to see me. He was hanging his head. He asked me to come to their place for dinner. I was so excited. I was going to get to spend time with my grand daughter. Then he asked me that when I came to dinner, would I give Katie and her mother a perm. I know I should have refused because I was being used, but I didn't. I even bought Katie's favorite wine. I got to hold my granddaughter for about a half an hour, then Katie put her to bed. What hurt worse, was that Phil Jr. would go pick up his father at the half way house to come to visit. He saw more of them than I did! I warned Phil Jr. that day that Kristen was born, not to leave his father alone with her, not even for a minute. That night I not only did the two perms, but Phil Jr. wanted a haircut. I did hair till midnight, and of course it was all free. I also had to work in the morning.

No matter where we lived, there was a coffee shop nearby, and were we were living now, was no exception. I used to get up a couple of hours earlier than I needed to so that I could have at least a couple of cups of coffee and sometimes breakfast before I went to work. One Monday morning I was drinking my coffee when all of a sudden, I got extremely hot, and like I couldn't breathe. I remember going to the door to get some air. The next thing I know, I was sitting in a booth, throwing up into a pan. I had passed out just outside the door. They owner of the diner called the paramedics. They checked me out and asked me if I wanted to go to the hospital, but I refused because I had no insurance. I asked one of my friends if she would call Betty and tell her that I was sick, and wouldn't be in. I went home and slept for six hours. The diner changed hands shortly after. The new owner and his wife were Puerto Rican and very hard to work for. He had a hard time keeping waitresses because he was so strict. One day he was without a waitress, he asked me if I would help his wife out. I didn't have to work that morning so

I agreed. His wife told me that her and I would be sharing tips. When it wasn't busy, I washed dishes. He closed at two, I had to sweep and mop the floor before I went home. He paid me at the end of the day. It ended up with him hiring me. I would work for him when I wasn't working at Betty's. I also worked the weekends. A lot of customers felt that it was unfair that I needed to share tips with the owner's wife. They started putting their tips under their plates. When I would clean the tables, I picked up the tip together with the plate. By doing that, we were mainly sharing tips left on the counter. There was also a pizza parlor in that little plaza. We'd go there either to eat in or take out. One time when I was still working in a nursing home, I was working third shift. I was sitting on the front steps waiting for my ride. Paul pulled up in front of the house and handed me a pizza that someone hadn't picked up to take to the girls at work.

# CHAPTER THIRTY-SEVEN

I bought a VCR, and a gadget called a VCR Plus that would allow me to tape one show while watching another. I love movies. I would buy a five pack of VCR tapes. The manager of the electronics store in the mall would put some in the back for me when they came on sale. I could put three movies on one tape. I bought a notebook, index cards, and a recipe box. I would right down the title of the movie and color code it as to what kind of movie it was, such as comedy, drama, etc. Each movie had a number and a color. I listed them by number in my notebook, and index cards. By the time we moved to Maine, I had taped over a thousand movies.

I also joined the fitness club in the mall. I loved doing aerobics. The instructor was amazed that I could do aerobics because I smoked. After aerobics class, I often soaked in the hot tub or grabbed a quick shower. I'd stop at the bakery and order a grapefruit juice to cool down before I went outside. In nine months I had lost fifty four pounds. I had been struggling with my weight since I gained the fifty pounds while I was pregnant with Phil Jr. It was even harder after my hysterectomy to keep the weight off. Betty was also on the heavy side. She put herself on a diet. By this time, I had put back some of the weight I lost after I stopped going to the fitness center. I stopped going because they went out of business. Betty and I joined the aerobics and exercise classes at the Girl's Club.

PJ was now seventeen, but looked twenty. He was a husky boy. He got a job at the outlet store in the mall. He met a girl who worked there and they started dating. She was twenty four and PJ told her that he was twenty one. His girlfriend cosigned for him to buy a brand new pickup truck. He would take me out to some back roads and an old parking lot to practice driving. One time he wanted me to drive back to town. A little ways down the road, I panicked and pulled over to the side of the road, without putting on my blinker. The car in back of me blew his horn at me. He even offered to let Earl and I take his truck when we went on vacation in Maine.

I wanted Earl to spend the day with me at Mystic Seaport and Aquarium. He didn't want to go, so he paid PJ to take me. On the way there, PJ asked me what I thought was a strange question. He asked me if Interstate 95 went all the way to Florida. I told him that I wasn't sure. We toured the seaport and of course I bought a sharp looking straw hat. PJ didn't want to go on the steamboat down the Mystic River. After some coaxing, he went with me. He was anxious to see the aquarium, so we drove there. It was beautiful and we watched the dolphin show. Finally it was time to head home. I didn't know it then, but that would be the last mother son outing we would share

About three weeks later, PJ told me that he was going on a weekend camping trip with his friends. He didn't come back to his girlfriend's after the weekend. About a month later I got a phone call from a woman police officer in Sarasota Florida. At first she was kind of cold to me on the phone. PJ had told her that his mother was the wicked witch of the west. PJ had these large brown eyes and could look you right in the face and lie his butt off. The officer and I talked a little more, then she asked me if I wanted to talk to PJ. I heard her in the background saying that she didn't want to hear any more of his lies. I talked to PJ, then the officer told me that they would send him by bus. Apparently the truck got repossessed in Florida. When he got back to Connecticut, he went to stay with my friend that groomed dogs. The finance company had been going after his girlfriend for payment on the truck, because she cosigned and she finally found out that PJ was still a minor. The girlfriend tried to get Earl and I to help her pay for the truck. One day, I ordered a grinder from the pizza shop. Paul the owner was giving me the cold shoulder. Finally, he asked me what kind of mother was I that I wouldn't help my son pay the insurance on his truck and that's why he lost it. I told Paul the truth. He said he had no idea that he was lying, he had told him the story with such an honest face. Another time he tried to pass a bad check at a gun shop. He needed an ID card. The owner was an ex cop and a notary republic. The owner would arrest his own mother. He wanted to come after me to cover the check, but Earl paid him. One Saturday night, the phone rang around two AM. It was the police station. They had PJ for creating a disturbance and needed a parent to pick him up. Our car wasn't running then. Earl said he'd go get him because he didn't want me walking the streets alone at that hour. I would have loved to see PJ's face when he saw his stepfather and not me.

# CHAPTER THIRTY-EIGHT

Even though I was married, I often felt lonely. Every year we'd have two big festivals, the Greek festival, and the Mum festival. Most of the time I went alone because Earl didn't want to go The last time I saw Aunt Emma was at the Greek Festival. She talked about Uncle Bill as if he were still alive. About the only thing Earl and I did together was going to the club to drink. I thought of leaving him several times because of the way he verbally abused when he was drunk, but I was afraid that I couldn't make it on my own. One time I almost lost my job at a nursing home for clocking in to work the third shift feeling no pain. They couldn't send me home because I rode with Sam. It would have taken her an hour to bring me home and get back to work. Another time I was too drunk to work, so I called in sick. Sam and I also picked up extra money by working for a temp agency. They would book us at different nursing homes that used them when they were short. One time we got out of work at seven AM and headed for the nursing home that the agency got for us on the first shift. The Director of Nurses came down on us for being an hour late. We explained to her that we had just gotten off our regular job at seven. The nurse said that she didn't allow her aides to work third and first shifts back to back, but she let us work the weekend anyway. Sam started dating Mark, the same guy that was stalking me. He was doing the same to Sam. He would peek in her window, follow us if we went out and even followed her car when we were going to work. By now, Buddy and Sam had broken up. I don't know why, but Sam ended up marrying him.

Amanda called me one day and wanted me to cosign for a loan for her. I was in no position to do it even if I wanted to. She was on city welfare, how was she going to pay back the loan. Besides, my gut instinct told me that she didn't want the loan for herself, but for her father. I know he put her up to asking me. When I told her I couldn't do it, she asked me what kind of a mother was I. That hurt, we didn't talk again for two years.

Earl and I were still going to Maine to stay with his sister for two weeks during the summer. Earl's brother was now in a nursing home forty miles away from home. Earl's sister didn't want him placed in the local nursing home. She was afraid that he'd be at "her" house all the time, and she didn't want that. His sister never knew that their father wanted to leave the house to Earl with the stipulation that his sister be allowed to live there as long as she lived. Earl turned it down, because his life was in Connecticut. He told Dad to give the house to his sister. She was an old maid and had taken care of their parents, but she always put herself first. She never missed a chance to throw it up in Earl's face, that it was her house and she could do what she wanted. Especially when they were both drunk. They were like fire and water. They couldn't go two weeks without getting into an argument. In fact Earl had gone eight years without going to see her. I loved the trip there. Earl and I were able to talk about different things and things that bothered us. It was on one of these trips, that I told him what Amanda had said to me, and how badly it hurt. Going home was an entirely different matter. On the trip up, we would travel during the night, getting there around noon time. On the way home, Earl wanted to leave about six in the morning to miss the rush hour traffic in Hartford. I didn't want to go home. I would stay in bed until he almost literally pulled me out. I'd cry in the car until we reached about Bangor. Then I knew that I had to face going home. From the first time Earl brought me to "the valley" I knew this was where I wanted to live. Earl said he'd never move back to Maine to starve again. Once we were home, I would settle into my daily routine.

I met a elderly woman, I don't remember where, but we became good friends. She lived in an elderly housing complex not to far from where I lived. Sometimes I'd take the car, though I was still very nervous about driving. I'd go for coffee and to play bingo. She introduced me to another friend of hers that also lived there. Gloria and I became very close friends, almost from the start. She told me that I reminded her of her daughter who lived in Maine. She also had a son around my age who was always chasing one dream or another. She had two other sons that lived in Texas. We became like mother and daughter. She was the closest person in my life that took the place of my mother. I'd give her perms, and cut Eddie's hair.

We drank coffee and smoked cigarettes. I grew to love her vey much, and Eddie was like an older brother that I always wished I had. My cat "Tigger" also took a liking to Eddie, even though he hid from strangers. Eddie wasn't particularly fond of cats. He called Tigger my "Chinese chicken." Eddie was the only one Tigger would stay with while we were in Maine. I think he sensed the close friendship Eddie and I shared. Tigger started doing that when Kristen was a toddler. She'd come to my place calling "kitty, kitty. kitty." only this kitty wanted no part of her. Her other grandmother had cats that let Kristen do almost anything she wanted to with them. She teethed on one of the cat's ears. One time she came, and Tigger's mother had just had another litter of kittens. I got her to sit in a chair, and let her hold one. After a few minutes, I told her it was time to give it back to its mommy. She got upset with me and told me she hated me, though I knew she didn't mean it. I always kept a jar of cookies on the table for her, like my grandmother had done for me.

Katie was pregnant again. Phil Jr. called and asked me if I could buy them a double stroller. Katie had a baby-sitting job that she had to walk to, and it was too far for Kristen to walk. I told him that I could put in a hundred dollars toward one.

That would have been enough if she wanted one from a local department store, but she wanted to get one at a expensive chain store for kids in the West Farms Mall. They had to put in another thirty dollars with my hundred. I didn't mind, for once I made my daughter-in-law happy. She had to show the stroller off to her friends. I tried not to be a meddling mother-in-law. I remembered how I felt when Phil's mother tried to take over. Actually my ex mother-in-law and I got along much better after I divorced her son, until Annie accused him of touching her and he went back to prison. She always felt that her grand daughter was lying. I don't entirely blame her for our not being close in the early years of my marriage to her son. I didn't know how you were supposed to act towards a mother. This time Katie had a boy. They named him Eric after one of their friends who was also going to be his godfather. I remember Kristen cried all during her christening, and fell asleep when she got in the car.

The same pattern after Eric was born. Katie was at her parents most of the time. I only got to hold Eric for a little while. Katie's sister now had a baby girl. One day while I was at Katie's parents' house. I saw Katie's niece wearing the dress Betty had bought for Kristen. I don't think Kristen ever wore it. But at least someone was wearing it.

Phil Jr. was like his father, he couldn't hang on to money. They were always moving because they'd get behind on the rent. They weren't good at paying bills either. While they were dating, Katie got fired from a convenience store where she was working for stealing. Her parents came to her rescue and got her out of trouble. Phil Jr. and Katie needed a car. Her parents cosigned so that they could buy a brand new Honda. They had a couple of accidents and finally totaled it. The bank put a lien on Katie's parents' house because the car wasn't paid for, and the kids were behind in the payments. Katie's father had been married before and had another family in Ohio. He would travel to Ohio sometimes once or twice a month. Katie's mother was a nurse in a local hospital.

They moved to a third floor apartment just around the corner from Earl and I. A couple of times Phil Jr. would ask to borrow our car. We'd let him, but Earl wasn't crazy about it. One time I was baby-sitting, when the landlord came looking for the rent. I explained to him, that I was just a baby-sitter. Super Bowl Sunday that year. Phil Jr. asked me if I could baby-sit so that they could go to their friend's Super Bowl party. Kristen was almost three, and Eric was five months. Of course I wanted to. I would get a few hours to enjoy my grand children. Kristen wouldn't eat the hot dogs and french fries Katie wanted her to have for supper. She loved blueberry yogurt and pop tarts. That's what she wanted for supper. Katie told me that they were having problems getting Kristen to sleep in her own bed. When I put her to bed, I read her a story. After the story I kissed her good night and told her that if she needed me, I would be in the living room. She fell asleep and never got up. Eric was no problem putting him to bed. He was dry and full and had his bottle. The kids were surprised when they got home that Kristen was asleep in her bed. One time Phil Jr. called me to tell me Kristen had threw all her bed linens out the third floor window. Then he asked me a question that's every mother's dream come true. He wanted to know if he was that bad at Kristen's age. Every mother wants her child to have a child just like they were.

Then one day, They came to tell me that they were moving to Ohio. Katie's parents had lost their house, and were moving to Ohio. At first I wasn't worried. The kids never had any money, and it takes money to move that far with two kids. Katie came to see me to ask if Phil Jr. could stay with me while she moved with her parents. She told me it would only be until they were settled, but I knew better. Besides it wasn't fair to Earl. He had already helped me raise the kids once, now it was time for him and I. The kids found a way. They sold what they didn't need and put the rest of their belonging in the moving truck. Katie and Phil Jr. and the kids would follow behind the truck in Katie's father's car.

I got to baby-sit one more time before they left. I had blueberry yogurt and pop tarts for her. They called me when they got there. They were going to stay with Katie's parents until they got their own place. It was going to be easy because Katie's father had gotten fired from Connecticut's largest newspaper where he had worked for many years. Her father had gotten Phil Jr. a job there, and they both got fired because they got into a fight at work. Katie's father really didn't like Phil Jr., even before that happened. Katie put Kristen on the phone. The first thing she said to me was that her father wouldn't give her any pop tarts. When Phil Jr. got back on the phone he told me it was because he had no money for them. Katie was pregnant for a third time when they moved. She had another boy. He was born in Ohio. They named him Corey. I never even got to see him. I couldn't go out to visit, because of not having enough money, or credit cards, and of course they never had money to come visit me. I felt cheated. I always thought that when the kids were raised, I'd have the large family I always dreamed of, complete with holiday gatherings, but it never happened. My friends would always invite Earl and I over for Thanksgiving, and sometimes Christmas, I always felt like I was on the outside looking in. I appreciated them asking us, but it still wasn't my family.

# CHAPTER THIRTY-NINE

I missed my grandchildren something awful. I threw myself into my work. At one point I had three jobs, a full time job, and two part time jobs. I worked at the local newspaper, which was a two minute walk from home. I was collating newspapers. You had to go in at two AM to six AM. Sometimes I'd over sleep, because I would lay down in the evening. I either went in late or not at all. Sometimes if there were a lot of sale papers you went in the afternoon. Sometimes the presses would break down, if they couldn't get them working, we went home early. I also took care of an elderly lady every other weekend from five PM till eleven thirty PM when her overnight aide arrived. She was a sweet lady. I had to fix her supper and sit with her while she ate because she choked easily. I'd washed up the dishes, and even if there was only one piece of paper in the waste basket, I had to out it in the trash barrel outside. She was terrified of her daughter-in-law who lived upstairs. One time she sent me to the basement for a can of white paint. There was a small nick in the floor board from her wheel chair. She wanted me to fill in the nick with the paint. After supper we'd watch the country music station on TV until her bedtime. After she went to bed, I'd fix her lunch for the next day. I didn't go to her funeral when she died, because I was too hung-over. Her daughter-in-law went up side of me and down the other the next time she saw me. I told her that I'd rather remember her alive.

One night Annie came to see me with her new second husband. She told me she was pregnant. I asked her when she was due, and by her answer, there was no way she was pregnant. She always had a very strong maternal instinct. She loved dolls and babies. One time when she was nine, she went into a strange lady's house, took her baby out of the playpen and into the stroller. She took the baby for a walk, and brought it back. The mother who was obviously scared out of her wits, wanted to have me arrested for kidnapping. When I explained to her that Annie had problems, and that she would never have harmed the baby, she calmed down. The next time Annie and Chuck came to see me, she was obviously very pregnant. Chuck told me that they were moving to Virginia so that his mother could help Annie with the baby. I was devastated. PJ had just took advantage of a major bus line's special, anywhere in the U. S. for ninety nine dollars. He went out west. My only child left in Connecticut was Amanda, and she was with her father. I wanted to move to Maine more than ever now, but Earl still wouldn't budge. He still was doing maintenance at the mall.

Gloria's daughter from Maine came to visit her. She wanted her mother to come to Maine and live with her. Gloria was a bad diabetic, and had trouble controlling her sugar. Sometimes she'd pass out. Gloria wanted me to move with them. Her daughter wanted her to help with the moving expenses, which Gloria couldn't do without my paycheck. I didn't really realize then, that she was using me, I just wanted to move to Maine. I was sure that if Earl saw that I was serious about moving, he'd fix the car and join me once he saw that I wasn't coming back. Earl watched me pack and never said a word. He didn't ask me not to go or even goodbye.

We had a good trip. We got to Nancy's late in the evening. The next day I called Earl's sister to see if I could stay with her. I didn't realize it was another fifty miles to my sister-in-law's. Her hearing was bad, and she couldn't make out what I was saying. She handed the phone over to her friend. She said that I couldn't stay with her because it would affect her Social Security, but she wanted me to come see her. Nancy had a room ready for her mother, and there was a spare room upstairs for me. The most important rule was that I couldn't smoke upstairs. Nancy had a teenage son. Her husband was a nice man, but I soon learned that Nancy was a difficult person to live with. I also felt guilty when my money ran out, that I couldn't pay room and board. I did the housework during the week, because Nancy worked. On Saturday it was her thing to give the house a good cleaning without any help. Also no one could touch her ice cream. Once in a while she'd offer me some. She brought me to the Employment Center to apply for jobs. She took me to where she worked to fill out an application. You had to take a difficult written test, because what they did was edit articles for different companies. I got the second highest score. A guy that got the better score got the job. I did get hired as a chamber maid in a large hotel next door to where Nancy worked. I had to go into work later than she, so she'd drop me at a Dunkin' Donuts shop. I had to walk up a big hill to get to work. I started to meet a couple of male friends at the donut shop. They'd give me a ride up the hill. I almost got into an affair with one of them. I would wait for Nancy outside the hotel because I got out earlier than she did. and ride home with her. At least now I could pay my way, though I hated the job. People are such slobs when they're on vacation. Not only that, but Mainers especially in Aroostook County didn't appreciate people moving from Connecticut to Maine. They felt that we were taking jobs away from them. I made a couple of friends, but I really didn't fit in. I would call Earl, and he'd be drunk every time I talked to him.

Gloria after a while moved into a senior housing complex in the center of town. She didn't live their long, because she couldn't make friends. To the tenants living there, she was an outsider. She moved into an apartment across the street. One day we went to this restaurant next door for coffee. The waitress was a good friend of mine from Connecticut. She had moved back because of family issues. She told me she'd ask her boss about hiring me. At the time he didn't need anyone. Sometimes I spent the night with Gloria. On Sundays, Nancy would pick us up for Sunday dinner and to watch a movie she rented. I started spending the weekends at Gloria's. All day Saturday we would spend the day doing our hair and nails just to go to bingo at the VFW club. Neither one of us ever won very much, but it was a night out.

It came time for me to find my own place. One day I did the laundry and washed a pair of Nancy's son's pants that weren't supposed to be washed. I almost ruined them. Her son was understandably upset, but calmed down when his mother said that the pants could be saved. Nancy's son and I often sat on the front lawn and talked. We'd watch the planes going to and leaving Loring Air Force Base. One day, we were in the kitchen, when I heard what I thought was the fire horn in town. Nancy's husband told us to come quietly outside. In the river across the street was a large bull moose. I had never seen a moose before. Nancy's husband would get drunk on scotch every weekend, which caused arguments between him and Nancy. Nancy told me once that she didn't want to like me, but she did. I started looking for an apartment. Nancy said that she didn't want me to take an apartment without her checking it out first. She didn't want me renting from a slum lord. We found a one room apartment with a half bath in a rooming house. The landlord was had moved back to Maine from Connecticut. His wife sewed. She said that if I took the apartment, she would make a bedspread and curtains for me. I could afford the weekly rent, and the room was nice. The only thing was that I'd have to go outside and up the stairs to take a shower. There was a large kitchen where you could fix your own food. Sometimes the roomers played cards in the kitchen. Nancy approved so I took the room. I applied at Mc Donald's because it was only a five minute walk. I think if I had been a Mainer, I would have got hired.

Then one day I got a call at Nancy's. The manager from Dunkin' Donuts wanted me to come in for an interview. I had filled out the application at the Employment Center. I went for the interview. The first thing he said to me was that I wasn't from around there. He said that people didn't use my kind of lingo up here. He wanted me to be manager for the two PM to eight PM shift. He wanted someone that was mature. I told him that I'd take the job. I could walk to and from work. I was supposed to start training in two weeks. The hotel wouldn't let me go without a thirty day notice. This was acceptable with the manager of the donut shop.

I was still calling Earl collect. I'd always ask him when he was coming to Maine. I told him that I was working. He never gave me a direct answer. I still believed that I could get him to make the move. One thing about Earl is that he's a creature of habit, and also very stubborn. I missed him terribly, and at times I thought of going home. I was nervous about taking the manager's job. Earl was afraid that he wouldn't be able to get a job here. He didn't want to live on just my paycheck, and he still had a couple of years before he could retire. One time he called and asked me to come home. As time went by, I began to realize that he wasn't going to make the move. He was enjoying the summer with his friends from the lodge. I decided to go back home. I went to the rooming house and they gave me my deposit back, which they didn't have to do. Then one night Earl called me from the pay phone at the lodge. He was pretty drunk. He must have ran out of quarters, because after a few minutes we were cut off. I decided to call him back in the morning when he'd be sober. I called collect and he refused to take my call. That changed my mind about going home. I went back to the rooming house and was able to get the same room. I still had a little more than a week at the hotel. All that time I didn't hear from Earl. Finally he called. He accused me of hanging up on him the last time he called. I explained that I hadn't that he must have run out of quarters. He apologized. He still wanted me to come home. I assumed that he had fixed the car and was going to come up and get me. The next Sunday, I waited all day on Nancy's sun porch anxious to see our car, but

186

it never came. On my second to last day of work at the hotel, Earl called. He wanted me home. I asked him to send me bus fare. He gave me a hard time about sending the money, but agreed. I went back to the rooming house to tell them that I wasn't taking the room, that I was going home. The landlord's wife talked to me about going back. She wanted to know if I really wanted to go back, or was it because I was afraid to make it on my own. She told me that even though I had paid two weeks rent, she could get the city to pay two weeks rent and a check for groceries and household supplies. I told her that I was going back, even though I knew she was right about being afraid to make it on my own. She told me this time, they couldn't give me my deposit back, because the bedspread and curtains were already made, and they'd have to rent the room to a female. I called the donut shop and apologized for the short notice, but I couldn't take the job. The next day I packed. Nancy was going to take me to the bus stop in the morning. The phone kept ringing. I knew it was the hotel wanting me to show up for work. I just let it ring. Finally it was time to say goodbye to Gloria and Nancy. I thanked them both for everything. Gloria told me to always keep pictures of Maine in my head. I got on the bus. As soon as it started to pull away, and I waved my last goodbye, my gut was telling me that I was making a mistake. I had to change buses in Houlton. A state trooper came on board to check all the passengers, to make sure nobody was on that was wanted by the police. We made a lot of stops in some small towns until we reached Bangor. I talked with a few passengers that sat next to me. I had a little money on me, but not much. I hadn't picked up my paycheck at the hotel. Earl had sent me just enough for bus fare. It's about an eighteen to twenty hour bus ride to Connecticut. We got to my stop in New Britian about forty five minutes early. It's in a bad section of New Britian. There's a diner nearby. I had enough money for a cup of coffee. After my coffee I waited outside the diner with my luggage. The cook would stick his head out the door every so often to check on me. Earl and his friend were on time to pick me up. they had no idea that the bus was early. Earl was so drunk, he was staggering. If I'd had the money, I would have took the next bus back to Maine. My instinct was right. This was a mistake. I should have been strong enough to make it on my own.

The apartment was spotless. There was a teacup and saucer with silk flowers in it on the kitchen table. For about three months, Earl treated me like a queen. A couple of months later, Gloria also came back to Connecticut. She got an apartment in the same Senior Housing Complex that she lived in before she left. Eddie wasn't supposed to, but he more or less lived with her. One day he brought her an artificial wooden fireplace that had logs that looked like they were burning when you plugged it in. The fireplace tools were also with it. Gloria loved it. She also collected butterflies and loved sci-fi. She read every book Stephen King who comes from Maine wrote. She also had pictures of the outside of his home in Bangor. The wrought iron gates had spiders and bates on them.

# CHAPTER FORTY

I couldn't take Earl's drinking. He never physically abused me, but emotionally and verbally he did. I thought of leaving for good, but didn't have a job that paid enough to support myself. It would take a lawyer to force Earl to pay me support. Also I had such a large family, that I didn't know if I could live alone.

I couldn't get my job back at Betty's. I'd been gone three months. The hairdresser that we bought the car from, worked for Betty for a short while, but quit because she couldn't smoke at her station. Betty's friend had taken over my clientele. Betty hired me to do shampoos, take out rollers, perm rollers, rinse out the perms and colors to help out the girls. I also did walk-ins when they came in. She paid me by the hour or commission which ever was higher. If business was slow, which wasn't often, I didn't go in. I went back to my habit of going to the coffee shop in the small plaza. A girlfriend of mine was helping out her best friend as a receptionist at her salon. She told me that she was also looking for a hairdresser. Her salon was in the main plaza in town, with a lot of volume. I called her for an interview. I could take the town bus to work. It stopped in the plaza every hour. The interview went well. She promised to teach me the latest styles and haircuts. I loved working at Betty's, but our clientele were mostly senior citizens. I hated telling Betty that I was leaving. She bought me a mum plant.

My first day at the new salon, I did my best to fit in, but I couldn't quite do it. After the first couple of weeks, the owner sent to work in her second shop, that was in a small plaza. I could still take the bus to work, but I'd have to walk like a quarter mile to the shop. My first day there was Halloween. I figured the other girls would be dresses up, so I went to work as a witch. Earl had brought me to work that day. When I got there, there was only the manager, and she wasn't in costume. I felt so out of place. I called Earl and asked him to bring me some jeans and a shirt. He did, but couldn't understand why I was upset about being the only one in costume. You remember Halloween was the holiday I hated the most. I know that if I had explained this to Betty why I hated dressing up for Halloween, she would have understood, and not asked me to.

Sometimes I went to the bakery that was in the plaza if I got there before Diane came to open the shop. There was almost any new business. Another hairdresser working there had a following, and of course so did Diane. There were very few walk-ins. Most of the time I spent cleaning, washing towels, and putting stock away. My neighbor downstairs started selling products for a weight loss company. I bought from her and we held meetings in a conference room in a motel chain. I brought my meals to work. Shortly after, I began to feel like I was being set up. All of a sudden, customers I did were coming back with complaints about their haircuts. I can see one or two dissatisfied customers. Sometimes they change their mind halfway through a haircut about how they wanted it cut. The other hairdresser could read a book when she wasn't busy. I was told I couldn't read a book or magazine while I was at the desk. I think the owner was hoping I'd quit, because she had no good reason to fire me. If she laid me off, she'd have tro pay unemployment because I was full time. I think she was offering these customers that were coming back, either free or reduced priced haircuts in her main shop. One time Diane was late and a customer that I had done before came in. I cut his hair. When Diane came in, I told her I did a customer. Her response was that of surprise, that I should have had him wait until she came in. One day at the coffee shop by my house, I saw my girlfriend that had been helping out the owner as a receptionist. The owner and her had been friends for a long time. She was visibly upset. She told me that she quit. She told me that she would check with the girls before she booked an appointment. The girls started complaining to the owner that my friend was overbooking them. She felt that she was set up.

The one thing they couldn't find fault with was my perms. Customers were telling me their perm was one of the best they had. Some customers sensed the tension in the shop, and picked up on the vibes as to what they were doing to me. They would compliment me on their haircut. I did one lady's young son's haircut. The next time she came in, she told me that her husband liked her son's haircut, and that he was hard to please. Paul and his wife came to visit me. I gave them each a haircut. We could do family for free. After they left, Diane had some crude remarks about what I talked about while I was doing them. Especially the time I talked about what Paul had said when he was little about the black kids in the project. Diane was doing a black person at the time, and yes I should have thought before I said it, but his wife was asking me questions about Paul when he was little I was always so on edge at work. Diane's customer didn't seem to be offended, actually she laughed when I told her about the situation.

Diane was making plans to buy her own shop, but she didn't want the owner to know about it. She left me in charge of the shop while she ran errands concerning her new shop. She even brought in a 13" television set. When the owner would call looking for Diane, I'd have to lie. The other hairdresser wasn't going to say anything, because she was going to work in Diane's shop. One Monday, Diane came to work and said that she had decided to quit smoking. I didn't want to tempt her, so I didn't smoke at work either. I thought that it might be a good time for me to quit as well. I kept an unopened pack on me, just in case I had bad withdrawal symptoms. Three months went by, and I was having the DT's especially when I was cutting hair. Diane said that it couldn't be because I wasn't smoking. She said the withdrawal symptoms didn't last that long.

Customers were still coming back, almost regularly.

I was always upset when Earl would pick me up from work. I began crying over nothing. People I knew started looking at me like I was going crazy. They'd say something to me and I'd start crying. I even called the owner once to tell her that I couldn't work for her anymore, but I was crying so hard, she told me she couldn't understand me and hung up.

The owner eventually found out about Diane's plans to open her own shop. The owner knew that a lot of customers would follow her because Diane was an excellent hairdresser. The owner came to our shop to find out for sure. She questioned me and the other hairdresser. Diane wasn't there when the owner came. The owner gave me a perm while waiting to face Diane when she came in. When Diane came in, they went into the back room. When they came out, Diane began packing her things, because she had been fired. The owner put her friend of twenty years in as manager of our shop. My haircuts were still being critized. The owner cut my hours down to seventeen hours a week. Anything under fifteen hours, she wouldn't have to pay unemployment. If she fired me without a good reason, I could take her to the labor board. I finally decided to quit, but I needed to give her a week's notice. That Saturday was my last day. As soon as she came in, the new manager started yelling at me for not doing anything, but I had just gotten in myself. She started going on about how the shop was dirty. She even got on the other hairdresser's case. Then she ripped her license off the wall, actually she tore it up, packed her things and left. I really believe that the owner and her friend were into drugs. Normal people don't act the way they did. The owner was also from Earl's hometown in Maine originally. When Earl picked me up I was crying uncontrollably. I worked at that shop for seven months, but it seemed more like a seven month prison sentence.

# CHAPTER FORTY-ONE

I needed another job. I picked up some money doing perms and haircuts for my friends at home. I answered an ad for the Visting Nurse's I got the job. One thing though, I hadn't driven in five years. My neighbor downstairs took in our car out on the back roads, to get me back behind the wheel. I hadn't forgotten how to drive, but I was still scared and nervous. A short time later, the couple downstairs told us that they were moving. I should have been happy, not because they were moving, but because Earl and I were going to get their apartment. It was on the second floor, larger, and had a small porch. I went to the rent to own store in the mall. I wanted a living room set that matched. I saw one that I fell in love with. The only thing was the coffee table and end tables that went with it had glass in the center. They were beautiful with a fancy milk glass border. Then I thought, what if by chance my grandchildren moved back, they might accidentally break the glass and get badly cut. Earl agreed with me, so I settled for practical, getting lamps that matched another sofa and couch.

My first day of training, I was able to walk to the office. I rode with the home health aide to her clients the rest of the day. I did this until my training was over. The Friday before I was to start on my own, I picked up my schedule. On Sunday, Earl and I made a dry run so that I would know how to get to my clients. Monday, I thought I only had one client. I did her, then went home. The car was acting funny. Earl was in the back yard checking it out when my supervisor called and wanted to know why I hadn't showed up to do my second client. I told her that I must have read my schedule wrong, and thought that I was done for the day. I told her Earl was checking out the car. He was able to fix the problem, but just to be safe, brought me to my next client. I gave the gentleman his bath, while the supervisor observed. I dressed him and gave him a shave. The family came in the room when I was done. The gentleman's daughter let out a big gasp. I had shaved this man's moustache that he'd worn for the last twenty years. She wasn't upset, just surprised, she didn't remember ever seeing him without it. I felt so bad, but it was gone. There was nothing I could do. They let me come back, so he became one of my clients. I was still feeling jittery and nervous. I wanted so much to feel like my old self again. One night I went out on the small porch and lit a cigarette It made me choke and gag, but I smoked it anyway. It had been four months, but I needed to know whether the way I was feeling was due to quiting smoking. I smoked a second one, and before long, I was smoking again, and I was back to my normal self. Earl eventually found out that I was smoking again, he wasn't happy, but didn't say anything. He had quit cold turkey fifteen years ago, but it took him two trys. The first time he went back to it after nine months because he had gained a lot of weight.

On a Saturday, I went to see Betty. I told her of my experience at the last shop. She told me that she had heard about the owner. I asked her why she didn't warn me. She said that she didn't want to stand in my way, of doing a younger clientele. I told her that I was now working for the Visiting Nurses. She surprised me by asking me if I wanted the same arrangement that we had before I left on Saturdays. She'd let me know if they weren't busy enough for me to come in, so I agreed. I was fortunate, I had good clients., but sometimes I had to put up with the families who thought that they had maid service. One family in particular. They would come for lunch, and leave a messy kitchen for me to clean up. I would do more housework than I was supposed to, like wash floors. I was only supposed to keep my client's living area clean and comfortable, but these clients appreciated the extra I did. I also did perms and haircuts on my weekends off. We only had to work one day out of the weekend twice a month. It was usually a short day, because the only clients that got weekend help was when they had no family to help them.

As good as the car I paid a hundred and fifty dollars for, it was time to send her to the bone-yard. The front end needed major repair, and the frame was rusted. Jane from Betty's, husband worked at a car dealership in the used car section. The dealership, especially the used car section, had a very bad reputation. Jane assured me that if I only dealt with her husband, I wouldn't get taken advantage of. It turned out that I wasn't able to deal with him, but his best friend. I wasn't sure that I wanted to do business with them now, but decided to look to see what they had on the lot. I did see a small Renault that I liked for its size and gas mileage, but couldn't make up my mind about buying it. The salesman was persistent, even calling Earl at the mall. Earl called me and asked me if I wanted the car. I finally agreed. Yet if I knew more about cars, I would have known that I was going to have problems with the car. Even driving out of the lot, the brake pedal was almost touching the floor. I'm surprised that Earl didn't notice it when he test drove it, unless they put enough brake fluid in to raise the brakes.

We were still coming to Maine for vacations. They would play videos of the Christmas parties in the boarding home where my sister-in-law and her friend played music. I still wanted to move to Maine more than ever, and the videos only made it worse, because I wanted to be part of them. I still cried when we had to leave. The sun and the dew coming off the St. John River was beautiful The sun made the river different shades of violet, pink, and blue. I was trying to save money to move to Maine. Every time I got close to three hundred saved, something would go wrong with the car, and would cost just about what I had saved. Earl had gone to Maine with a friend of his. I got stuck in the parking lot of a grocery store. A trucker tried to get it started, but couldn't. I took the bus home and called the garage to have it towed. The next day was my birthday, and I was alone. Earl was still in Maine. He didn't even call to wish me a happy birthday. I was hurt. I called him and told him about the car. All he did was bitch me out.

The VNA told me they were giving me a year and a half old child. I wasn't sure whether I wanted to take the case. If it was a child, it was serious, but curiosity killed the cat. I figured that I'd at least go once. The foster mother was a licensed practical nurse. She worked at a hospital that had a special needs children's ward. She brought Ernie home, so that he could be part of her family. She had three teenage children of her own, two boys and a girl. Ernie had cerebral palsy. He was my last client of the day. She wanted me to get him ready for bed, like give him a sponge bath and put hid pj's on. After I was done, I sat in the rocking chair. I sang to him and read to him. After awhile Chris the foster mother said that I just didn't have to stay in the nursery. He was the most handsome little guy I had ever seen, with his Hispanic heritage. I decided I wanted to take the case I went the first thing in the morning, for his bath and to dress him. Sometimes I was nervous getting him in and out of the tub, because I was afraid my knees would give out and I had a terrible fear of dropping him. I waited until I was on my feet before I picked him up and wrapped him in a towel. He couldn't use the baby bath, because there was nothing to support him or strap him in. Sometimes he rode the handicap bus to Easter Seals for therapy. Chris and her husband John began to treat me almost like one of the family. I taught Ernie the itsy bitsy spider game. He would laugh out loud. He communicated by using his eyes. He loved TV, especially Barney. I taped the Barney concert for him at home. He'd look at me when it came to the intermission part, because he wanted me to fast forward it. They began to have a problem with Ernie concerning the living room TV set. He wanted his programs all the time, which made it hard on Chris's children when there was something they wanted to watch. Chris and John put a VCR/TV combo set in the nursery for Ernie. I became very attached to Ernie. I think at times Chris was jealous, of my taking her place with Ernie. They were planning on adopting him. The last thing I would want to do was take her place. When I came to Maine on vacation, I bought Ernie a pair of Barney pajamas, and Barney high top sneakers.

Chris and John were strict Baptists. His family was from the Bible Belt of West Virginia. Their kids went to a school run by their church. They were only allowed to go to functions held by the church. They never had any friends over. I went to church with them one Sunday, even though I was Catholic. Ernie went to the church nursery. I was surprised how close it was to the Catholic religion. Then after the service, there was a large tank of water on the stage. A couple were going to be baptized. The minister was in the tank of water. He baptized the couple. A couple of minutes later to my astonishment, he was walking down the aisle bone dry! I knew that I had seen him inside the tank. John noticing my surprise explained that the minister had been wearing waders.

The next child that came was a two month old baby boy. He had been taken away from his parents at two weeks, because they were trying to feed him cut up carrots. He was a fetal alcohol syndrome baby. If expectant mothers could only understand what even one drink can do to their unborn child. I sometimes did respite care for Chris and John so they could get away. Chris' children knew just about as much as to how to take care of these kids as she did. A nurse came in from eleven to seven for Alec the weekends they were away. They had Alec until he was thirteen months. His first steps were to me. Then a couple that were friends with Chris and John, thought they'd like to adopt Alec. They had Alec for a few months, then changed their minds. Alec wound up back in the system.

Their next child was a girl born at twenty four weeks. She was in the hospital for three months, then her mother took her home. She wasn't home a week, when the mother gave up her parental rights. The baby had started choking, and the mother was afraid she was going to die. But that's not what Mary had in mind. Chris brought her home when she was around a year. She'd never look at you directly, but she knew what was going on. She sure wasn't going to let 50 feet of oxygen hose slow her down. One morning Chris went to check on her, and she was gray. Somehow she wasn't getting enough oxygen. Chris revived her, but it gave the whole family a scare. Chris wanted to install a generator. She needed permission from all the members of the association that governed the housing complex. Chris had a hard time, getting it to pass, but she finally did. The next step was to get the state to pay for it. They needed it in case they lost power. Chris got her generator. They also had to wait until Mary was deaf, because she didn't seem to react to sounds.

Her next child was a boy with Down's Syndrome. I often went to the pediatrician with Chris to help her with the kids. I also took a five week course held by the hospital for respite care givers. I learned how to feed Ernie from the tube in his stomach. I learned CPR for children. It was very valuable knowledge to add to what I knew as a CNA.

Not all my clients were a bed of roses. I had one client that lived in a rest home. He was very good to me, it was his future grandson-in-law that was the problem. One time he made a point of checking my client's wallet while I was there, hoping to accuse me of stealing money. Other things also happened. He accused me of not giving my client a bath because the soap was dry. Well it was summer, and I wasn't going to leave the soap in the bath water to melt. He also gave the nurses who went there a hard time, and he wasn't even family yet. I felt so for the girl that was going to marry him. The last straw was when he threw a pair of my client's pants at me that I was going to put on him, shouting at me that they were too small. When I left that day, my client said to me that they had found a way to get rid of me too. I was so upset, I drove straight to the office and told them of the abuse I was getting from the boyfriend. They changed me.

Then I got a lady that liked to sit in her front window and spy on her neighbors across the street. She had curtains that you could see out, but you couldn't see in. She also liked to place bets on horse races by off track betting. She got the racing form, to chose her horses. One time she cut this horse's name out of the racing form. The name of the horse was "Roses For Anne Marie" The horse placed third in show.

One Christmas Chris and her family gave me a sweatshirt with the footprints of Ernie, Maey, and Alec on it. Across the top she wrote, "Helping Hands help little feet grow". I felt special, then I realized that all the people involved in the children's care got the same sweatshirt, only different colors. I had Ernie for four years. Then I couldn't be his home health aide anymore because he needed to have a trach put in and I wasn't qualified to care for him anymore. I had grown very attached to him, maybe too much so. Chris and John began talking about eventually selling their house and moving to West Virginia where his family was. Their oldest daughter would graduate from high school soon, and wanted to go to a bible college down south. I suffered severely from separation anxiety. It seemed anyone I ever got close to had either left me or died. The latter, I know that they had no control over. I tried to stay away. It lasted for about a month. One Sunday afternoon, I was out driving, when before I realized it, I was parked in front of Chris and John's. I went in to visit them and spend time with Ernie. They invited Earl and

I for Thanksgiving dinner that year. Seeing Ernie hooked up to a breathing machine made Earl uncomfortable because he felt for the child. He used to hold him sometimes when I needed Earl to pick me up. Sometimes Earl did odd jobs and needed the car. He would work around my schedule. Once or twice he dropped me off and the client wasn't home, and hadn't called to cancel. After that, Earl would wait to make sure they were home before he left.

# CHAPTER FORTY-TWO

Gloria and I were becoming very close. We saw each other almost everyday. If we didn't see each other, she'd call me when she got up from her nap at five o'clock. She never hung up without telling me she loved me. I began to tell my kids I loved them before I hung up when they called. Gloria's health was getting worse. Her diabetes also led to trouble with her heart. She needed a home health aide three days a week. The only one she'd have was me., so the office gave her to me as a client. One day I left her apartment a few minutes late because we were talking. Good thing my next client was only across the street at the other senior complex. When I got home from work that night Gloria called me. She said that she felt bad because she didn't tell me she loved me before I left that day. She said what if I had an accident or died before she could tell me she loved me. I was still giving her perms, and cutting Eddie's hair. Gloria was the closest thing that I had for a mother. I went to play bingo at her place every week with her.

I still hadn't forgotten about wanting to move to Maine. I was still trying to save money, and my car kept eating it up in repairs. One day, I had a minor accident. I wasn't hurt, but my fender had a gash going along the side of it. I was shook up. Eddie happened to be across the street and saw the accident. He moved the car out of the line of traffic to the side of the road. He said that he'd explain to Earl that it wasn't my fault, that a parked truck had blocked my view of on coming traffic. The owner of the truck got a ticket for unsafe parking, I just got a warning. I still had afternoon clients to do, I called the office and tried to get the rest of the day off. My supervisor asked me if I was hurt or if my car was un-drivable, I told her no. She told me that I needed to finish my day. I wanted Earl to drive me around the rest of the day, but he wouldn't. I had no choice but to get behind the wheel again.

Another client that made a big impression in my life was a male client who was originally from Maine, in the next town over from Earl's home town. He lived with his daughter, son-in-law, and grown grandson. He had been operated on each side of his neck because of clogged arties. They did one side, then a month later, they did the other. In the beginning, I was there for eight hours, because his family all worked. All they expected of me was his care and to change his bed, and clean his room. I was there so long, I also did housework. and laundry. I knew what it felt like to work all day, then have to clean when you came home. Earl liked it because he had the car all day. He asked me to call him "Pepe" They had a small white dog. We fell in love with each other. She loved to go to the mailbox with me. I'd bring her dog biscuits. Pepe and I spent a lot of time talking. Once he asked me how I got involved with a frenchman. After a while my time got cut from eight hours to six, and later four.

Pepe one day remembered that his brother and Earl had left for the army from the same place and day. They were both only eighteen years old then. Pepe wanted to set something up so that they could see each other again. Pepe told me when his brother was coming to visit, and wanted Earl there at the same time. Earl didn't want to disappoint him by refusing, seeing how excited Pepe was about the meeting. He also knew how well the family treated me and appreciated the extra work I did. The two men met and it went very well. On the way home, Earl admitted that he didn't remember pepe's brother, but he was glad that it made pepe happy.

Even though Pepe loved living with his daughter, he told his son-in-law that he wanted to move to a rehab center in Maine, near his son. Apparently Pepe and his son had a strained relationship because of his son's wife. He was hoping that by moving back he could get close to his son before he died. His son-in-law and grandson took a weekend to bring Pepe to Maine, even though they thought it was a bad mistake. His son came to the boarding home a couple of times to visit him. The first time he bought him a rocking chair. Pepe never got what he was hoping for.

When we went to Maine on vacation, Earl, my sister-in-law and I went to visit Pepe. My sister-in-law who was an old maid was always joking about looking for a boyfriend. She genuinely liked Pepe. I brought him a video of the "Honeymooners" which he loved to watch. He also liked Red Skeleton.

The next time we went to Maine, I didn't stop to see Pepe. Nursing homes and hospitals made Earl uncomfortable. In November, his daughter called me and told me that Pepe passed away. I told her how sorry I was, and felt guilty about not visiting him the last time I was in Maine. She told me not to feel that way, that Pepe knew how I felt about him.

Another patient I got close to decided one day that she wasn't going to get out of bed anymore. She had problems with her husband's drinking. She had left him once because of it, but came back. She had given up. She told me that God had sent her an angel. I don't know about that, but that's what she believed. She didn't want me to start her care until I'd had my coffee. I drank my coffee black, and told her that I could still drink my coffee while I was doing her. Her health became steadily worse. Then it came to the point where she was dying. She didn't want me to leave when it was time. She asked me to stay with her. The family called the office and got me permission to stay until the nurse came. She died shortly after I left. I asked my supervisor if I could have enough time off to attend her funeral. Considering how I feel about funerals, I felt I needed to go to this one. At first my supervisor wasn't going to give me the time off. She told me that I couldn't go to all my patient's funerals. I told her I understood this, but this was important to me. She finally agreed.

# CHAPTER FORTY-THREE

I still wanted to move to Maine. I was still was saving money to make the move. Earl hadn't been home for Christmas in years. We talked about it, and I told him that would be the best Christmas present he could give me. He said he'd think it over. He finally agreed. I think he thought that if I got a taste of a northern Maine winter, I wouldn't want to move there anymore. The weather was predicting a winter storm that would cover all of New England. I didn't want Earl to hear the weather report. Eddie was at the house to take care of Tigger. He kept playing videos so that Earl wouldn't hear about the storm. We left for Maine. We didn't hit any snow until Fort Fairfield, but the wind was blowing, and blew the snow off the road. We still had another fifty miles to go. We got to Madawaska ahead of the storm. By nightfall, it was snowing heavily. The next morning, Earl went out to shovel out the walkways and our car. After he got the car shoveled out, he tried to start it. It wouldn't start. One of my sister-in-law's friend came with a tarp and a heater like the ones they use in potato houses. It warmed up the engine, but it wouldn't stay running, so Gary gave Earl a jump. After that he kept the car covered with the tarp.

Christmas Day was a winter wonderland of fresh white snow, and bitterly cold. I walked to the one store that was open with Earl's ex niece. I had dressed warm, but still stood by the wood stove to warm up when we got back to my sister-in-law's. We opened gifts. I had wanted a keyboard that was on sale at a local department store. Earl and his sister had gone halves to get it for me. His sister also gave me a ten pack of video tapes. We went to Christmas dinner at Earl's sister's best friend's house, and opened more gifts. It was the kind of Christmas I'd had always dreamed of. I had gotten two weeks off from work. Eddie called the day before we were supposed to leave. He told us not to leave because there was an ice storm coming that would cover all six states. I called my supervisor and told her the storm would cover all the states that we had to drive through. I told her I would be back as soon as possible. Naturally, I wasn't disappointed that we couldn't leave. I got to stay an extra week. It didn't deter me from still wanting to Move to Maine.

Summer was finally here. Eddie decided that he wanted to move his mother to Texas to be with her other two sons. One night him and I drove to the truck stop. He wanted to pick up a road map. We had chili for supper, and I bought a radio that looked like a nickelodeon. I got it a a reduced price because it was a demo. When we got back to Gloria's, she seemed upset that we didn't ask her to come with us. The reason we didn't, was because we thought it would be too much for her. I promised her that I'd get the car Sunday, and we'd bring her then. Sunday afternoon, Gloria, Eddie and I went to eat at the truckstop. It was hot that day. Gloria and I went out to the car, Eddie said that he'd meet us in a few minutes. He wanted to finish his video game. We waited and waited, and still Eddie didn't come out. The heat was really bothering Gloria, and I was afraid that she might have a sugar reaction. I went back into the truck stop to get Eddie. I balled him out on the way to the car. Gloria's doctor told Eddie that she'd never survive the trip by car. He'd have to fly her out there, which he didn't have the money for. Again they suggested that I go with them, but I said that I couldn't. The week that followed was very strange. On Wednesday, Gloria went out for the day with some friends, something she never did. She always laid down from three to five o'clock. I went Thursday to give her shower as her home health aide. She was in bed, eating chocolate like there was no tomorrow. Instead, she wanted me to go to the drugstore and pick up her prescriptions, and to hurry back. Before I left, she told me again not to forget her prescriptions. I assured her I wouldn't. When I got back, she told me to call 911. The ambulance came. They worked on her for quite awhile before they left for the hospital. Eddie called me very early Friday morning, to tell me that Gloria had passed away. Apparently she had a heart attack in her sleep. I had to go to work, even though I was terribly upset. To make matters worse, my first patient lived in Gloria's building. I couldn't hold back the tears anymore. I called my supervisor, and told her what had happened and that mentally I was in no shape to work. She told me to come to the office so that we could talk. It was only a short walk from the mall to Gloria's building. My patient called Earl to come and get me because he didn't want me driving. Earl came and drove me to the office and waited in the car while I went in to talk to my supervisor. I explained to her the close relationship that Gloria and I had, and that we had lived together in Maine. She said that I shouldn't have taken her for a client, but I explained that Gloria wouldn't have taken anyone else. She let me go home. Earl went back to work. I fell asleep on the couch. I saw Gloria in a cloud. She was dressed up complete with earrings and her purse. Gloria always wore earrings. She told me that she was alright, but she didn't want to go without telling me she loved me. Then she was gone. She had never been to my apartment because I lived on the second floor. Gloria had a habit of always being late. We used to joke that she'd be late for her own funeral. Gloria was cremated. Her children arranged a memorial service for three o'clock. We had to wait because Gloria's ashes hadn't arrived yet. True to form, she was late for her own funeral. Finally the doorbell rang and it was the UPS guy carrying a box. As Eddie signed for the box, he told the guy that it was about time he got there, because his mother was in the box. The guy's face went as white as a sheet. He quickly turned around, and almost ran out the door. Gloria wanted her ashes spread in a meadow in her home town in Maine. Her son

206

wanted the tools that went to the fireplace. Nobody wanted the fireplace, so I asked Nancy and Eddie if I could have it. Eddie said that Gloria would want me to have it. Gloria had given me a gray leather cigarette case with a compartment for matches. It had a flower painted on the front. I don't know how many times I almost lost it, but it always found its way back to me. I still have it.

I even had my stepmother as a patient. I could have refused, but decided that I could be professional.

# CHAPTER FORTY-FOUR

I guess I was driving the customers at the coffee shop and the beauty salon nuts with my talk about moving to Maine They were kind enough not to tell me so. I think that I was just trying to convince myself that it was the right move for Earl and I.

PJ came back from California. He was staying at the his friend the dog groomer. Her and I weren't friends anymore since she knew where Paul was and didn't tell me for eight months. PJ was drunk. I asked him to leave and not to come back unless he was sober. He left. I was trying to use the "tough love" method on him. He came back the next day and he was sober. We had a nice visit. I didn't know that it would be the last time I would see him.

A couple of days. later, our apartment had been broken into. My VCR and fifty dollars I had saved in an envelope in my dresser drawer were missing. Earl said that a pair of diamond earrings that he had been planning to give me as a anniversary present were missing. Earl told once that one day he would put diamonds in my ears. I knew that it had been PJ that broke into our apartment, because my paperwork on my patients that I had had in a drawer were in my brief case, even my home health aide certificate. that had been in the drawer. Only someone who knew me and my schedule would know how important those papers were. He used Earl's tools to disconnect the VCR. He got it out of the house in a overnight bag I got as a free gift at a hair show. The fifty dollars was my move to Maine fund. I was beginning to think that it wasn't meant to be. The dog groomer bought the VCR from him, knowing full well that it was stolen. He used the money to go to Texas

# CHAPTER FORTY-FIVE

The next summer we went to Maine. On the way home, Earl said the car was acting funny. We hadn't reached Houlton yet, where we would get on the turnpike. Earl wanted to turn around and go back to his sister's and get the car checked out. He didn't want to break down on the turnpike. Of course I wasn't disappointed that we had to turn back. I got to spend another couple of days. I loved my job, but hated Connecticut, especially since the kids were scattered all over the country. My job was only eight hours of my day. Earl couldn't understand why I would give up a job making $9. 50 an hour to move to Maine and make $5. 00 an hour. I also felt that I was the one that had to leave Ernie, before they moved down south and he left me.

That year, I got a real big income tax refund. I had enough money now, and what I could add to it from my paycheck to make the move.

We went to Maine that summer. I asked Earl repeatedly if we could look at apartments. He kept putting me off, until the last week of vacation. We looked at a couple of places, but they were too small for our furniture and all the stuff we had. I went to the local nursing home and spoke to the director of nurses. She explained the job requirements, and patient assignments. They also had split shifts, 7AM to 11AM and 3:30PM to 8PM. I would have to take the CNA course over again, because I hadn't done any CNA work in four years. I had just missed the grandfather clause by two months. She assured me that I could get in the next CNA class starting in September. I assumed it worked like Connecticut, you work half a day, and go to class the other half. Finally we found a two bedroom apartment that we both liked. The only drawback was that it was on the second floor, and Earl was hoping for a first floor apartment. It turned out that he and the landlady were distant cousins. I told her we had a cat, but I would have given him up at the time to take the apartment. She told us that we could bring him. I gave her a security deposit. The day we were leaving, I called the nursing home just to be sure that I'd have a job

This time I didn't cry when we left for home because I knew that I was coming back in a month to live. I still wasn't absolutely sure that this was the right move. I knew I wanted it, but I wasn't sure about Earl. Was he agreeing to the move to please me, or afraid I'd make the move without him. We were in Mid Maine, when smoke started coming out from under the hood. Earl pulled over to the side of the road and opened the hood. A big cloud of smoke came billowing out. There was a young couple in a pickup truck behind us. They pulled up in back of our car. They had a mobile phone in the truck and called a garage. They followed us to the garage to make sure we made it. They didn't have a mechanic on duty because it was Saturday. They towed our car to a garage in the next town. It so happened that it was the owner's Saturday to work. If the other mechanic had been working, he would have closed the garage early. To me, it was God's way of telling me that we were making the right move. We ate at a diner next door while they worked on our car. The engine was burnt, and he didn't know if he could get another one. If he could, it would cost more than the car was worth. I had already put enough money into it. We told him to junk the car. I had enough money to get us home by bus, but that would have cut into our moving money. He told us to wait at the garage, while he went to his parent's house. He said that they liked to take trips, and might take us back to Madawaska or home to Connecticut, which ever we wanted. A short time later, the owner and a van pulled into the garage. The owner introduced us to his parents. They said that they would bring us home. We just had to pay for the gas, tolls, and our food. They brought us right to the house. We asked them if they wanted to spend the night, but said they'd sleep at their other son's place in Kennebunk. We thanked them and for awhile kept in touch.

# CHAPTER FORTY-SIX

Earl did most of the packing, I guess he didn't think I'd do it right. I bought a collar and leash for Tigger. He had never been outside, except to lay on the small roof of the downstairs porch. I walked him around the back yard a little each day, so he'd get used to walking on a leash. Finally, it was time to rent the twenty four foot moving truck. It cost Earl almost a hundred dollars to empty a garage he was renting and take what he didn't want to the dump. It was Labor Day weekend. One of our friends from the coffee shop went with us to drive the truck to the house. If I could have waited until Tuesday, the day after Labor Day, it would have been a couple of hundred dollars less for the truck. Eddie and a couple of our friends were coming with us to help drive and unload the truck once we got there. They all worked, so Labor Day weekend was the only time they had off. After the truck was unloaded, they'd head back. Eddie had me give him a haircut for the last time. John, who had worked third shift and his two boys helped pack the truck. As they were packing the truck, I couldn't find Tigger anywhere. He was afraid of strangers. One of John's boys spotted him hiding in a industrial mop bucket Earl had in the closet. John gave me a ride to his house so that I could have one last visit with Ernie, Chris, and their daughter Becky. Ernie fell asleep in my arms. After awhile, the nurse came for him. Chris told me not to tell him that I wasn't going to see him anymore. Even though he had cerebal palsy, he understood everything that was going on around him. I kissed him on the forehead and handed him to the nurse so that she could give him his feeding. I went in the nursery to say one last goodbye and keep a picture of him in my heart for always. John came for me when they were done packing the truck.

We were going to travel during the night, like we always did when we went on vacation. We ate our last grinders at Paul's Pizza. I wanted Tigger to ride in the cab with Eddie, Earl, and I but there wasn't enough room. He had to ride in the cat carrier in the back of the truck. Eddie assured me that he'd have enough air. Every time we stopped, we took him out of the carrier and walked him around. Eddie's two friends were following us in their pick up truck. Earl, Eddie, and his two friends took turns sleeping while the other one drove. We stopped often, just for coffee. Eddie and Earl were both glad that I could stay awake and talk to them while they were driving. I couldn't drive a vehicle that large and that heavy. Finally, at least to me, we crossed the state line and into Massachusetts. Connecticut was now behind me. Eddie would sometimes start to nod off, on the dark strip of highway in Massachusetts. I'd give him a quick nudge. It was daylight when we hit New Hampshire. You're only in New Hampshire for thirty miles. I could smell the ocean air. Then at last, the Portsmouth bridge. Half is the New Hampshire border, the other half Maine's. We were now in Maine. We stopped at the first open gas station, for gas, food, bathroom, and coffee. When I took Tigger out this time, I realized that I had forgotten his litter box. The attendant gave me a plastic pan filled halfway with speedy dry. I put it on the ground, but he wouldn't use it. He also hadn't eaten in awhile. We still had another seven or eight hours of traveling. Earl took the wheel, and Eddie got as comfortable as possible to try to get some sleep. The cushions in the truck weren't padded, and my butt was getting pretty sore. We stopped more often to stretch. At one stop I got my whoopie pie and Tigger's favorite flavor of cat food. He still wouldn't eat or use the cat box. Each mile was bringing me closer to my new home and new life.

It took us fourteen hours to get to Madawaska. We stopped at my sister-in-law's first. She took a couple of pictures of us and the truck. Then we went to our apartment to unload the truck. A guy walking by stopped and helped bring stuff upstairs. I carried the light boxes and clothes. When the truck was empty, I gave Eddie a large hug and kiss, telling him that I was going to miss him. I hugged and thanked the other two guys, then they left to go back. They all had to work the next day. I whispered to myself, Mom(Gloria) I'm here. Madawaska is so many feet above sea level and it takes you awhile to get used to the altitude. When everything quieted down, Tigger ate so fast he burped. He also needed the cat box. We had to stay with Earl's sister for three days until we got our electricity and phone hooked up. We bought a ten dollar phone after Earl realized that he had left our phone under the front seat of Eddie's friend's pick up. I had paid quite a bit for that phone. It was a see through phone with a neon nite light. Earl told me that Eddie forgot to give it to us on purpose. I called Eddie and asked him to mail the phone to me. While I had him on the phone he asked me if I would register a car for him here in Maine. Apparently he was unable to register a car in Connecticut. I told him that it was impossible because I had no way of getting to Motor Vehicles, which was forty miles away. Another one of Earl's friends followed us in his car to drop the moving truck at the nearest dealer. I got some of my deposit back.

As usual, Earl had to do most of the unpacking and putting things where he wanted them. If I put something in the wrong place, he'd move it and tell me to do something else. He was disappointed that he couldn't put the refrigerator where he wanted it, because it was too tall and wouldn't clear the cupboard. The kitchen was large with plenty of cabinets. The living room had a large window that caught the morning sun. Our bedroom was good-sized and the extra bedroom, Earl set up as his office. Sometimes in the evening, we'd take a walk to his sister's which was about a twenty minute walk. If you looked across the river to Edmunston, it was a large area of round lights.

I started the CNA class in mid September. Even though you were taking the class, it didn't mean that you were guaranteed a job. One woman had to drop out because she didn't have a high school diploma which was required. I got nervous, because I didn't have one either. There was a woman in my class that had worked with me at the Visiting Nurses. She had moved up from Connecticut a year before me. We became close friends. I confided in her that I didn't have a high school diploma or GED. A few classes later, the Director of Nurses who was teaching the class, said that sometimes important papers get lost when you move. It told me that she knew I didn't have a diploma. I couldn't enroll in the GED class at Adult Ed because I would have gotten her in trouble.

Still I needed a job. I walked to a restaurant just on the outskirts of town. It didn't seem that far by car, but it had to be at least four miles. It was raining. I finally got there. The woman that interviewed me wrote a few things down on a guest check pad. I told her that I had done waitressing before. When I left, I turned around and looked in the window. The woman tore up the piece of paper. She could have just told me there were no openings, and that she couldn't hire me. Now I had to walk back. Earl's sister's neighbor picked me up just as I got back into town and brought me home. The next place I went was to a catering service, which was near the nursing home. The woman there was much more polite and suggested I look for CNA work because that was where I had the most experience. I told her I was already in the class at the nursing home. I answered an ad in the newspaper. This young couple with a newborn was looking for a sitter. It wasn't far from home, but the interview went awkward. I explained how I had raised five children, and knew CPR for babies. I think the young mother was feeling guilty about having to leave her newborn with a stranger, which I understood. I got a nice card from them in the mail thanking me for answering their ad.

We lived on Earl's Social Security check. We bought food for groceries that would give us leftovers. I could walk to my CNA classes. I studied hard. It was beginning to get cold. At break, everyone who smoked rushed out the front door of the nursing home to get in the corner, out of the wind. Then in December, the DON hired me, and my girlfriend got hired the next day. We both got the split shift, four hours in the morning, and four hours in the afternoon, except if we had class that night. The other aides were pleased, because I knew the job, and just had to get to know the patients. I started to pick up a few words and simple sentences in French. Before we moved here, Earl's sister's friend would tell me to repeat words in French, knowing full well I didn't know what they meant. Some of the words they taught me were swear words. One day my patient as I was helping her with her breakfast, told me in French that she had a stomach ache. I thought that I'd tell the nurse in French about her stomach ache. It came out that I told the nurse that she had a sore ass. The aides and the nurse all began laughing. I swore that I wouldn't try to speak French again, though I did. Most of the patients spoke both English and French. Only a few from the back settlements spoke only French.

I was nervous working the morning shift. I was afraid that I wouldn't get my assignment done by lunch. In Connecticut, our patient assignment consisted of ten residents if we were full staffed. We could have as many as twelve. I would spend my lunch break making my beds many times. Here our assignment were six to eight residents. I was especially nervous when it was my day to do whirlpool baths. I mentioned this to the charge nurse one day. She said she didn't care how fast I could do a resident, but how well I did them. That put me more at ease.

I had to walk to work. Sometimes we slept at my sister-in-law's because it was closer to work. I loved the smell of burning wood in the cold crisp air. I bought a full face ski mask, because my face got so cold. Sometimes someone going to work would pick me up. I didn't have to walk anymore once I got to know my co workers. Some had to go right past our apartment and they'd pick me up, and bring me home. Donna picked me up for class, and sometimes dropped me off at the end of my street.

The aides loved it when it came time for our class to do the clinical part of the course, because they had extra help with their residents in the afternoon. It came time to take our test. The two weeks we had to wait to get the results back from Augusta were agonizing. Finally, I got my score. I passed with a ninety two. I got my hair done at a local salon. The hairdresser had a hard time with my hair because it was so straight. Donna and I bought new outfits for the party. We had our certification party at a local restaurant. We were allowed to bring a guest. Of course Earl came. Donna relaxed after Earl ordered a beer, because she didn't want her husband to be the only one drinking.

PJ called once while I was at work. Earl said he sounded okay. A few months passed, when he called again. This time he told Earl for me to go "f" myself. Earl told him never to call again.

I soon learned that the nursing home was a very stressful place to work. There were a few cliques. There was a very overweight aide that lived next door to Earl's sister, who thought she could have control over anyone she chose. She had worked there fifteen years when I started. She would enjoy picking on new aides that got hired. Often she brought them to tears, and they'd quit. The rule was three warnings in a year, then you were fired. This aide always got two warnings, but never the third. The patients that wanted me to do them, would say they wanted the "English girl".

The next year I was put on third shift. One day I got a call from Cynthia. PJ had been in an accident. Somehow, she was the one he could remember, though she hadn't been part of his life growing up. He had been walking alongside the road during a blinding rainstorm, and got hit by a car. He was thrown thirty five feet. He was bleeding on the left side of his brain. I had no way of getting to Texas. I also didn't have the money or credit cards. They wouldn't have kept my job open for me. I called him everyday. I spoke to the neurosurgeon on the phone. By the grace of God, the bleeding stopped on its own, and he wouldn't need an operation. I gave the doctor what medical history I had for PJ. I also told him that PJ drank heavily. The doctor told me that PJ was drunk when he got hit. He said that if PJ had been sober he would have died. Paul was driving tractor trailer at this time. He was in California on a run, when he heard of the accident. He went straight to Texas and the hospital to see his brother. Paul said the first thing PJ asked him was how I was. PJ needed to stay in the hospital for extensive rehabilitation. He needed to learn how to walk again and other motor skills. Instead, he just walked out of the hospital against medical advice. It seemed as though God was giving him a second chance at life. I prayed that he would take it. I felt so guilty, and still do, that I couldn't be there with him. I think some of my coworkers didn't believe me about PJ's accident. I think they thought any good mother would have went to be near her son. Believe me, if it was humanly possible I would have been there.

# CHAPTER FORTY-SEVEN

I made friends with a woman who did volunteer work at the nursing home. She was a few years older than me. I would help her out with the residents during activities. I'd go to her house for coffee. She had a live-in boyfriend that didn't like company, except if they were his friends. He and his friends played music. Sometimes they would join Earl's sister and her friend when the played music at the boarding home. I went to these parties if I wasn't working, and sometimes danced with the residents. Roxanne though everyone called her Roxie and I would sometimes go to a town twenty five miles away just to grocery shop. We also stopped at the coffee shop there. We also went across to Canada to the dollar store there. We did these things so that we could talk freely and enjoy shopping together. Roxie and I both smoked, but she was a chain smoker. She had a wicked cough and also coughed up mucus, but she still wouldn't quit. We had Thanksgiving at Roxie's that year. Her grown son joined us. I would sometimes tell Roxie a little bit about my life. She'd laugh, and say that I should write a book.

I worked with a girl whose husband would drop her off at work, then hang around town until her shift was over to save gas. She didn't drive. They lived a good distance from town, and couldn't afford to make four trips a day, five days a week. One night the police found him dead in his car that was parked in a store parking lot. I surprised the Director of Nurses when I told her I would go with her and a couple of other aides to his wake and funeral. She knew how I felt about funerals, but I also felt that now she was alone, and needed our support.

219

The aide that lost her husband, had to quit because she had no transportation. That left a position on second shift open. The DON gave me the position. She said I had done my time on third shift. The overweight aide, her best friend, and another aide always worked together on the same floor. The charge nurse on the third floor wanted to break up the trio. She went to the DON and talked it over with her. She succeeded. One of the aides got changed to days, and I was the unfortunate one that had to work with the other two. The overweight one got it into her head that she was going to make my life miserable. Her friend was the complete opposite of her. I think she was a little afraid of her heavyset friend. This woman also had a cake decorating business beside working forty hours at the home. She made beautiful cakes, but she was also expensive.

We could only call in sick twice in a six month period. If you called in too often, they cut your hours, if there was enough staff to cover. I would only call in if I thought I was too sick to finish my shift. The DON would sometimes gave me a warning if I was calling in too much, or cut my hours. I never called in because I went out Friday night and partied, like some did. The heavyset one would turn me in if she saw me doing something against the rules, for instance, putting a patient that was two assist, in and out of bed by myself. Sometimes I had to, because her and I were supposed to be working together, but she did her own thing and wouldn't help me, unless the nurse made her. She even threatened the DON. The Director of Nurses was renting from the heavyset aide's brother. She told the DON that she could have her evicted, anytime she wanted. The DON decided to buy a house. There was another aide that I had worked with several times before with no problems. Suddenly, that changed. She was really nasty with me. In fact she embarrassed me in front of a patient's family that was really good to me. I knew that she was trying to work three jobs. She also became really friendly with the heavyset aide. I don't know if she was responsible for the drastic change in this girl's personality, or maybe she was on drugs. It got so bad, that I ended up reporting her.

In our small town, all the streets are numbered from First to Twenty-Fifth Ave. The streets on the other side of Main Street were part of the same Ave, up to Thirteenth, The avenues that went to the paper mill were called north of what number avenue they connected to. We don't even have a traffic light in town. You can't get lost in our small town.

Early that spring, Earl saw an ad in the classifieds of our local paper for a car that he was interested in buying. He saw the words Fifth Ave in the ad, and thought the owner must live on Fifth Avenue near his sister's. He called the number and the car was a Chrysler Fifth Avenue. When he saw the car, and test drove it, he called me all excited. He wanted to buy the car. It only had one owner. They were asking a thousand dollars, but we had nine hundred in cash and they accepted the offer. The owner loved that car, and really didn't want to sell it. He had just retired, and his wife wanted a brand new car. It had never been driven in the winter, because they spent the winters in Florida. I liked the car also. It was silver gray with red velour interior. I used to tease Earl that he loved the car more than me. He always liked big heavy cars. We drove the car for three years before we had to put any money into it.

I always knew when Earl had been to the bar while I was working, because the first thing he would ask me when he picked me up, was how did it go. He'd also had a peppermint in his mouth. Sometimes on the Friday nights that I worked till eight, we'd go to the dance downstairs of the hotel. I loved to dance. It was getting to a point where sometimes I'd tell Earl to ask someone else to dance, because I'd get very tired and short of breath. When Earl was drinking, he'd want to dance every dance. Other times, he'd be at the hotel bar all the time I was at work. He'd stop there after he picked me up. I'd be just starting to relax and have fun, we'd have to leave because he couldn't drink anymore. One afternoon, I was home. The hospital called to say that Earl's brother had been admitted and he was in very serious condition. I walked down to the bar to tell Earl. Earl was feeling pretty good, so I told him I was driving to the hospital, not only that, but he was too upset to drive. On the trip home, Earl talked me into letting him drive. His brother had a feeding tube inserted in his stomach. When he was well enough he went back to the nursing home. A few months later, he got a staph infection around the incision and died. At the funeral, Earl's sister collected all the sympathy cards. The first thing she looked for was if there was any money in the card. What money she got, she didn't share with Earl, even though him and I were the ones that visited him regularly. One night just after Christmas, Earl was at the bar as usual. While he was out, he stopped and bought some marked down Christmas ornaments. He was almost to the top of our stairs, when he fell all the way down. I felt the house shake and went outside to see what happened. Earl was at the bottom of the stairs. At first I thought he was unconscious, but no, he got himself up and climbed the stairs. His jacket protected him from breaking anything but one Christmas ornament

One morning I got a phone call. The girl on the other end, told me not to hang up on her, that she wasn't a crazy person, but that we might be related. I knew I had a half sister out there somewhere. She told me that she had gone to a fortune teller. The woman told her that she would find a sibling in a cold climate. She didn't know whether it would be two hours, two days, or two months, but the number 2 was very important. It took her two weeks to find me. We talked for awhile. She told me that she, Cynthia, and Victoria had set up a time and place to meet. Cynthia called me and sent me so many pictures of what she was going to wear. She wanted to look as good as Victoria. Her inferiority complex was kicking in again.

In February, Paul called me. He asked me why I had to move to the top of the world. He was driving tractor trailer and he was up here to pick up a load of potatoes. He was in Houlton, and had some time to be able to come see us. He wanted directions. We gave him the directions to the outskirts of our town, and Earl arranged a place to meet to bring him the rest of the way. It so happened that our main street was blocked off for the snow mobile parade. Earl had to bring him the back way. Paul had to get that big truck around some tight corners. We talked for awhile, and then we took Paul to the hotel. Earl and Paul played pool. Roxie was there and I introduced her to our son. Time went to quickly. Soon he had to leave. I couldn't stop crying for quite awhile after he left. It had been so long since I had seen him, and didn't know when I'd see him again.

One night Earl picked me up and brought me to his sister's. He had been drinking quite a bit. He said he'd be back, he was going to go home and feed the cats. He had been gone about ten minutes, when the phone rang. Earl was at the police station. He'd had a minor accident at an intersection. The cop knew he had been drinking, so he was arrested. Earl told the cop to go, and that he'd follow him to the station in our car. The cop asked me if I had been drinking too. I told him that I had just got out of work. I had to walk to where our car was parked on the side of the road, and drove to the police station to get Earl. Maine has a very strict drunk driving law. A first offense was a mandatory forty eight hour jail term. I went to court with Earl. The judge asked him if there was any medical reason why he couldn't go to jail. Earl answered no, and he had to go wait in a room until after court to be transported to the Houlton Jail. Houlton was about two hundred miles away. I cleaned the house from top to bottom, and spoke to Earl on the phone. It was November and the night before I had to go pick Earl up at the truck stop in Houlton, we had freezing rain. I had to borrow twenty dollars from his sister to gas up. I had never driven that far by myself. I had to leave around six o'clock in the morning. I was so nervous. I put my cigarettes and lighter in a cup in the compartment between the seats, so that I could reach them easily. I also made a large mug of coffee and had my cassette tapes handy. I started out. I had to pull over to the side of the road several times after a tractor trailer splashed my windshield with muddy water. I finally made it on time. Earl was anxiously waiting for me. He didn't even want to wait for me to have a cup of coffee at the truck stop. He told me that he couldn't even see outside, and that he had given most of his food to another prisoner. On the drive back, he began to criticize my driving. I told him that I had gotten there to pick him up, and if my driving made him nervous, he could walk or hitch hike home. He wanted to stop at a small store just before we got home to get our town's newspaper. He wanted to see if his name was in there before he saw his sister. We stopped at his sister's for a few minutes before going home. I had never seen him cry. He was sore all over from the hard beds. A couple of hours after we got home, the DON called me and asked me to come into work. I told her I was tired after driving five hours, and that Earl was very upset and needed me. He stopped drinking for quite awhile afterward. I didn't think he'd ever drink and drive again, but about a year later, that's what he was doing.

# CHAPTER FORTY-EIGHT

They hired a woman around my age that was also from Connecticut. We became friends because we had a lot in common, in more ways than one that I would find out a few months later. In October this woman had to take an emergency leave. Her mother was dying in Connecticut. Earl picked me up from my three to eight shift one night while this woman was gone. We were almost home Earl told me he had some bad news to tell me. I don't know where it came from and neither did he when I said to him "The bitch is dead." He asked me how I knew, and I couldn't answer him, it just came out. He told me that Cynthia had called him to tell him our mother died of a heart attack in New Britian, Ct. I could have gone to Ct. for her funeral, because I'd have three days off with pay. I told the Director of Nurses that my brother-in-laws were going to drive up to get me. I had no intention of going to her funeral. I was glad she was dead. I would have felt like a hypocrite if I went because I wasn't sorry. Now I realize that it was a big mistake my not going. She wouldn't have been able to hear me, but at least I could have told her how I felt about what she did to me. I would have had some closure. I stayed in the apartment with the shades down and didn't answer my phone for those three days. I always wished that she'd die alone, that's how much I hated her. After talking to Cynthia, I found out that I got my wish. Then I felt guilty because my wish came true. When I came back to work, the DON asked me how and when I got home. I told her my sisters chipped in for plane fare. I think she knew that I never left Maine. When the other woman came back, I think the DON asked her if it was true that my mother died. I got money from a fund that you signed up for if you wanted to. They would take whatever amount you wanted from your paycheck.

When I saw my friend when she got back, I told her that I was very sorry for her loss. Then I told her that my mother had died a day after hers. Come to find out, the two women knew each other. Their pictures were side by side in the obituary column of the newspaper. After talking, she realized that I was my mother's oldest daughter. She and my mother had worked together in a nursing home in New Britian. I thought it odd that we had no relationship what so ever, yet my mother and I did the same kind of work. I tried to get information from my friend, like did my mother ever mention her daughters. She told me how my mother was grandmotherly with her children. I was angry and also jealous. What was wrong with us, we needed her too. My friend began to avoid talking to me about her. A short time later, she quit and moved back to Connecticut. At first I thought that she might have been my half sister. I knew that my Dad had to sign papers for my mother to be able to give that baby up for adoption, because they were still legally married at the time.

My friend Donna and her husband bought a mobile home. Her husband's father allowed them to put the trailer on a half acre of his land. She quit the nursing home, to go to work in the nursing home three minutes from her new home. The stress at work was getting worse. Donna told me that there were a couple of positions opening up in a couple of weeks. I called the Director of Nurses there to set up an interview. The interview went well, and she said that she would get back to me. I enrolled in a medical terminology class, that was being taught by our Director of Nurses. She made a comment that her and the other Director of Nurses did what they had to do to keep their aides. I didn't hear back from the other Director of Nurses, so I called her. She told me that one aide had changed her mind about quitting, and then the other position had already been filled. I know my DON stopped me from getting the job. I applied for another job in a town twenty five miles away. If I had got the job, it meant that we would have to move to that town. They called, and I had the job if I wanted it. I talked to Earl. He's a creature of habit, and hates change. He didn't want to move again, so I turned down the job.

I took the three day medication aide class. One aide from another nursing home took a clear dislike to me, after I answered many of the questions. I think she thought that I thought that I knew more than her. Anyway, I passed the course. I mainly worked the second shift. Sometimes I did the third shift. There was an aide that had hurt her back and couldn't work on the nursing wings anymore. They changed her to boarding. One evening we were both on break. I told her that she was lucky that they had a job for her. Well, she took what I said the wrong way. She reported me the person in charge of boarding. She told this person that she was afraid to work with me. When they called me into the office, I tried to explain that I was glad that this aide was still able to work here. I called this aide at home on Saturday and explained what I meant. I told her that I wouldn't hurt her like that. This aide wouldn't hurt a fly. We talked for awhile, and after that we became good friends. After that they would only put me on the third shift to pass meds, and only when no other med aides wanted the shift. One time though that I was working the second shift, I accidentally gave a patient the wrong pill, I was afraid to report it to the charge nurse. It was only an iron pill, but I still should have told the nurse. I was afraid the patient would tell the day nurse, but she never did. Shortly after both her and her roommate moved to a boarding home closer to where they lived. They were only here until two beds became open, and where they still could be roommates.

One evening I was working on nursing. I had a very traumatic experience. We had a patient that could be difficult and demanding, but him and I got along well. I think it was partly because we were both English. Sometimes if I had time before supper trays came up, I would go to his room, and we'd talk. Whenever I had him for a patient on the three to eight shift, I was always fifteen or twenty minutes late punching out, because he had a strict and long routine for getting ready for bed. This evening, he was my patient. After supper, we were to walk him from his wheelchair to the bathroom which was close, then from the bathroom to his bed. He was on oxygen all the time. This evening his two sons arrived from downstate to visit him. They left for supper. I went to take him to the bathroom after supper. I was waiting for him to tell me he was done, instead he told me to hurry and get him into bed. I was walking him to his bed. We were almost there, when he collapsed, and was turning gray. I lowered him to the floor and was cradling his head. I pressed his buzzer three times indicating that I needed help. The med aide finally came in, and started to bitch me out, but quickly called the charge nurse. The nurse and a couple of other aides came in to get him into bed. I was crying. The nurse sent me out of the room. He died a couple of minutes later. I blamed myself, for making him walk to bed. Nobody had said on report at the beginning of the shift, that he had trouble walking the distance between his wheelchair and his bed. If they had, I never would have had him walk. I thought of his sons, and the shock they would feel, when they came back from having their supper. Later, I told the charge nurse why I was upset, and that I blamed myself. She told me that he was probably just waited to die until after he saw his sons. I wanted to go home, but she wouldn't let me go home. She didn't make me wash him, though that would have been part of my assignment. The med aide working that night, lived in the house across from me. A male aide that worked with us lived in the house on the other side of her. The next morning, I was still pretty upset. It wasn't anything that Earl wanted to hear or talk about. This patient had once been Earl's math teacher. I knocked on the male aide's door and asked him if he had time for coffee, and I needed to talk. I needed to talk to someone who would understand what I was feeling. The med aide saw me go to his apartment. Soon after there was a rumor going around that the male aide and I were having a affair. The funny part was, this male aide was gay.

A few months later, the med aide and her husband that lived in the next house moved out after living there ten years. Earl had told the landlord when we first started renting from them, that if a first floor apartment came open he wanted it. We got the apartment. A couple of Earl's friends helped him move the heavy furniture. The things that Earl told me to unpack and put away, he rearranged. I never liked the apartment because there was no privacy. You had to share a small front porch with the family next door. You couldn't have company on your side of the porch and talk privately. You looked out your living room window and could see inside the apartment of the next house. At first I got along with the people next door. Their daughter worked at the nursing home with me. They were heavy drinkers. In the summer, they'd sit on their side of the porch drinking coffee brandy all day and into the evening. One night they went out barhopping in town. Apparently, his wife made a fool out of herself. A rumor started that I supposedly was telling everyone about it, which wasn't true. After that, she made it a point to make my life hell. She even threatened my company when she was drunk. I was stuck at home a whole summer, because Earl had the car all day. He'd be at his sister's working in the garden. He wouldn't come home until it started getting dark.

I also had started building up credit awhile before we moved to the first floor. I eventually had four credit cards. I would buy Earl expensive gifts on credit. One time he said to me,

"Whose going to pay these credit card bills if you get sick?"

I was only forty nine, I wasn't going to get sick. Our twentieth anniversary was coming up. I ordered a beautiful light blue pants suit that cost me seventy five dollars. I had never spent that much on an outfit before. Also blue was Earl's favorite color I didn't let Earl see the outfit until we were ready to go out. His expression told me that the outfit was worth every penny I paid for it. We went to a nice restaurant by the lake for supper.

# CHAPTER FORTY-NINE

In another border town twenty five miles north of here, on the first Saturday in March, they hold the CAN-AM dog sled races. It's a smaller version of Alaska's Iderod. Mushers come from all over the country. There are three different legs of the race, the longest being 250 miles. I talked Earl into taking me. He wasn't crazy about going because it was cold. They offer free coffee and hot coaco. It's exciting watching the dogs barking and anxious to get running. I got some good pictures as the teams raced past where I was standing. We stayed until the last team was on its way.

I had to work the next Monday evening. The aide that I was working with, were putting a patient to bed. He was very thin. We had to use a hoyer lift to get him up and put him in bed. I had a hold of his legs, so that he wouldn't slide out. The door was closed and the room was stuffy. After we had him in bed, I began to feel faint. I splashed some cold water on my face, but it didn't seem to help. The girl I was working with, said I was as white as a sheet. She told me that she could finish the patient and for me to go sit at the desk for a few minutes. I hadn't eaten supper, so I thought that my blood sugar might be low. I asked the med aide for a cup of orange juice. I drank the juice and still didn't feel right. I got up to sit in a chair under a ceiling fan. That's the last thing I remember. The heavyset aide couldn't wait to call my friend Donna to tell her what happened to me. Donna went up one side of her and down the other. She told her that she was the major cause of my stress. When I came to, I was on the floor covered with a sheet. My co workers were standing all around me. The EMTs were working on me.

The nurse took off my uniform and underwear because I had vomited and soiled myself. She put me in a johnny. The EMTs got me onto a stretcher and out to the ambulance. My blood pressure was really low, and they were trying to get it up with medication, but it wasn't working. I still had the dry heaves. They decided to take me to the hospital across the border, because it was only five miles away, and our closest hospital was twenty five miles away. This time of year, we have frost heaves in the road, which would have slowed them down. They were afraid that I wouldn't make it that far. I got excellent care in their emergency room. My nurse and a couple of aides who were Canadian, came to visit me in the ER when they got off work. The ER nurse told me that they were admitting me because there was something wrong with my blood work. The doctor told me that I had a vagal attack. The Vagus nerve runs from your brain to the rest of your body. It controls many of your systems, including heart and lungs. When I got to my room, I had a male nurse that didn't speak English. The next morning, I rang the buzzer for an aide. I was reaching for a cup of water from my nightstand and accidentally spilled it on the floor. The aide came in, I showed him the water. He looked at it, left and never came back. The girl I was working with came to see me later that morning. She told me that she had taken my clothes to her house and washed them. She came back in the afternoon and brought me a soda. I got to see my doctor about six o'clock. I told her that I was feeling better, and wanted to go home. The doctor suggested that I stay another day, but I told her I could rest better at home, so she discharged me. The girl who I had worked with brought me home. Earl was very upset because the hospital wouldn't give him very much information on my condition, they also wanted a thousand dollar down payment on my bill, because I had no insurance. After I had been home a couple of days, one of the EMTs that worked on me called to see how I was doing. I thought that was very nice of him to care that much.

The doctor had told me not to go back to work for a week. My first day back, I was sitting at a table in the dayroom, listening to report I again began to feel like passing out. It so happened that my doctor was at the nursing home at the time doing his monthly patients. He told the nurse to give me a nitro, and call the ambulance. Again the ambulance took me to the hospital across. Donna came to see me in the ER. I told her that I didn't want to be admitted to this hospital again. I asked her to call my doctor and get me transported to the hospital on our side. My doctor agreed. I was still having chest pain, so they got me stabilized and then put on the intensive care unit. My doctor contacted a larger hospital in Bangor to see if they had a bed for me on their heart unit. He had me transported to Bangor by ambulance. The ambulance takes the back roads until they can get on the turnpike in Houlton. In Bangor, the doctor told me that I had suffered a mild heart attack. They were going to do a catherization. They were going to insert a wire in my thigh with a small camera on the end to see what was going on in my heart. When they injected the dye, I felt like I passing out. I told the nurse. The cardiologist said that they were going insert a stent to keep the artery open. I had to stay overnight and go home the next day. Earl paid one of his friends to come pick me up. His friend took me out to eat on the way home, and we stopped at the PX in Bangor. He was a veteran and could get cigarettes a lot cheaper.

Every few months, I would have chest pain. I'd get admitted. The doctor sent me to Bangor again. They checked out my stent, and it was still open. Sometimes the artery can clog up again in three to six months after the stent is put in. Earl's friend didn't show up to bring me home, though he told Earl he would. I stayed overnight at the Ronald Mc Donald house. One of the volunteers bought me a bus ticket from Bangor to Caribou. The bus would get into Caribou around ten o'clock at night. Earl paid the heavyset aide to pick me up at the bus stop. She and the girl I had worked with when I had my first attack came together. They were really good friends, because the girl was dating the heavyset one's single brother. It was Mother's Day. They wanted to eat at Subway before going home. I told them I'd wait in the car, because I had no money. She told me she was going to buy my sandwich for Mother's Day.

I went back to work when the doctor said I could I was working the three to eight shift. My partner and I were doing a patient, when she asked me if I felt good. She told me my lips were blue. She told the nurse that she thought I should go home, and the nurse agreed. They wouldn't let me come back to work. They sent me the money in my profit sharing plan, and listed me as retired, yet I never signed any papers saying that I was retiring. Again, we were just living on Earl's Social Security check. I hadn't applied for my Maine state hairdressing licence when we moved here. I would have needed to go back to school for five hundred hours. Also I didn't speak French, and here it was an advantage to be bilingual. Also, this town had more hairdressers, than Carter had liver pills.

A few weeks later, the DON knocked on our door. She had a box of food, and told me there were two more boxes out in the truck. The front of the first box was decorated and had a get well soon wish on it. The DON made sure I knew that she had bought the turkey. The head cook said they never had collected that much food for an employee before. Of course it was needed and greatly appreciated.

# CHAPTER FIFTY

While I was in the hospital in Bangor having a stent put in my heart, Earl was in the hospital in northern Maine having a liver biopsy. He called, and we talked to each other from our hospital beds. I had a couple of more episodes of chest pain. They were angina attacks. On one of these hospitalizations, a nurse noticed that I had stopped breathing while I slept. My oxygen stat was very low. The doctor ordered some breathing tests. I was diagnosed with COPD (Chronic Obstructive Pulmonary Disease. ) He put me on oxygen 24/7. I also had to go to Presque Isle for two nights in a row to be tested for sleep apnea. I was told that I was one of the severest cases he had. My regular doctor also prescribed a hospital bed, because I also had acid reflux disease. I couldn't breathe laying flat. I would cough. He also suggested that I have a life alert system installed and go to cardio rehab for twelve weeks. It was summer and hot. The power windows on our car didn't work, and the air conditioning was disconnected. Before I could go anywhere, I had to open all four doors for awhile so the inside of the car would be cooler. I drove the twenty five miles that way to the hospital all summer.

I could no longer work. It was a good thing that we lived on the first floor now, because I had trouble climbing stairs. The state paid Earl's Medicare premium, and considered him my caregiver. I applied for Social Security Disability Income. Of course the first time I was denied. I got a woman lawyer who was an advocate for women's rights. Her office was in Presque Isle. You had to climb a long flight of stairs to get to her office. There was no elevator in the building. Earl would hold the door open at the bottom of the stairs, so that there would be more air while I climbed the stairs. The lawyer told us that if you could easily climb the stairs, you didn't need disability. She told me to gather together all my medical records. By this time, I had been in the hospital several times. I was finally diagnosed with Coronary Heart Disease. The first time we went to court, the judge asked me most of the questions. I told him that I had tried to go back to work three times. My oxygen tank ran out, and the bailiff went to get Earl so he could get another one from the car. Earl couldn't be in the courtroom with me and my attorney. When I had answered all the judge's questions, he told me to wait outside the courtroom while he spoke to my attorney. On my way out, the bailiff whispered to me that I had done a good job, and was sure I had won my case. My attorney came out a few minutes later, and told me I won

Now that I was going to get a disability check, we had another problem. We were over income to get help with my medical bills from the state. I would have to pay the first fifteen thousand in a six month period. Then the state would help. After the six months, I had to pay the first fifteen thousand for this six month period. In other words I was responsible for thirty thousand dollars of my medical bills a year. My social worker suggested that one of us move out so that we would have different addresses. At the time, it was something neither one of us wanted to do. We had been together over twenty years.

A week after my birthday, Cynthia and our half sister came up for the weekend. Cynthia was familiar with the area, because her second husband was from northern Maine. They had a belated birthday party for me, giving me several silly gifts. They bought me a nightgown exactly like theirs. Earl took a picture of us in our matching nightgowns. I introduced my sisters to Roxie because Barb wanted to go across the border shopping. We took her to the dollar store and she was able to buy everything she needed for the Easter baskets she was going to make for about fifteen dollars. They took turns cooking their favorite meals. Earl usually ended up doing the dishes. They slept in our bedroom, and Earl slept in the recliner. I was embarrassed that I had to wear Depends, and that Earl had to help me fasten them. I didn't want my sisters to know, so I waited till after they went to bed to put one on. Over all, it was a great weekend. Barb said she'd come up again to visit me.

A few months later, our landlord knocked on the door. She was looking for the rent, which surprised me, because it was another week before it was due. Then she told me that we were three months behind in the rent. She saw the look of surprise on my face. I had no idea, that we owed back rent. I began to panic. All I could think of was being evicted and out on the street again. I confronted Earl when he came home. He got as mad as a hornet, saying that the money went to taking care of me. At the time, the state was paying my medical bills, and his medicare premium. All he had to do was feed me and put a roof over my head. He stopped talking to me. Oh, he cooked, and tended to my needs, but he stayed in the bedroom all the time he was home. There was a TV in the bedroom. He did this for a month. I lost twelve pounds that month, which was a good thing, but its how I lost it. One night Earl was in the bedroom as usual, It was summer, so all the windows were open. I went into the bedroom and told Earl that we needed to talk about this. His face got as red as a beet, and he put his fist back to hit me. It was the first time I had ever been afraid of him. I called Roxie, and she came to pick me up. She brought me to her house for awhile. She couldn't put me up for the night, because now her oldest son was living with her and her boyfriend. I told her that I'd be safe for the night. She told me to call her if I wasn't. I told her that I was going to move out. Roxie came the next morning, and we went apartment hunting. The nice places had waiting lists, and a couple of landlords we couldn't reach. Roxie brought me home around noon. I checked for apartments in our local newspaper. I called this woman, and she told me that she had a one bedroom apartment open. She came to pick me up because Earl had the car. I liked the apartment. It had a large kitchen and bedroom. The living room was very small. It had a large porch that I didn't have to share with anyone. I could also have Tigger. I was going to leave Penny with Earl. The best part was that I could afford the rent. I could also apply for Section 8 so I took the apartment. Donna was supposed to pick me and bring me to the General Manager's office. I thought she forgot, so I hooked up a oxygen tank and walked. It was July and hot. I had to rest several times on the park benches in town. I finally got there. She gave me a voucher for my first months rent, one for groceries, and one for cleaning supplies. She arranged for a truck from a local furniture store, to move my furniture that I absolutely needed. Then she gave me a ride home. I had to wait in the apartment for the phone company to install my phone. I continued moving some of my stuff with our car. I brought Tigger to the apartment when I was ready to start living there. He walked around the apartment for three days meowing. I didn't realize it at the time, but he was waiting for Penny to come. He finally settled in. Earl helped me pack the car. He told all our friends that I moved out so that I could get help from the state with my medical expenses. A few days later, I asked him if he wanted to see the apartment. He bought me a plastic patio table and four chairs to use as a kitchen table and chairs. He also bought me a set of pots and pans and a few other items I needed. I don't know how he did it, but he talked me into letting him keep the car at his place.

Shortly after I moved out, he told me that he was taking Penny to the animal shelter, because she was peeing on his bed. All he would have had to do was keep the bedroom door closed. I think he did it to get back at me for moving out. I would have taken her if I thought I could afford two cats. Also at the time I adopted Penny, he didn't want another cat. He told me that it was either the cat or him. I knew he wouldn't leave me over a cat. I put her inside my coat, and home went. After she got used to the house, she attached herself to Earl.

# CHAPTER FIFTY-ONE

I guess I let Earl keep the car, because he was getting older, and where he lived was on top of a big hill. Also he needed it to take his sister to the doctor and run errands for her. He came to see me just about every day. Once in a while, he'd sleep over. I finally got my back pay from Social Security. Earl told me that 27" TVs were on sale at the local department store. He took me to get one. Then he told me that he had put one on lay-away, so I paid the balance so that he could get it out.

I knew that I needed mental help to deal with the issues in my life I went to the mental health clinic and registered. I went to an sexual abuse group and I was seeing a therapist. One day the counselor for our sexual abuse group took all of us on a outing. We went to this place that a local business man had built for a person in his life who had cancer. It was a religious shrine around a pool. It was beautiful. We ate lunch and talked. I took pictures, making sure that no one in the group was in the pictures. It was a confidentiality issue. After awhile the group broke up because the counselor who was also a hairdresser was quitting. She wanted to devout more time to her family and her business.

My therapist who was a male started seeing me once a week. At every visit I acted like everything was going good, and I was okay. Then he suggested that I see him every two weeks. I still was acting like I was fine, oh we talked a little about Earl's drinking, and why I moved out. Then he suggested we meet once a month, and if everything was still okay, every six months. I had a hard time letting myself trust him. The last therapist that I saw in Connecticut and was making progress with, changed jobs. I thought about it for a whole week. I finally came to the decision that if he was going to help me, I had to tell him what happened to me. It was so horrible, I didn't think anyone would believe me. Also it had been drummed in my head that everyone had their own problems and didn't care about yours. I began to tell him about my mother on our next visit. He told me that he was running a evening group for women who suffered from post traumatic stress. He thought that I would benefit from this group. Earl brought me to my evening group sessions. Most of the time he just dropped me off. Sometimes I was glad that he didn't come in. The apartment would be dark when I went inside. After one particularly stressful session, Earl dropped me off. I went inside and locked the door. The apartment was dark. All of a sudden, I felt like I was screaming, but nothing was coming out. A few sessions later, the therapist suggested that I write my feelings down in a journal. I took his suggestion. As I was writing in my journal, I realized that I had been through enough to write a book. I kept writing in my journal, but also started my autobiography. I felt that if someone read my story and that I survived, maybe someone else who had or was being abused, would seek help and also become a survivor.

# CHAPTER FIFTY-TWO

While I was writing my book, they assigned me to another therapist, because mine was going to cut his hours, so that he could go back to school. I finished the book, and also put it on audio cassettes. I asked a local merchant if I could display the audio version in his store to sell it for me. I had even drew a cover free hand. It was of a little girl locked in a closet, with only a light bulb hanging from the ceiling. Cynthia saw it and told me the cover gave her the creeps. I left the cassettes in his store for awhile, but they didn't sell, so I picked them up. I wrapped a copy of the audio cassette book and put a picture of me on the back, like a real author to give to the male therapist. The girl at the desk said she'd give it to him the next day he worked. One day I happen to be in the waiting room waiting for my therapist to see me. The male therapist called me into an empty room. He told me that he wasn't allowed to accept gifts from clients. I think he got the impression that I gave it to him because I had a crush on him. I think we were both embarrassed. I just wanted to show him that I had started a goal, and finished it. I saw an ad in a magazine from a publisher. I sent them my typed out manuscript. I never had typing classes, so it was full of white out and paper clips. I got it back in two weeks, in the same condition I sent it. That rejection hurt.

Roxie and I were still getting together for coffee or a trip to Van Buren and across the border for shopping. The aide that worked in bordering at the nursing home would also come visit me. One day she picked me up. There was a light rain falling, but we decided to go to the local carnival anyway. We didn't stay long. We left and my friend wanted to go for a ride. She loved to drive. We drove all the way out to the Allagash. I had my camcorder with me. We we went to the buffalo farm. Earl had promised to take me but never did. At the farm were buffalo, deer, goats, moose and other wild animals. We recorded each other petting and feeding the animals. After we stopped at this rustic little restaurant. They let me video tape the dining room, which was decorated like a hunting cabin. After we ate we went to the river. We sat on rocks and skipped rocks and talked. Her marriage had been a abusive one. She was now divorced. She walked away with nothing. He got the house. and also turned their daughter against her. Shortly after their divorce, her ex husband got his arm caught in a fan at work, and lost half his arm. She moved back in to take care of him, taking a leave of absence from work. It was a good afternoon. Some time later, she began to date the son of one of the residents. They eventually got married after his mom died. They moved downstate. I thought here was another good friend that moved away. They were happy at first, then his personality began to change. She would call me and tell me that sometimes she was afraid to go home. About two years later, he died of a brain tumor. She moved back north, into her house. I saw her again while she was working in the nursing home where my sister-in-law was a patient.

# CHAPTER FIFTY-THREE

About a year before I moved out, Tigger's fur would mat on his back. I'd cut the mats off, until breathing in the cat hair was too much for me. A friend would sometimes shave his back for me. Also, his skin was dry. I thought it was the change in climate causing it, because he didn't act sick. One time I brought him to a groomer that did cats for a special bath, and to shave his back. When we brought him home, Penny wouldn't let him anywhere near our bedroom. She perched herself in the doorway and wouldn't move. To her, he didn't smell like Tigger. That was in April. The next year about a week before my birthday, Tigger stopped eating. I called the mobile vet. He checked him out, and ruled out what wasn't wrong. He gave me an antibiotic to give him. The next day Tuesday, the vet called me back. I told him that Tigger seemed better, he was eating again. I gave him his pill Wednesday afternoon. About a half hour later, he threw up bile. Thursday again he wasn't eating. I even gave him our tuna fish which he loved. He ate a tiny bit. Thursday night he hid in my bedroom closet in a laundry basket. I took the laundry basket out of the closet with him in it, so that I could keep a close eye on him. He didn't even sleep on my pillow at the top of my head, like he always did. I called the vet, and he told me to get him to the closest animal hospital which was in Caribou, forty miles away. The vet's wife who also was his assistant, talked to me for awhile, trying to calm me down. I think she and the vet knew what was wrong with Tigger. I called Earl. He came right away, and we left for the hospital. The vet there called me the next day, asking me what Tigger's favorite food was. I told her about the tuna fish. That night she called back, and told me that they had to force feed him, but he seemed a little better. I called on Sunday, and they told me that I could come visit him, but Earl didn't have the gas. That night, the vet asked my permission to operate on Tigger. I gave my consent. After the operation, she called and said that he was beginning to wake up. When I went to the hospital, she'd show me how they were feeding him. I called the hospital at seven Monday morning. Tigger had died about an hour before. She told me that she wouldn't charge me for the biopsy, because she wanted to know why he died. I swear to God that I heard him meow around six that morning, as if to tell me goodbye. I was so consumed with grief, that I forgot that Earl was hurting too. He loved Tigger as much as I did. I cried more for him than I did some people. Tigger had died of liver cancer. It was already in the ducts, and there was no way to save him. Earl said he died because I gave the vet permission to operate on him. My landlady and her husband had to stop by that evening to check on something. She knew that I had been crying. I think she thought that Earl had abused me, because she was once an abused wife.

That first night without Tigger made me crazy. I couldn't stand the quiet. The next day, I called Earl and told him that I wanted to go to the animal shelter and adopt another cat. We went to the shelter where he had brought Penny. I told him that I wanted a female, because I wasn't ready for another male. Earl saw this calico cat up in the rafters. He said that she was the one. She was about two years old. I gave a donation, and brought her home. I named her Callie. Her coat was dry and coarse. She mooched food, until she realized that she was going to get enough to eat. Soon, her coat was soft. I took good care of her, but was afraid to let myself get close to her. She attached herself to Earl. The next month, Roxie's cat had kittens. I went to see them. I fell in love with a buff colored male. I brought him home when he was old enough to leave his mother. I named him Buffer. I used to call him" Bug" for a nickname. I would hook two cat leashes together and hook up Callie and Buff to the railing in the summer, so that they could be with me on the porch. I'd walk Callie on a leash two or three times a day up and down my dead end street. Sometimes we'd take the trail. When she was ready to go home, she'd just turn around and head for home. She had what the vet called a "kennel cough" which was common in shelter animals. The vet was surprised that Buff didn't catch it. I hooked Callie on a leash, because she was a real pretty cat, and I thought someone might come and pick her up. She walked very well on a leash. Eventually, I let her come and go as she pleased. By now, the neighbors knew that she belonged to me. Callie wasn't afraid of strangers. She'd follow people walking on the street. She really like the ten year old boy that lived upstairs. If she was outside in the morning when he left for school, she'd follow him to the bus stop. When he got on the bus he'd tell her to go home, and she would. Sometimes, she'd be waiting for him to get off the bus in the afternoon. One thing though, I couldn't go to bed until Callie and Buff were in for the night.

One time Callie didn't come home for two days. I walked up and down the street calling her name several times, thinking she was in the field. Earl did the same thing. One the second night, she came out of the bushes when Earl called her. A couple of months later, Earl and I had just come home from going out to dinner. I was sitting on the couch, when all of a sudden, this tiny kitten crawled out from under the couch. We checked to see if there were any more, but this was the only one we found. When we adopted Callie, the woman told us that she was spayed. Well obviously she wasn't. I decided to keep him. He was yellow and white. I named him "Benji". All of this will tie in later on.

Cynthia and her husband stopped in for a visit on one of their trips to visit his family.

# CHAPTER FIFTY-FOUR

I made two more trips to Bangor for my heart. On the second trip the cardiologist took me to the operating room twice. The second day the doctor explained to me that he was going to do a fairly new procedure. He was going to insert radiation into my stent. He explained that it keeps the stent open for longer periods of time. When Earl dropped me off home from picking me up in Bangor, I went to use the microwave. Believe it or not, it zapped! But it still didn't stop my episodes of chest pain. I was in Bangor and napping when the cardiologist that was assigned to me came in while doing his rounds. He kicked my bed to wake me up to tell me he'd be doing my catherization. He had no bedside manners at all. The next day, he said he couldn't get the wire with the camera through my thigh, so he was going to use my right arm. Later, that day, when my supper tray came, I must have raised my arm just enough. Blood came spurting out where the wire had gone in. It scared my roommate. We both rang our buzzers. My male nurse came in, and when he saw my arm, yelled for more help. I passed out from the loss of blood. Five nurses worked on me to get the bleeding stopped. My nurse told me that he was going to report this to my doctor. He never came to see me. I had already got my discharge orders when I got back to my room. He could have at least come to check me out and reassure me that everything was alright. I called Earl and asked him to come and get me before they killed me. He left Madawaska at five the next morning. He called me from Houlton to tell me he'd be there in a couple of hours. I told my primary care physician about my experience. She was upset over the way they treated me.

She called Northeast Cardiologists to tell them that they at least owed me an apology. Unfortunately about six months later, I needed to go back to Bangor. I was scared. This time I had a very nice older and experienced doctor. In the recovery room, I asked the nurse if I could see my doctor to ask him a couple of questions. She told me that she would page him. He came to my room. I asked him if I needed to be on all the meds that I was on. Up north, you have to change doctors about every two years because they don't stay. Each new doctor prescribed a new med. At the time, I was taking twenty nine different pills. He agreed with me, and took me off what medication I didn't need.

My half sister sent me a basket of flowers after I came home.

My half sister and her thirteen year old son came up to visit me for the weekend. My nephew Bill made friends with the boy that was living upstairs at the time. We took her to my sister-in-law's so she could meet her. They liked each other right away. I took them to the Block House in Fort Kent which is an historical site. We took a lot of pictures. We did a lot of shopping. She spoiled me rotten. She put it all on her credit card. We also did a lot of drinking, and crying over our mother. Earl took her to our American Legion, because her husband was commander of theirs.

Bill was disappointed that we couldn't go to Canada. I wasn't sure of my way across, and we couldn't get in touch with Roxie to go with us. When she got back home, she found a set of lighthouse dinnerware. She asked a friend of hers who was coming up to bring them to me. It would have cost her more to ship it to me than she paid for the dinnerware.

# CHAPTER FIFTY-FIVE

I signed up at Adult Ed for some basic computer classes. I didn't know the layout of the high school, and didn't have my oxygen. I climbed a couple of flights of stairs, looking for the classroom before I asked somebody. By this time I was out of breath. When I found someone to ask, I was only a couple of doors away. It was a ten week course. I enjoyed it, and believe it or not, I was one of the youngest in the class. The class was made up of mainly seniors.

That summer, as I was sitting on my porch with the cats listening to music, I thought, I wrote a book that was non fiction, because I lived it, what could I do with fiction. I took subjects I liked, history and animals. I got a notebook and a pen with erasable ink from the house. I don't know why I chose to write about Alaska. I had never been there. I follow their Iderod race on TV every year. All I knew about Alaska, is what little I read and seen on TV. I worked with a hairdresser that had taken one of their cruises. She showed us pictures and described its beautiful glaciers, icebergs and sea life.

I decided that I'd start with a boy who had lost his father in a ice fishing accident in the late 1870's. He, being the eldest child, was responsible for taking care of his younger siblings and helping his mother. I decided that I'd follow this family from generation to generation over a span of a hundred years, using history to show the passage of time. I had wrote about twenty seven pages of my book. That night I left it on the coffee table to continue to work on it the next day. When I got up the next morning, Earl said I shocked him. I'm thinking to myself, what did I do now. He asked me how did I know so much about Alaska. I told him I didn't, only what I read, watched on TV, and what people who had been there told me. He told me it was good, and to run with it. I wrote out my first draft, then typed out what I had written, then finally I put it on a floppy disc. Even when I was satisfied enough with the book to put it on a disc, I would still make changes. When it was finished, I got on the internet looking for publishers for first time authors. I came across Publish America. Their logo caught my eye. It read "we pay authors." This was right up my alley, because I was on a limited income. I emailed my book to their acquisitions department. I received an email from them that I would receive an answer in two to four weeks. The first week went by, and nothing. The same thing on the second week. The waiting is the hardest, believe me. I also knew the longer it took for them to get back to me, the better chance I had. The third week, and still nothing. One night into the fourth week, I was checking my emails. There it was, "The Land of the Midnight Sun, Alaska, Our Last Frontier" was going to be published! I was an author! I wanted to call all my friends, but it was eleven o'clock at night. They sent me my contract and other forms, but most importantly, I received my first dollar as an author! My landlady bought a copy of my book and had me sign it. After my new book was out, I called our local newspaper and got an interview and my picture holding up a copy of my book. PA also offers a free website to its authors.

I loved writing and typing. It seemed to relax me. I was still in therapy. I was diagnosed with post traumatic stress, depression, anxiety, and panic attacks. I had to go to the emergency room a few more times for chest pain. They kept me for observation. They turned out to be severe panic attacks. I told the doctors and nurses about my book.

Cynthia sent me some of my baby pictures. Aunt Emma had passed away, and she was helping one of our cousins go through her things. I showed them to my therapist. From the pictures, it looked like the June Cleaver family, but it was far from the truth.

Earl and I were still having problems. Sometimes he'd be drunk, and walk out on me and I wouldn't see or hear from him until he thought I'd been punished enough.

I began another book on a subject that I'm very passionate about, The Holocaust. Earl could have been a great help to me, because he took part in liberating some of the camps. It was a subject he didn't want to talk about, and said it was something I didn't want to know what he saw. I did a lot of research concerning the Holocaust. I even included the Nuremburg trials. I wanted the younger generations growing up to know that this atrocity did happen, and the civilized world wasn't going to tolerate it. I invented a Polish family that lived prior to World War II, that lived through Hitler's reign of terror and eventually got sent to the camps. I chose a Polish family, partly because my paternal grandparents immigrated to this country from Warsaw just after the first World War, and because Poland's natural resources and location were of vital importance for Germany to conquer Europe. It took two years, but I finished "The Holocaust: Poles the Forgotten Victims". I submitted it again to Publish America. They agreed to publish it. They did email me saying that I would need to get written permission from the author of one of the websites that I had gotten information from. Fortunately, the website had the author's email address. I emailed him, explaining that I had written a book on the Holocaust and had taken some information from his website concerning the Warsaw ghetto. I told him that I needed his written permission to use it. He consented, asking only two things from me, acknowledgment of his website, and that I send him a copy of my book for his personal library. He was a rabbi in Houston, Texas. He hadn't been part of the Holocaust, but had relatives who were. I kept my end of the bargain. Also here I am, with only a ninth grade education, with two published books under my belt.

After "The Holocaust: Poles: The Forgotten Victims" came out, I kept bugging our local television station for an interview. The station covered all of Aroostook County and parts of New Brunswick, Canada. Finally on my birthday, the manager agreed to set up a televised interview with me. We did it at our public library on Good Friday. I made the six o'clock news! I donated a copy of each book to the library.

# CHAPTER FIFTY-SIX

We had to junk the silver Chrysler, because the work that needed to be done was more than the car was worth. Not only that, the car was seventeen years old. My landlady's husband had a car dealership. I'd heard that he had a bad reputation as a businessman, but I thought that his wife and I being friends, she wouldn't let him screw me. He even agreed to let us make the payments to him, so that we wouldn't need to get a car loan. The car was fifteen hundred dollars. If we wanted the car, Earl would pay him one hundred and fifty dollars a month for twelve months. We bought the car in December. The car was a 1987 Ford Topaz. When I went to see if it was what I wanted, I was shocked. The car looked like showroom. By the end of December, the car started to show signs of rust. It's caused by the salt they use on the road. Plus a part needed to be replaced. The dealer agreed to fix the car and all we had to do was buy the part. He told Earl if he wasn't satisfied, we could pick another car. Earl looked under the car while it was on the lift, and felt satisfied. It was my car, but Earl kept it at his place. I rarely got to drive it.

I thought that my landlady and husband really made it easy for us to own a car. I called Mary Ann to tell her I loved the car. I also wrote a thank you message and put in our local newspaper. I didn't mention that Earl was helping me by making the payments. I didn't think I could because I was getting benefits from the state. If someone reported that he was helping me, my benefits might be cut. When Earl read the thank you note in the paper, he was livid. He accused me of not giving him credit for anything he did for me, that I was just using him. Then he walked out, and again it was awhile before he called and came back.

Earl's sister had to go to a rehab center in Van Buren. We visited her often. On one of the trips home, I asked Earl if we could stop at the Acadian Village. I had my camcorder with me. Earl stopped, but wouldn't go in with me. It was a hot day. He parked under a tree and waited for me. First you went into a large house that was filled with Acadian culture and artifacts. The Acadian culture and French language are very strong in northern Maine. Its people work hard to keep their heritage alive. The lady let me use my camcorder. After the museum, you went into houses, from the very first family on down. The first house was the Roy house. It consisted of one room with a dirt floor, fireplace and meager furniture. Each house progressed from the last one. All the first Acadian families were represented. I went into the one room schoolhouse and church. I noticed that in each of the newer houses, there was an organ. Before I left, I bought a hat from the gift shop. We have a small museum in town. Earl brought me there and showed me some of his mother's wood carvings on display there. Every year a different family takes part in the Acadian Festival which is held the last week of June and lasts for four days. The host family has a large family reunion. A re-enactment of the landing of the first Acadians takes place on the shore of the St. John River. A canoe occupies a priest, Indians, and Acadian settlers.

One night Callie didn't come home. She didn't come home the second day either. Earl went up and down the street calling her name, but he couldn't find her. A third night went by. I was getting worried that something might have happened to her. I prayed to St. Anthony to help me find her. The fourth afternoon, I opened the door to go get the mail, and there she was. I called Earl right a way to tell him she was home. Three months later, she had five kittens. So for awhile, I had eight cats. I wanted to keep one, but I already had three. We gave the kittens to a woman who ran a clean shelter for cats, mostly strays. She promised that she'd give my babies to good homes. She only had them three days, and they all got adopted. After, I called my vet and had her spayed. Believe it or not, she was pregnant again. This time she was carrying three. It was still early, so the vet aborted them

# CHAPTER FIFTY-SEVEN

It was a beautiful summer day. My landlady's handyman who lived in Canada, was working around the buildings. The tool shed was next door to my building. He had his radio on the grass tuned to a French station. Callie was laying down in the grass next to the radio. I joked with the handyman that he was trying to teach my cat French. He laughed. That afternoon, Earl and I went to visit his sister at the rehab center. She was doing better. She was off the nursing floor and into the boarding unit. On the way home I told Earl that I would love to go inside an old church Mount du Carmel that had been restored and was now a museum. It had twin dome-shaped belfries with an angel on each one blowing a trumpet. They had painted the domes with a special gold paint that would hold up through our long harsh winters. It was free to go inside, but they appreciated donations. Earl gave a donation. Earl showed me a Acadian house his mother had carved out of wood. It even had tiny furniture. There were also horses and sleighs that she had carved. She loved horses, and even owned one. Climbing stairs is very hard for me. It makes me very short of breath. After I had seen everything on the first floor, I climbed the stairs to the first balcony. After looking at everything, against Earl's wishes, I climbed the second flight of stairs to the second balcony. By, now, I really was having trouble to breathe, and the dust made it even worse. I climbed down to the first floor, collected some literature and we left for home. On the way home, I began having chest pain. After we got home, I rested awhile to see if the pain would go away. It didn't so Earl called the ambulance.

They admitted me and did some tests. The doctor decided that I needed to go to Bangor.

In Bangor, my roommate and I became quick friends. I called Earl when I was to be discharged to pick me up. My roommate lived in Mars Hill which was on our way. She asked if her and her husband who was staying at the Ronald McDonald house during her hospital stay if they could get a ride home with us. I told her yes, without talking it over with Earl. When Earl got there, I found that I couldn't go home, because it was too late for the medical company to deliver a tank of oxygen for my ride home. The nurse said that we could stay at a hotel associated with the hospital. I was excited about that, but not for long. I wasn't allowed to be on oxygen in the hotel. My room mate's husband offered to share his room at the Ronald McDonald house with Earl for the night. Earl didn't sleep very well. The next day, they delivered my oxygen tank, so I could go home. My room mate wasn't ready to be discharged yet. On the ride home, Earl told me that I should have talked to him before agreeing to give them a ride. He said that it was a great responsibility on his shoulders with two sick women in the car. Apparently my room mate and her husband didn't have a car. We still exchange Christmas cards every year. We also communicate on Facebook.

Earl called me while I was in the hospital in Fort Kent to tell me that Callie hadn't been home for a couple of days, and that none of the neighbors had seen her. Callie had a habit of sitting by my downstairs neighbor's door, waiting for her to come out and pet her. Earl told me not to worry, that he'd keep looking for her. I was in the hospital a total of six days, three days in Fort Kent, and the three days in Bangor. On the ride home, it was pouring rain. We were getting the aftermath of hurricane Katrina. Earl told me that Callie still hadn't come home. She had never been gone this long before, and she wouldn't have stayed out in the pouring rain. The rain finally stopped, and I was able to sit on the porch again. I kept looking at the tool shed, remembering that the handyman had been in and out of there the day I went to the hospital. I went to look inside the windows, but they were so dirty and covered with cobwebs I couldn't see through them. My gut told me she had got locked in there. I told this to my therapist on my next visit. By now, nine days had gone by. My therapist told me to follow my instinct. I called my landlady to tell her that I thought Callie had accidentally got locked in the shed. She told me that she doubted it, but would come up after lunch and check. Earl wanted to go visit his sister and didn't want to go alone. We left before the landlady came. When I got home, Mary Ann called me to tell me that Callie was inside the shed. She came out when she opened the door. Mary Ann picked her up and set her on the porch, but she ran off. She told me to just call her and she'd come home. I went outside and called her name a couple of times. Suddenly she came running up the bank and to the house. She had lost weight, but otherwise seemed fine. The roof of the shed had been leaking, so Mary Ann had put a bucket inside the shed to catch the water. Thankfully, the heat wave we had broke. She must have drank from the water in the pail, and ate bugs and mice.

A nurse I had worked with, lived a couple of houses up the street. She'd come and visit me on the porch or in my house. She'd check my feet for swelling. One day she came with a stray black kitten. She was treating him for ear mites. I helped her hold him while she put mineral oil and a Q tip in his ears to clean them. Eventually his ears were clear. She wanted to go down state to visit her daughter, and one of her cats didn't get along with the kitten. I offered to take care of him while she was gone. I had let him out before with my cats and he always came back. One night I let him out after supper, but he didn't come back. My friend came back, and she drove around looking for him, while I checked with the neighbors. We never found him. We think the people that left him in the first place, came back for him.

After that, I wanted a black cat. Earl believed that black cats were bad luck. I called my friend at the animal shelter. Someone had dropped off two black kittens on her doorstep. She gave me one of the kittens on Thursday. He ate and played until Sunday night. He wasn't acting right. By Monday, I knew he was sick. That night I called my friend at the shelter. She said she'd come the first thing in the morning and we'd bring him to her vet across. In the meantime, I tried to get liquids into him. I had named him "Boo" because it was close to Halloween. Joyce came the first thing the next morning. Boo was so weak, we didn't even put him in a carrier. I held him in my lap. He took his last breath before we got to the vet. The vet said he died from distemper, even though Joyce had given him a shot. It just didn't have time to take full effect. Even though I only had him three days, I still cried. I even wrote a short poem about him. The person that adopted the other kitten died the same way, and on the same day. Joyce said that she had a black female cat that was about six months old. I named her "Beauty" I didn't let her outside. Now, I had four cats. I'm not really a cat fancier. I prefer dogs. Now, thinking back, in my mind I wanted to find another "Tigger."

# CHAPTER FIFTY-EIGHT

I decided that it was time for me to keep a promise I made to my Dad which now seemed a lifetime ago. I enrolled in the Adult Ed GED class. I thought it would be like high school, with the teacher teaching the class as a whole, but it wasn't. The students would come in, take a seat, and continue where they had left off at the last class. The teacher was the same one who taught the computer class. She sat at the desk and was there to answer questions, or give you some help if you needed it. I had to take a pretest to see where my strengths and weaknesses were. I could have told him what my weaknesses were, science and math.

My first class, I took a seat next to a heavy set woman. She told me that I needed to take a binder and a small notebook for a journal. She told me the first thing we did in class, was to write in our journals. We introduced ourselves to each other. Her name was Myra. One of the teachers came up to me and asked me if I wanted to join a reading club that she ran one night a week at the library. I told her that I would, but wouldn't have transportation to get there. Myra said that she went, and offered to bring me and give me a ride home. So I joined the group. We were given three children's books to read and to discuss at the next meeting. We also got to keep the books. They served refreshments and got a ten minute break. I enjoyed the class. Sometimes, I didn't get all my books read, but lucky for me, there was a gentleman in the class that liked to talk. Myra and I became friends.

One day the head of Adult Ed gave us a practice test. I passed it. I already had my credits for reading, social studies, and science which were combined in one test., and reading comprehension. This test was on math. I didn't score high, but I passed. A month later, she gave us another practice test. I thought it was strange that she had given me the same test as last time. I was almost finished the test, when she grabbed it away from me, saying that she had given me the wrong test. Then she made the remark that I didn't do so well anyway in a snotty way. I ran out of the classroom, I was crying, and angry that she had insulted me that way. My teacher followed me out, trying to calm me down, and have me go back to class. I told her that I was through, that I didn't need the GED anyway. Myra was in another room taking her science test. I went out to her car and had a cigarette to wait for her. My teacher followed me out to the car, but I still wouldn't change my mind. Finally, Myra came out. She told me that our teacher told her that I needed her. I told her what happened and why I was upset. Myra drove me all over town until I calmed down. She talked me into going back to class. The head of Adult Ed met us at the door. She apologized and had me come to her office. We went over the mistakes I had made on the first test.

Myra and I also joined a cooking class held at the high school one night a week. Sometimes the teacher would pick a number, and if you guessed right, you won a prize. I never won. Myra did a couple of times. A woman from our reading group was also in the class. She often won a prize. Around Christmas, the teacher taught us how to make homemade Christmas gifts, such as ingredients to make homemade soup, in a decorated jar, and cake in a cup. I was going to give my soup in a jar to Earl for Christmas.

It was Christmas time. We had a Christmas party at Adult Ed. Earl came with me. The gentleman from our reading group was also studying to get his GED. He brought his wife. Myra didn't come. We ate, sang carols, and played games. I won a large fruit basket that I gave to Earl.

# CHAPTER FIFTY-NINE

It was the week before Christmas. One night about three thirty in the morning, the man that lived in the apartment in front of me, was ranting and raving and pounding on my door, yelling at me to open the door. It was the first time that I was afraid to live alone. After about ten minutes later I heard him go stomping off my porch. That was on a Wednesday. That Saturday was the Saturday before Christmas. The neighborhood kids were outside playing, when that same man was ranting up and down the street with a beer bottle in each hand. The kids were scared so they came running into my apartment. Also that afternoon, a circuit breaker went out about three times in a row. After the third time of coming to reset the circuit breaker, my landlady called a friend of hers to check out the breaker box. He told me my outlet in the kitchen was overloaded, but all that was plugged in was my toaster and coffee pot. I had spent the day cleaning. That evening after all the cats were in, I was watching TV and telling myself how good the house looked. I went to bed my usual time. About two in the morning, someone was pounding on my door. I didn't answer it because I thought that it was my neighbor again. I could hear a man ask why I wouldn't open the door. Then my upstairs neighbor shouted for me to open the door, that the house was on fire! I slipped on my bathrobe and opened the door. Flames were coming down the stairs from the second floor. I went back into the apartment to get my cats. They were my babies. The only one I found was Buff. I carried him out to the porch, but he was scared and jumped out of my arms. He went back in the house. I went back in to get some shoes on and kept calling the cats' names. The fireman finally convinced me that I had to get out. He said that they'd leave the door open so they could get out. I was on the first floor, but the way the house was built on a hill. Iron poles held the porch up, and there was a wrought iron railing. I still don't know why I didn't throw Buff over the porch to the firemen below. There was also a tank of liquid oxygen in my apartment that could have blown sky high! I had to climb down a ladder to the ground and into the ambulance. By now I was having chest pain. My upstairs neighbor and her ten year old son were also in the ambulance. Her teenage daughter wasn't home at the time, but got home just as the ambulance was leaving. She was drunk and high. They admitted us for smoke inhalation. My neighbor's son only stayed overnight. He went to stay with his aunt until his mother was discharged. Myra a nd her live-in boyfriend Jim came to visit me in the hospital as soon as they learned that it was me that got burned out. They offered to let me stay with them until I got settled. Earl was telling our friends that I'd have to stay with him now. I know I hurt him when I told him that I was going to stay with Myra and her family. It was hard enough for me to move out the first time. It would have been even harder the second time. When I was discharged, my room mate's daughter gave me ten dollars. I felt strange taking money from a stranger, but she said that it came from the heart.

The first thing Earl did the morning after the fire, was go to the apartment to see if he could find the cats. Callie saw his car and came running out from under the porch of the next house. She jumped right in the car. She must have followed my neighbor's son down the four steps leading to my apartment. He couldn't find the other three cats, though he kept going back to look.

Myra had a two and a half year old daughter and a thirteen year old son. My oxygen company came to set me up with a concentrator, CAP machine, also a nebulizer. The first night I was there Myra's daughter got up during the night. She saw me on the couch with my mask on. She ran to her parent's room to tell them about the mask. My oxygen company had also taken up a collection for me. There were lamps, a TV a coffee mug filled with Christmas candy and other things. Donations of food, clothes, and money were coming to Myra's everyday. Earl helped out with food and cat food for Callie and Myra's cats. Callie wouldn't come out from under one of the dressers, except to use the cat box. She began to warm up to Jim, and would sometimes lay on his chest. I also got help from the Red Cross, and The Salvation Army. There were vouchers for clothes, and essentials. I had lost everything. Myra took me shopping and sometimes I'd have her get something she wanted. I remember getting upset when we were shopping. I had picked out a two year calendar with dolphins and whales. When we got to the cashier, she said that the calendar wasn't included in the voucher. I was in tears. The cashier rang up the calendar anyway. I got upset again when Earl came to visit me at Myra's I had lost the Christmas jar of home made soup ingredients that I had made for him in cooking class. Myra gave Earl the one she made. My first night at class after the fire, none of the clothes I was wearing were mine.

The general manager helped me out again. She called the owner of a subsidized apartment building for elderly and handicapped to see if they had any openings. I needed first floor. They had a one bedroom ready to rent. Myra brought me to see it and fill out the paper work. The town paid my deposit and two vouchers for household supplies and food. Our local grocery store gave me a gift card for one hundred dollars. At this apartment building, small pets were welcome. Myra and Jim went to the thrift store to see what they could get me for furniture. They got me a couch, chair, some end tables,. and a dresser. My oxygen company replaced my hospital bed. Complete strangers were donating dishes, silverware, two microwaves, pots and pans. Within a week after the fire, because of my community and neighboring communities, I had enough to set up housekeeping again. The pastor of a small church collected over a hundred and eighty dollars from his small congregation. He had been my downstairs neighbor before he bought his house. I planned on moving into my new apartment on the third of January. Myra and Jim went to the apartment and arranged the furniture. A mutual friend of both of us, went and cleaned and put stuff away.

Christmas Day, Myra, Jim, their daughter, Earl, and I went to the Christmas dinner and festivities at the K of C hall. I asked one of the people in charge if I could get up and thank everyone for everything they did for me, and that it meant even more because it came from the heart. Their generosity taught me the real meaning of Christmas. People were still coming up to me to ask me what I needed. After Christmas, Myra and Jim took me to my new apartment. They told me that they wanted to be sure that I liked the way they put the furniture. When we got to my door, they told me to close my eyes. They unlocked the door, and led me inside. They told me to open my eyes. They had decorated a four foot Christmas tree for me. It was the most beautiful tree I had ever seen. We went back to the general manager's office to pick over stuff that was left after Christmas.

The week after Christmas, we had a severe snow storm. If no one had taken in the other three cats, there was no possible way they could have survived outside. During that week, I was looking at the pet section of the classifieds in our local paper. A Canadian breeder had puppies for sale. He spoke very little English, so a friend of mine who was visiting Myra, talked to him. We made arrangements to look at the puppies the next day. I wanted a male. When we got to the breeder's he went upstairs and brought down a black ten week old toy poodle. It was the only male he had. He began to lick my face as soon as I held him. Myra's daughter wanted to hold him. I said yes, but I was nervous that she might hurt him because she was so young. She held him so gently, I was surprised. I told the breeder that this was the puppy I wanted. He wanted to get paid in Canadian money. I gave him a hundred and ten dollar deposit, thinking he'd let me take the puppy. I told him I'd come back on the third with the balance, but he said no. I got very upset. I had to wait nine days to get my puppy.

On New Years Eve, Earl came for awhile. The rest of us made a resolution to quit smoking. We all tried, but none of us succeeded. Finally, the third was here. I went to the credit union and got the balance for my puppy changed into Canadian money. Then we went across. The breeder filled out the paperwork. He had to pay two different taxes, which he charged me, but explained that I would get one of the taxes back. All I had to do was show the custom officer his papers. They would give me an address to mail the form to get my refund. He also gave me a bag of dry puppy food. It was very cold, so I put the puppy inside my coat. At the border, I had to bring him inside. The women officers were passing him around, remarking how cute he was. They told me that he had to be in quarantine for two weeks, meaning he couldn't cross the border for that period of time. It was the same thing on the American side. Finally, we were back at Myra's. I visited for awhile, then packed our stuff, and brought my new family to our new home. I named my puppy "Noel". I just didn't ever want to forget the true meaning of Christmas ever again. Noel, is Christmas in French.

# CHAPTER SIXTY

When I got to my apartment door, there was a Christmas card and the word "welcome" taped to my door. I looked around my new home. I almost felt like I was living in a boarding home, because most of the tenants were elderly. There were also two call bells in the apartment. When you pulled the cord, the light outside your door went on and a buzzer went off. I thought that it was connected to the police and fire department and would come immediately when the buzzer went off. The first night in the apartment, Callie was playing with the cord by my bed, and the buzzer went off. I kept waiting for the fire department or an ambulance to show up, but neither did. Then I learned they wouldn't come unless they were called. I taped the cord to the wall after that.

The tenants were also giving me things like knick knacks and other things to make it look more like home. One morning there was a boom box outside my door with no name. My neighbor gave me a stereo set, complete with a turn table, cassette, and a CD player that played five CDs at once. People were still bringing me clothes, and coats. I almost got off on the wrong foot with one neighbor. Noel was only ten weeks old, and I had him in the hallway with me without a leash. This lady started to scold me, that he was supposed to be on a leash. Well about that time, Noel lifted his leg against the wall and peed. I hadn't had the time to housebreak him yet. Then the lady looked at him and said, "But oh! He's just a baby!"

They been friends ever since. She loves him, and him her. She's an animal lover, though she doesn't have a pet of her own. She always has pet treats. It didn't take long for Noel to know this. If he got out of the apartment on me, he'd go straight to her door and bark. Sometimes, she'd leave her door ajar. Noel would push on the door, go in and into the treat bag. Then he'd run to the dayroom to eat it.

He was the hardest dog I ever tried to housebreak. I'd put down newspapers and puppy pads, because it was still winter and too cold to take him out When he missed the puppy pad, I'd scold him and put him in the cat carrier for about five minutes. He got along alright with Calie. She was getting older, and always didn't want to play with him. She'd find a place to sleep where he couldn't reach her. When we went to visit Myra, it was like packing a diaper bag for a baby. I had to bring the puppy pads, newspapers, his favorite toy, and dog food. The first three days I had him home he wouldn't eat the puppy chow from the breeder. I bought can puppy food at the store, and mixed it with the dry. He ate it that way, and still does, though he's a finicky eater. Spring finally came, and I'd take him outside for a walk. Once he learned that he could mark his territory, he house broke. He had to go through his puppy shots twice, because I understood from the breeder's paperwork, that he had his last shot in January. I called the vet in February, thinking he'd get his next shot, but she explained to me that he was supposed to have had it in January. Maine has a program for seniors and handicapped people who have pets to make it affordable on a fixed income to have them spayed or neutered. When Noel was six months, I used this program to have him neutered. Earl paid for his license. Noel also began to suffer from separation anxiety.

The gentleman that was in our reading group also lived here. I would ride back and forth to school with him. He and his wife and teenage son and I became good friends All I had left to pass was math. I struggled with Algebra and Geometry. I didn't have them in school. When it came time to take my test for math, I made the mistake of spending too much time on one problem, which the instructor told us not to do. The test was in two parts and you were timed. I ended up leaving four questions blank, because I took too much time on one problem. I only needed a 410 to pass, because my other grades were high. When I got my results, I missed passing by ten points. They asked me to speak at our graduation, even though I wasn't graduating. My teacher wanted me to speak on "The Cost of Freedom". I got a standing ovation. One thing I'm not, is a quitter. I went back to Adult Ed in the fall. I had a very good teacher. She was patient, and explained each step in Alegbra. I had an easier time with Geometry. It came time to take the test again. This time I took an anxiety pill before I took the test. This time I didn't leave anything blank. One day my teacher called, and asked me if I was sitting down. I passed with ten points to spare. At graduation, all the graduates got a red rose corsage from the head of Adult Ed. I had my GED at fifty seven years old. The next fall I took a couple of college entrance courses. There was a man in my class who was short. He got a lot of teasing from the other classmates that he had worked with at the mill. He always had an answer for them though. His dad had died, and he still missed him terribly. It showed in some of the essays he wrote. Then around the middle of the year, his mother was hit by a truck crossing Main Street. She wasn't the same after the accident. In January we had to take our exams. Joey was in a good mood and joking with the rest of us. He apologized to me for talking shop with his friends because I was the only female. I told him how luckier could I be being the only woman in the same room with six good looking guys. Our last essay had to be read in front of the class. They teased Joey because they couldn't see his head over the podium. Joey went and got a chair and stood on it behind the podium. His essay was on the danger of driving while talking on a cell phone. That would be the last time I'd ever see him. In February his finance broke up with him. He committed suicide one afternoon at his parents' cabin on the lake. Every time I see someone talking on a cell phone while driving, I think of him. Nobody knew how badly he was hurting, because he covered it up so well and only showed his sense of humor.

# CHAPTER SIXTY-ONE

After I got settled, I started another book. It was a tragic love story about a Negro slave and his master's daughter who fall in love It dealt with the issue of slavery, the Underground Railroad, and The Civil War. I titled the book "Forbidden Love" I changed publishers. My book got excepted by a New York literary publisher. This book was edited professionally, though I needed to invest some money. They made my book into an ebook when it was completed. It took me four years to complete the book, because of the research and because I was spending a lot of time at Myra and Jim's house. I was beginning to love their little girl like an adopted grand daughter. I spoiled her like grand mothers do.

Noel and Maggie would play together. They'd chase each other all over the house. Maggie had a favorite toy that she took everywhere. It was a stuffed dog named "Woofie" Of all the toys that child had, Noel would want her woofie. Maggie also still had a pacifier. They would play keep away, and would you believe that Noel would get it in his mouth the right way. One day Myra and I were shopping. She bought Noel his own package of pacifiers, but he still wanted Maggie's He would hide them. One night Jim rolled over in bed and felt something hard. It was Maggie's pacifier. Noel had hidden it in their bed. Of course I did a lot of free baby-sitting. One time I was baby-sitting, and Maggie bit me. I was so upset with her. I put her in time out, and went in Myra's bedroom to have a cigarette, because that was the only room where we could smoke. Myra's oldest son, didn't like the smell of smoke. When her time was up, I let her out. I went back in the bedroom. When I came out, Maggie was sitting on the couch watching TV. I told her that I couldn't talk to her right then, because I was still upset with her. Sometimes, Noel and I would stay overnight. When we came home, Noel would be so tired, he'd crash for a day. I also spent money helping them out when I could. Jim couldn't hang on to money. Myra only had math to pass for her GED, but she dropped out. I was really getting attached to their daughter, but the separation anxiety was beginning to set in. I was afraid that I'd love this little girl so much, then they'd move away. They kept telling me that they weren't going anywhere, but I had heard that before. We spent a lot of time together, including the kids' birthdays and holidays.

One time Myra had asked me to baby-sit Maggie a couple of months in advance for a doctor's appointment she had in Presque Isle. Her friend, the town manager was going to bring her because her boyfriend had an appointment in Presque Isle around the same time. Jim wanted to go along. I figured that I'd have to baby-sit for about five hours at the most. Myra told me what to make for Maggie and her son's supper. Her thirteen year old son was very fussy and wouldn't eat a lot of things. The night before I was to baby-sit, Myra told me to come earlier than I thought I needed to. She told me that they were going to make a day out of going to Presque Isle which is sixty miles away. I told her that I hadn't planned on baby-sitting the whole day, and that she should have told me about their plans when she asked me to baby-sit. Myra knew I was upset with her, but it was too late for her to get another sitter, so I agreed. Maggie was good until after her shows were over. We went outside to sit on the porch. I hooked Myra's dog outside on a leash. The teenage girl next door came out to see Maggie and pet the dog. I had told Maggie more than once not to unhook the dog. The girl next door went inside. What does Maggie do, she unhooks the dog. The dog starts running back and forth down their busy street with Maggie running after him. Finally they both headed for the house. Both her and the dog got there before me. By the time I reached their porch, I couldn't breathe. Maggie was sitting on her swing set. She looked at me and said, "You're not talking to me Annie?"

She remembered what I told her the day she bit me two years ago. A friend came by, and said he'd help me baby-sit until Myra and Jim got back, but he had to go home for a minute. He only lived three houses away. Myra and Jim got back before their friend returned. I called Earl to come pick me up. I kissed Maggie good bye and left. Myra called me at home wanting to know why I didn't tell them I was leaving. I told her that I still was upset, and I'd call her back when I calmed down, which I did. I told her that I'd only baby-sit Maggie for a half hour or an hour at the most. She was hard to handle because she didn't have much discipline from her parents. Myra said she understood, and we remained friends. Jim was calling me his second mom, and Myra and I were getting as close as mother and daughter. She had lost her mother at a young age.

One day I was at Myra's and she needed to go to the store. She asked me to go with her. As a young dog, Noel would take off running if he got outside. It was July. Myra's son opened the door for someone, and Noel got out. Jim chased Noel around the block a couple of times in his bare feet Finally, there were some workmen sitting outside at the high school, eating lunch. Noel smelled the food and headed toward them with Jim yelling at them to grab Noel. The bottoms of Jim's feet got burnt. He'd get out quite a bit when I was at Myra's. We'd have to call Earl, if we couldn't catch him because he was the only one Noel would listen to. Another day I was at Myra's. I took Noel across the street to a field to go to the bathroom. Myra's dog Sammy always followed me. This day Noel and I had come back across the street. Sammy was still in the field. I called him and he came running. He was in the middle of the street when a car hit him. In fact it went over him twice. I just started screaming "No No!". I loved the dog as much as I loved Noel. Jim's cousin heard me scream and came running out. He got a towel and picked Sammy up and brought him inside. Myra was crying hysterically. She called her friend to take her and Sammy to the vet. When they got back, Myra said that Sammy didn't make it. I couldn't stop crying. I blamed myself, though everyone said it wasn't my fault. Even Maggie tried to comfort me. I felt that if I hadn't called him, he'd be still alive. Jim said he had a habit of chasing cars. About six months later, Myra and Jim came to see me, but they weren't alone. They had with them a medium-sized red Chow /Collie mix dog. She was about seven months old. I almost fell over backwards when they told me her name was "Sammi" Maggie had asked them when they were going to get another Sammy, so they went to the animal shelter to look for a dog. When Jim heard that this dog's name was Sammi, he said she's the one.

Myra came to see me one day. She gave me back the first manuscript that I wrote and got rejected. She had asked me if she could read it. She had it before the fire, that's why I didn't lose it. My therapist kept telling me that it got saved for a reason, that it was meant to be rewritten only a different way.

# CHAPTER SIXTY-TWO

Bob the gentleman from my reading group, his wife Candy, and their nineteen year old son Barry, and I became good friends. Bob and Earl even liked each other. I think Bob had great respect for Earl's age. If I wanted to get out of the apartment for awhile, Noel and I would go upstairs to visit. After we got to know each other better, I explained to them why I had severe separation anxiety. I told them that it was hard for me to trust friendships, because something always happened. The five of us started going to Presque Isle on the first of the month shopping, because they had a Walmart with a grocery store. It was cheaper and better quality fruits and vegetables than our store in town. We'd also go out to eat.

About a year later, in October we were having an Indian summer. Bob wanted to take a trip to Bar Harbor when they got their checks. He wanted to find the West Quiddy lighthouse. He said that he had always wanted to see it. They asked me if I wanted to go with them, because they knew that I collected lighthouses. Earl babysat Noel. The day we went, we had to stop at Bangor International Airport to pick up Barry's old girlfriend and her newborn son. Barry wasn't the father, but they had dated before in high school. They had been talking on the phone, and they decided to try again to have a relationship. We stopped at an outlet store in Brewer. I bought a hoodie, hat, two tee shirts, soap in the shape of a lighthouse, and a lighthouse coffee mug for just under fifty dollars. We stayed overnight in Bangor, and split the cost of the hotel room. We had the baby in our room, and Barry and his girlfriend shared another room, because they both smoked, though Barry's parents weren't supposed to know he was smoking. The next day we went to Bar Harbor. We asked about the West Quiddy lighthouse, but nobody seemed to know where it was. We toured the shops. I took pictures. I bought some dolphin wind chimes, and a thermometer in the shape of a black poodle. One of the shopkeepers told us of the Bass Harbor Light which was only about a half hour away. She gave us directions. We found the Bass Harbor Light. It sat on a cliff. The was a long staircase that led down to a flat rock. It was a good vantage point to take pictures. I only had a one time use camera. Going down the many steps was no problem. I took my pictures. Now I had to make it up the stairs and to where Bob had parked the van. Candy stayed in the van, because she was very heavyset and couldn't walk that far. By stopping to rest at each landing, I made it to the top of the stairs, though my chest hurt and I was very short of breath. When I got to the van, I laid down on the back seat and took a nitro pill. It worked. My chest pain went away. Bob and Bill joined us shortly after. They had found another path to the lighthouse which was much easier. Then it was time to head for home. I still don't know how, but we got lost. We traveled at least ten miles of dirt road that was under construction. We ended up in Calis at the border patrol station. He gave us the right route to take north. We got home around two in the morning.

That March, Bob and Candy came to visit Earl and I. They said they had some bad news to tell us. In April, they were moving back to California where they had lived before moving to Maine. Bob said his mother was ill, and he needed to go back and take care of her. Then their plans changed. They were leaving in two weeks. The night before they left, they invited Earl and I up to their apartment for pizza. The next day they left, knowing that they were forecasting a bad snowstorm. They left a lot of things behind. Candy gave me a few things that she wanted me to have. Earl picked over things he wanted. They left that afternoon, with the van loaded, and pulling a small

UHaul trailer that was filled to the max. They stayed overnight in Bangor, but left before I95 was even plowed. In Augusta, their transmission caught fire. A fellow traveler stopped to make sure they got out of the van safely, because all three were very large people. They needed to leave most of their stuff to pay the garage bill. The mechanic said he only could fix it good enough to get them to California. The van only made it as far as Colorado. Candy called and emailed me often in the beginning, and then it got less and less, and now its been two years since I heard from them.

# CHAPTER SIXTY-THREE

I was watching Maggie grow up. I was there her first day of school to wave goodbye as she got on the school bus. Myra and I were bawling our eyes out. But as she got older, her temper tantrums increased in intensity. Her home life was so unstable. She went to bed one night and her big brother was there. She got up in the morning, and he was gone. Myra had no control of her fourteen year old son, He was getting into trouble with the law, and refused to go to school. After breaking probation twice, the state placed him in a foster home. Myra and Jim would break up and a new girlfriend would move in with him, and Myra was in love with someone else Then they'd get back together. Maggie started seeing therapists and put on medication. It took a while with try this and try that to get her on the right medication. She loved school and didn't have any behavior problems there. She loved being with the other kids, because till now, she had only been around adults. I was the one stable person in her life. They moved a lot but not very far, it was either down the street or around the corner. Jim always moved close enough to Myra when they weren't together so that Maggie could see her mother anytime she wanted. Myra couldn't cope with Maggie on her own. Jim's disability finally came through after a four year struggle. Maggie was put on Jim's Social Security as her primary care giver.

One night I called Jim to see if I could see Maggie. He told me sure, and suggested that I spend the night. He and Myra were together at this time, and they had another couple who they were friends with, living with them. I knew that Myra, her friend that lived with her and her friend that was no longer the town's general manager were going to Bangor for the weekend. I thought that Myra's son, and their male roommate would be there. My neighbor drove me there and I gave him for five dollars for bringing me. I walked in the house with Noel to find out that Maggie and Jim were the only ones home. The other men had gone to the general manager's house for the night to take care of the cats and dogs, because she ran an animal shelter, mainly for stray cats, and only a few dogs. I didn't know what to do, it would have cost me another five dollars for my neighbor to come and bring me home, which I didn't have. I put Maggie to bed. Jim had a love seat that opened up into a bed, and he made the bed up for me. Oh I trusted Jim, after all he was young enough to be my son, and Myra wouldn't have cared, I was worried about how it would look. All I had in my bed that night was Noel, the friend's huge dog, and three cats. I guess Earl had called me at home around six o'clock in the morning, and couldn't reach me. He called me at Jim's around ten o'clock even though he hated him. He called to tell me that his sister had died at five o'clock that morning. She had been in the local nursing home for the last two years. I saw her a month before she died. I had gone with Myra and Jim to visit Jim's grandmother. I didn't feel right not going to see her while I was there. It had been two years since I last saw her. Earl never went because he held a grudge against her. We didn't even go to her funeral. One thing about Earl, if you hurt him badly, he'll never forgive you. A neighbor stopped by Jim's to say hi, and I asked her for a ride home.

One Fourth of July, Myra was bringing Noel and I home during a thunderstorm. We were almost to my place when we saw this tiny kitten alongside the road meowing and soaking wet. There was a field there. Either he had been born in the field or someone dropped him off. We couldn't leave him there, so I got out and picked him up and brought him in the car. Myra said that she couldn't keep him because Jim would have a fit. They already had seven cats. I took him home, dried him off and fed him. I tried to find a home for him, but I couldn't. It's been four years and I still have him. I named him "Papatoots. "

So this was my relationship with this family. I spent a lot of time there. Sometimes I'd stay three or four days. Especially, if Earl and I were on the outs. One time He walked out on me and I asked him for my house keys back. When I got up the next morning I found his set of keys hooked to Noel's leash. This time I stayed at Myra and Jim's for two weeks. Myra had broken off her relationship, and Jim had kicked his girlfriend out. They were back together again and happy. Maggie was happy that she had her mommy and daddy together again. My neighbor came there to see me once to ask me to come home She was taking care of the cats if I couldn't get home. I left Earl's keys under my doormat so she could get in. I told her I'd think about it. I was depressed and didn't want to be alone. I finally went home. I was determined that I wasn't going to call Earl. I hadn't done anything wrong. Almost always, when Earl and I had a fight, I was the one who called him first. The first Thursday I was home, Earl went to bingo at our building. We had bingo every Thursday evening. I didn't go because I didn't have any money. I saw him in the day room when I took Noel out. I was hoping Noel wouldn't see him. I couldn't understand why he was there, when he had told me that he didn't want to see me or talk to me again. He knew darn well that I might be at bingo. I know he saw me take the dog out. The next Thursday, I went to bingo. The regulars always sat at the same table every week. The tenants that sat at our table arranged it so that Earl and I had to sit next to each other. A couple of times our hands touched, but neither of us spoke to the other. The next week, when Annie called, I told her how much I missed Earl, but I wasn't giving in. The next day, Earl called me. We talked and made up. He came that night and stayed over. For awhile it was good, it always was, then slowly it drifts back to the old pattern. Life with Earl was an emotional roller coaster. I think Earl thought that now that we were back together, I wouldn't go to Myra and Jim's anymore. But he was wrong. I wasn't going to let him dictate where I could or couldn't go. I was still in therapy and also group therapy. Slowly I was getting stronger.

One winter I had spent the night at Myra and Jim's. I sleep with my mouth open. I didn't have my CPAP machine with me. At five o'clock in the morning, I was taking Noel outside. When we got to the bottom of the stairs, I noticed something pink in Noel's mouth. I went to see what it was. He had my top denture in his mouth. It must have fallen out while I was sleeping. He was looking for a place to bury them in the snow. I only had a top denture, because before the fire. I had a bad habit of leaving my bottom denture all over the house. My cat Benji was still a kitten then. One night I decided to put them in the denture cup where they belonged. The denture cup was on the second shelf of the open linen closet, but apparently I didn't notice that the cover hadn't closed tight. The next morning, I go to put them in and the cup was empty. Benji had climbed up on the bathroom sink. From there, he could reach the cup. He must have played with them. I went to the bathroom, and when I flushed the toilet, it overflowed. Benji had tossed my bottom denture into the toilet. I called my half sister to tell her. She told me that if they had gone into the toilet, it would have overflowed. She laughed when I told her it did. To be sure, Earl looked all over for them, even pulling out the stove and washer and dryer. My landlady had a plumber come with a snake, but came up empty. I thought, I might as well face it, my denture was floating down the St. John River somewhere.

# CHAPTER SIXTY-FOUR

I hadn't heard from Paul in almost two years. Annie calls me almost every day. But this day, I wished with all my heart that she hadn't. Paul had called her. He hadn't heard from PJ in two years, which was unusual, because they always got in touch with each other on their birthday. Paul told Annie that he decided to find PJ. He called the Amerillo, Texas Police Department, because that was the last place he knew that PJ lived. He explained that he was his brother, and was looking for him. An officer checked his records. He told Paul that PJ had died three years earlier from a blood clot in his stomach that had burst. Paul was so upset, that he wasn't able to call me and tell me, so he asked Annie if she would. Annie was crying, when she called me. After she calmed down a little, she told me that she'd call Amerillo and get a copy of the police report. I couldn't grasp it, my baby was dead. Why we didn't find out right away, because PJ had told the friends who knew him was that he had been raised in a foster home. A child is not supposed to die before his parents. He was only thirty four years old. I never got a chance to say good bye. In the back of my mind, I knew that if he didn't change his lifestyle, he would die young. I always thought that he might be murdered or die of a drug overdose. But he died of natural causes the report said due to many years of heavy drinking. He bled out before the EMTS could get to him. My therapist helped me get through this, though in my heart, I didn't want to believe it or accept it. A year ago, Annie sent me a picture of PJ. It was a memorial card.

Paul took it very hard. He began drinking very heavily. His twenty one year marriage would end in a divorce. One night when I was at Myra and Jim's Annie called me there. She told me that Paul had called her and asked her to tell me that he loved me, but had to say good bye. I dropped the phone, crying hysterically. I had already lost one son, I couldn't bear to lose another one. Myra and Jim took me to see my therapist the next day. She told me that she was going to admit me in the Physic ward, so that I'd get the help and support I needed. I told them that I didn't want to talk to Earl if he called. Myra and Jim took care of Noel, and came to my apartment to take care of the cats. Paul called me, and he was sober. I told him that I wouldn't want to live anymore if he killed himself. I knew that Annie and Amanda would be very hurt, but they'd be okay. Phil Jr. I hadn't heard from him since the fire. Before the fire he was calling me at least once a week. Myra called every night. I got a lot of support through individual and group therapy. I was on oxygen 24/7 because the oxygen in my blood was low. I was there seven days, but I felt much better. The doctor suggested that I stay with Myra and Jim for a couple of days before going home because they were a support system for me. The first night at Myra's I felt hurt, because Noel didn't come to bed with me. He had slept with Myra all week, and he went in their bed. He came to sleep with me after awhile. I think he was mad at me for leaving him.

About a year went by with Paul calling me occasionally. Then he began calling me almost every weekend, drunk. It always was the same story, that he wanted to be with his brother, and that he had been to Iraq, and had to kill people that never did anything to him, and that he just wanted to find a woman to love him. Until now, I had never known he was in the service. He said that he served four years, but didn't tell me because he didn't want me to worry. He was living with someone now, and they'd be arguing while he was on the phone. Earl wouldn't talk to Paul on the phone when he was drunk. I felt like I was dealing with our son on my own. I really could of used Earl's help and support. All Earl would say was that Paul was going to end up committing suicide. Some weekends I was dealing with two drunks, Earl and Paul. It was very hard on me. At one session with my psychiatrist, I made a comment that I wished everyone would just leave me the hell alone. He suggested that I go to the Crisis Center in Presque Isle. I told him that I wouldn't go unless my animals were taken care of. He tried to call Earl, but there was no answer. He called the Crisis Center, and they had a bed for me. The state would pay for a taxi to bring me there, but not home. At home I finally got a hold of Earl. I told him that I needed to go to the Crisis Unit and that I'd be there about five days. He agreed to stay at my place and take care of Noel and the cats.

It took the taxi over three hours to come from Caribou to my place to pick me up because of the blinding rain. On the way to Pesque Isle the rain had let up some. I got there about eleven thirty that night. It was two AM before I got to bed after filling out all the paper work. I got to talk to the staff individually and we'd have group twice a day. You could smoke outside on the porch, but you always had to ask for a lighter. I made a couple of friends. I had told one of the staff that I was a author and had published three books. I also told her about first writing my autobiography and how it had got rejected. I also told her how I still had it, and had lost everything else I had written in the fire. She told me that that manuscript got saved for a reason, and maybe it was meant to be rewritten. I was there five days. One of the staff gave me a ride home. Noel couldn't be happier to see me. As usual Earl had the house spotless which meant a lot. When I saw my regular therapist, she agreed with what the staff member had told me about rewriting my autobiography. To be honest I had thought about it, but wasn't sure I wanted to relive the bad memories. That night, I was checking my emails. I couldn't believe the email from my first publisher. They said that now that I was an established author, they wanted to offer me a contract to write my autobiography. They gave me six months to write it. Of course I got right back to them and signed the contract. It was going to cost me anything, I'd be crazy to turn an opportunity like this down. This is what you're reading. Partly I got myself known as a author by blogging. My publisher told me one of the great ways to promote my ebook was to flood the internet. I've even written some poetry on a poetry web site.

I can't tell you this is the end, because it won't be as long as I'm on this earth. I work everyday on the coping skills I'm learning in group therapy, my shrink, and my therapist. My goal for writing this book is that maybe someone will see themselves in me and seek professional help. Abuse, no matter what form it takes, is NEVER OKAY. It's not love. It's CONTROL. Good luck, you're in my prayers.

Thank you for reading

Mary Bernard Shay.

# Would you like to see your manuscript become a book?

**If you are interested in becoming a PublishAmerica author, please submit your manuscript for possible publication to us at:**

**acquisitions@publishamerica.com**

**You may also mail in your manuscript to:**

**PublishAmerica
PO Box 151
Frederick, MD 21705**

# www.publishamerica.com